Philosophical Theology and Christian Doctrine

Exploring the Philosophy of Religion

Series editor: Michael L. Peterson, Chair of the Department of Philosophy, Asbury College

This is a series of individual volumes on classic and contemporary themes in the philosophy of religion. Each volume introduces, examines, and discusses the main problems and arguments related to each topic. Each book also considers some important positions of major philosophers, offers thoughtful critiques, articulates new positions, and indicates fruitful directions for further investigation.

1   *Problems of Religious Diversity* Paul J. Griffiths
2   *The Divine Attributes* Joshua Hoffman and Gary S. Rosenkrantz
3   *Philosophical Theology and Christian Doctrine* Brian Hebblethwaite

Philosophical Theology and Christian Doctrine

Brian Hebblethwaite

Blackwell Publishing

BLACKWELL PUBLISHING
350 Main Street, Malden, MA 02148-5020, USA
108 Cowley Road, Oxford OX4 1JF, UK
550 Swanston Street, Carlton, Victoria 3053, Australia

First published 2005 by Blackwell Publishing Ltd

Library of Congress Cataloging-in-Publication Data

Hebblethwaite, Brian.
   Philosophical theology and Christian doctrine / Brian Hebblethwaite.
      p. cm. — (Exploring the philosophy of religion ; 3)
   Includes bibliographical references and index.
      ISBN 0-631-21151-9 (hardcover : alk. paper) — ISBN 0-631-21152-7 (pbk. : alk. paper) 1. Theology, Doctrinal. 2. Philosophical theology. I. Title. II. Series.

BT75.3.H43 2005
230'.01—dc22

2004021625

A catalogue record for this title is available from the British Library.

Set in 10.5/11.5pt Bembo
by Kolam Information Services Pvt. Ltd., Pondicherry, India
Printed and bound in the United Kingdom
by TJ International Ltd, Padstow, Cornwall

The publisher's policy is to use permanent paper from mills that operate a sustainable forestry policy, and which has been manufactured from pulp processed using acid-free and elementary chlorine-free practices. Furthermore, the publisher ensures that the text paper and cover board used have met acceptable environmental accreditation standards.

For further information on
Blackwell Publishing, visit our website:
www.blackwellpublishing.com

For Douglas Hedley

Contents

Series Editor's Preface   viii

Preface   x

Acknowledgements   xi

1   Philosophy of Religion and Theology   1

2   Revelation   16

3   Creation   35

4   Incarnation   57

5   Trinity   75

6   Salvation   91

7   The Consummation of All Things   108

8   Other Themes in Christian Doctrine   127

Notes   146

A Brief Guide to Further Reading   169

Index   171

Series Editor's Preface

Philosophy of religion is experiencing a kind of renaissance. From the last quarter of the twentieth century to the present, we have witnessed remarkably vigorous activity among philosophers interested in religion. We are likewise seeing college and university students seeking courses in philosophy of religion at an unprecedented rate. To reach this point, philosophy of religion had to weather the harsh and hostile intellectual climate that persisted through most of the nineteenth and twentieth centuries. Absolute Idealism depersonalized deity, naturalism supplanted a religious worldview, and positivism deprived theological claims of cognitive status. Yet, partly because of incisive critiques of these viewpoints and partly because of new, first-rate studies of religious concepts and beliefs, this field of inquiry has once again come to the fore.

The Exploring the Philosophy of Religion series, then, comes into a very exciting arena. The books it contains treat some of the most important topics in the field. Since the renewal of interest in religion has occurred largely among Anglo-American philosophers committed to the best in the analytic tradition, these works will tend to reflect that approach. To be sure, some helpful general introductions and anthologies are available for those wanting a survey, and there are many good cutting-edge monographs dealing with technical issues in this burgeoning area. However, the books in this series are designed to occupy that relatively vacant middle ground in the literature between elementary texts and pioneer works. They discuss their stated topics in a way that acquaints the reader with all the relevant ideas and options, while pointing out which ones seem most reasonable. Each volume, therefore, constitutes a focused, intensive introduction to the issue and serves as a model of how one might actually go about developing an informed position.

Philosophy of religion is dynamic and growing. The issues it addresses are of primary significance for understanding the divine, ourselves, and our place in the universe. With this sense of magnitude, the present series has been conceived to offer something to all who want to think deeply about the issues: serious undergraduates, graduate students, divinity and theology students, professional philosophers, and even thoughtful, educated lay persons.

Michael L. Peterson

Preface

My aim in this book is to survey and comment on recent work by Anglo-American philosophers of religion in the analytic tradition on the doctrines of the Christian creed. There are good reasons for restricting the book's scope, for the most part, to this tradition, as I trust the first chapter will make clear. The principal reason is that philosophical analysis is really no more than a tool for exploring and clarifying a set of ideas. It does not in any way attempt to impose an alien system on Christian theology. It simply takes a given subject matter, in this case, the doctrines of the creed, and examines them for their meaning and plausibility. The skills and methods of philosophical analysis have been applied to these doctrines, in the work surveyed here, chiefly in order to probe and explain their coherence. Whether or not they are true is another matter. But their truth or falsity cannot be fairly assessed until we have as clear and profound a picture as possible of what it is that they are claiming to be true.

The central chapters of the book, chapters 3–7, are devoted to discussion of the way in which philosophical analysis has been applied to the five core doctrines of Creation, Incarnation, Trinity, Salvation and Eschatology (the ultimate future of creation, as Christianity envisages it). But these chapters are prefaced and supplemented by chapters on revelation and providence (or special divine action), since these themes are pervasive themes, presupposed and exemplified throughout the Christian creeds. Moreover the themes of revelation and providence have been subjected to just as much philosophical scrutiny as the core doctrines themselves by the philosophers of religion whose work is under examination here.

The great virtue of the work surveyed in this book is its clarity. I hope that, when readers see how Christian doctrine can be, and has been, scrutinized in this way, they will be encouraged to explore these matters further for themselves.

Acknowledgements

I am grateful to the editor of this series and to a number of readers for Blackwell for their helpful comments on the first draft of this book. I have tried to take account of their advice in revising the text. I have borrowed and reworked some parts of my essay, 'The Communication of Divine Revelation', from Alan G. Padgett (ed.), *Reason and the Christian Religion. Essays in Honour of Richard Swinburne* (Oxford: Clarendon Press, 1994), pp. 143–60 for chapter 2; some parts of my essay 'Does the doctrine of the atonement make moral sense?', from Brian Hebblethwaite, *Ethics and Religion in a Pluralistic Age* (Edinburgh: T. & T. Clark, 1997), pp. 77–93 for chapter 6; and some parts of my book, *The Christian Hope* (Basingstoke: Marshall, Morgan & Scott, 1984) and articles on 'Immortality' and 'Soul' from Adrian Hastings (ed.), *The Oxford Companion to Christian Thought* (Oxford: Oxford University Press, 2000), for chapter 7. I am grateful to the publishers for permitting me to do this.

CHAPTER ONE

Philosophy of Religion and Theology

1.1 The Changing Scene in the Philosophy of Religion

When I began the study of the philosophy of religion in the 1960s, the subject had two main emphases: a historical element, largely devoted to the interaction, sometimes positive, sometimes negative, between western philosophy and the Christian religion, certainly from Plato to Kant, but then very much in the British and later Anglo-American, empiricist tradition; and a topic-oriented element, where we learned to wrestle with the standard problems of the philosophy of religion: arguments for the existence of God, the concept of God, miracle and providence, the problem of evil, the soul and immortality and the relation between faith and reason. At that time, the subject was dominated by the need to respond to the logical positivist critique of metaphysics and theology as basically meaningless. Inevitably, much of the work was defensive in character, typified by attempts to counter Antony Flew's challenge, in his article 'Theology and Falsification',[1] to show what detectable difference religious language made. Did not talk about God 'die the death of a thousand qualifications'? The meaningfulness of religious language was one of our principal concerns.

But already the whole subject was beginning to be lifted out of this rather narrow, dry, empiricist context, not least through the influence of the later Wittgenstein.[2] Wittgenstein is very hard to interpret aright. But his insistence that we should look not for the meaning but for the use of key words and phrases in fields we are interested in, and his insistence on taking account of the contexts in life and practice of what we say, have been enormously influential on the philosophy of religion as on many other areas of philosophical concern. One way in which this has been applied is typified by the work of D. Z. Phillips,[3] who has urged a complete break with empiricism and an exploration, rather, of the forms of life in which religious language is embedded. But Phillips has done this in a way which has led him to be accused of fideism and of a basically non–cognitivist analysis of religious language that refuses to face up to the old questions of sense and reference, certainly where the reality of God is concerned. And whether Phillips himself is to be understood this way or not, there has unquestionably been a marked growth in what has come to be called anti-realist or non-realist approaches within religion itself. This is typified by the work of my former colleague in Cambridge, Don Cupitt, and his *Sea of Faith* network.[4] The realism/anti-realism debate, itself of great importance in contemporary Anglo-American philosophy, is one of the key issues in the philosophy of religion today.

A second major development, stemming from the late 1960s and early '70s, has been the way in which philosophy of religion has come to be pursued in the context of the comparative study of religions. This development, associated with figures such as Ninian Smart[5] and John Hick,[6] has made it impossible to restrict one's interest to the debate between western philosophy and the Christian religion. The data for philosophical scrutiny and analysis now come from the study of religion worldwide. And issues such as the conflicting truth-claims of the religions and the possibility of developing a philosophy of religious pluralism, and critiques of this, have also become central topics in the discipline today.

But at the same time a third major development has been the huge increase in the application of the techniques of philosophical analysis to the central doctrines of the Christian faith. This may perhaps be called, in a stricter sense than was customary earlier, philosophical theology. It was already exemplified in the 1960s by the later work of Austin Farrer in Oxford;[7] but one of the most striking features of the discipline in more recent decades has been the quantity and quality of this kind of work on both sides of the Atlantic. In England this is most prominent in the work of Richard Swinburne, who has moved on from his well-known philosophy of religion books,[8] via his Gifford Lectures on the soul,[9] to a series of four major books on philosophical theology.[10] Swinburne's work has raised the level of sheer philosophical professionalism in handling theological themes. But there has been a comparable and much more extensive development in the United States through the extraordinary growth industry of the Society of Christian Philosophers, with their numerous regional meetings, often held in conjunction with the American Philosophical Association, and their first-rate journal, *Faith and Philosophy*, where much of their best work is to be found. Senior figures there include William Alston, Alvin Plantinga, Nicholas Wolterstorff and George Mavrodes; and a younger group includes T. V. Morris, William Wainwright, William Hasker and many others.

It is the third of these recent developments in the philosophy of religion that forms the subject matter of this book. I intend to offer a survey of the contributions being made by Anglo-American philosophers of religion to the analysis and explanation of the central doctrines of the Christian creed. The survey is bound to be selective, but I hope that it will demonstrate the continuing usefulness of philosophy for theology today. I shall also, of course, be attempting some evaluation of the diverse material surveyed here. My own understanding of the doctrines of the creed will inevitably emerge.

1.2   Tensions Between Philosophy of Religion and Theology

A number of felt difficulties with the whole project must be considered and discussed before we get down to business. In the first place, it has to be admitted that philosophical analyses, and even defences, of Christian doctrine are often not welcomed with open arms by systematic theologians in theology departments or Church seminaries. At times, the latter suggest, in the spirit of Blaise Pascal,[11] that the God of the philosophers has little or nothing to do with the God of Abraham, Isaac and Jacob. Theologians voice the suspicion that the philosophers are applying their analytic tools to an idol, a reification of their own construction. Conversely, they hold the living God simply not to be susceptible to analytic scrutiny. The mystery of God, as worshipped and adored in the community of faith, is beyond the capacity of the human, philosophic mind to analyse. This tension has been noted between the theologians and the philosophers in Oxford and in Notre Dame, and I have witnessed it myself at the American Academy of Religion, where outright hostility was expressed to members of the Society of Christian Philosophers.

Two recent published instances of this tension may be cited. A debate took place between 1989 and 1995 in the journal *Faith and Philosophy*, initiated by the liberal theologian Gordon Kaufman, over just this question of whether theologians should take any notice of, or show any interest in, the work of philosophers of religion such as Plantinga, Wolterstorff and Swinburne. Philosophers working on the meaning and truth of Christian doctrine, so Kaufman avers, are simply presupposing traditional theistic conceptions and formulations. They lack sensitivity to the significance of religious pluralism, to the symbolic and culturally relative nature of all talk about the mystery of God, and to the at least partial responsibility of traditional Christianity for the great evils of the twentieth century. The philosophers appear to be just fiddling while Rome burns.[12] In their reply,

Eleonore Stump and Norman Kretzmann, while repudiating the last of these claims, point out the inconsistencies in Kaufman's dogmatic espousal of pluralist, relativist claims. Questions of rationality and truth are implicit in Kaufman's own agnosticism. So Stump and Kretzmann urge the liberal theologians to return from their wanderings and take seriously the traditional doctrines of the Christian faith.[13] James Keller responds with a defence of Kaufman, urging the practical priorities of Christian faith, and defending the theologians' right to concentrate on how religious belief contributes to the transformation of life rather than on the details of Nicene trinitarianism or Chalcedonian Christology.[14] William Hasker replies to this defence by pointing out how Christian understanding of such transformation ('salvation') is itself bound up with Christian doctrine and cannot escape the questions of truth and rationality that exercise the philosophers. He also comments on the fact that many centres of theological study are dominated by the more liberal types of theology, while the Christian philosophers tend to be more orthodox.[15] To this comment we shall return. James Keller returns to the fray with an eirenic defence of the theologians' right to focus on how people live as Christians.[16]

An English version of this tension is to be found in chapter 8 of Maurice Wiles's book, *A Shared Search*.[17] The chapter is entitled, 'The Reasonableness of Christianity'. It articulates Wiles's perplexity about how work in the philosophy of religion and work in theology ought to be related. One aspect of the philosophical approach criticized by Wiles – and this is the aspect of particular concern to us here – is the excessively rationalistic approach of writers such as Swinburne. Swinburne is accused of an over-literal approach to the doctrine of God, a failure to do justice to the analogical nature of all talk of God and to its rootedness in long traditions of experience and interpretation.

We need to be aware that Wiles, like Kaufman, is a liberal theologian, though not such an extreme one; and it might be thought that the tensions under review are felt most strongly by theologians who have come, for a variety of reasons, to adopt a revisionist approach to the traditional doctrines of the Church, as both Wiles and Kaufman have done to the doctrines of the Trinity and Incarnation. Equally we might suppose that the early Swinburne (and Wiles considers here only his *The Coherence of Theism* and *Faith and Reason*) is at the extreme end of the spectrum of rational approaches to the analysis of Christian doctrine. In his later philosophical theology books, Swinburne shows a greater sensitivity to history and tradition and to the analogical nature of religious language, as we shall see. Again, we note that Wiles speaks much more warmly of the work of Basil Mitchell, the philosopher of religion with whom Wiles held for many years a seminar in

Oxford on the relationship between philosophy and theology, and also of the work of Keith Ward, the philosopher of religion who succeeded Wiles as Regius Professor of Divinity in Oxford. Mitchell's own view on the relation between theology and philosophy will be considered later in this chapter; and, in the next, we shall be examining the debate between Wiles and Mitchell over whether Christianity needs a revelation. The work of Keith Ward will also feature prominently in the surveys of philosophical reflection on Christian doctrine that form the bulk of this book.

But it would be a mistake to suppose that the tensions between philosophy of religion and theology are most acutely felt by liberal theologians. As Hasker notes, the dominance of liberal theology in centres of theological education is on the wane. Recent decades have seen a marked recovery of traditional trinitarian theology in both Catholic and Protestant schools. But this has not led to much in the way of a rapprochement between the philosophers and the theologians. This is largely due to the influence of Karl Barth, the recovery of whose powerful, revelation-based, theology lies at the heart of recent developments. Barth's strong opposition to natural theology and to any 'points of connection' between theology and philosophy has reinforced and sustained the theologians' suspicion of the Christian philosophers, even where they share a commitment to mainstream Christian doctrine. This comes out most clearly in the influential work of Thomas F. Torrance, the Scottish Barthian dogmatician, who, in his *Theological Science*, insists that a theology that is true to its proper object – God's self-revelation in Jesus Christ – will have its own logic, inaccessible to the natural human mind.[18] But this is an extreme position. It is one thing to insist that the nature of the object under discussion be allowed to determine our approach to it and to control our knowledge and experience of it. It is quite another to suppose that, in the case of our knowledge of God, this means a private logic internal to the response of faith. Theology cannot be protected from debate and criticism in this way. However much we must indeed respect the mystery of God, what theologians say and what creeds affirm are expressed in human language and are the result of human rational reflection. As such, they can and ought to be discussed, as Wolfhart Pannenberg puts it, 'without reservation, in the context of critical rationality'.[19]

So, while philosophers of religion must indeed be careful to do justice to what theologians say about the context and the traditions out of which their doctrines come and about the special nature of their primary subject matter, God, theologians, for their part, must be prepared to listen to and argue with philosophical comment on, and critique of, what they say. A major purpose of this book is to encourage both sides to respect each other and learn from each other.

1.3 Historical and Linguistic Sensitivity

A little more may be said here about the need for historical and linguistic sensitivity on the part of philosophers attempting to examine and reflect on Christian doctrine. Of course, theologians themselves can manifest historical and linguistic insensitivity. Wedded to a particular school – say, that of Thomism (the systematic theology derived from St Thomas Aquinas) – they may attempt to teach a rigid, inflexible 'orthodoxy' that ignores the medieval background, the particular factors shaping St Thomas's thought, and the difficulties of appropriating a system of ideas and a technical vocabulary across eight centuries of development and change. Students of religion, too, can manifest comparable insensitivity. Attempting to apply the methods of phenomenology, by bracketing questions of truth and reality and comparing and classifying key elements in religious life and thought across the globe and throughout recorded history, they can fail to appreciate the historical embeddedness and particularity of the phenomena under scrutiny. Pannenberg has criticized both theologians and phenomenologists for just such historical insensitivity.[20] But remember that it was Pannenberg who insisted on Christian theology being discussed 'without reservation in the context of critical rationality'. Historical sensitivity must not be used as a device to block philosophical analysis.

After all, philosophers are well placed to combine history and analysis. Students of ancient philosophy, for example, are used to using all the methods of historical research in order to explore the distant worlds of Plato and Aristotle in their own setting, and at the same time to using all the methods of conceptual and metaphysical investigation in order to appropriate what is of lasting significance in the thought of the ancient philosophers for philosophy today – and that includes the philosophy of religion. In a similar manner, philosophers explore the later worlds of medieval thought for what is of enduring import in the synthesis of ancient philosophy and the Jewish, Christian and Islamic traditions. (We shall be considering the work of such scholars as Eleonore Stump and Norman Kretzmann in this connection in subsequent chapters.) The critical philosophies of the Enlightenment may also be scrutinized and assessed for what still illuminates contemporary understanding of the world and human life. Only if historical sensitivity is held to shut off past worlds from present appropriation completely, as seems to be the case in Denis Nineham's work, for example,[21] does there arise an insuperable gulf between history and philosophy. The work surveyed in this book will provide a clear refutation of this overly sceptical and pessimistic view.

Linguistic sensitivity is something that is also needed by theologians and philosophers if the subject matter of Christian doctrine is to be explored appropriately 'in the context of critical rationality'. Philosophers trained in the analytic tradition ought to be well placed to show such sensitivity. Mid-twentieth-century analytic philosophy was known as 'linguistic philosophy'; and attention to ordinary language and its nuances of meaning is the hallmark of this school. But such attention misses the mark if religious language, especially talk about God, is treated as operating at the same level as everyday talk about the natural and human worlds. Justice has to be done to the unique nature of the transcendent object of theological enquiry. Both Wiles and Swinburne, in the debate described in the previous section, refer to and accept the analogical nature of human speech about God. In the chapters that follow we shall again and again come back to the 'way of analogy', by which, it is claimed, just because human beings are made in the image of God, language that has its home in the human context may be used, albeit in a stretched and undoubtedly inadequate way, to speak about God and God's relation to the world.

1.4 Problems of Accessibility

Some further reflections on the question of the accessibility of Christian doctrine to philosophical scrutiny may be called for at this point. Can the view that these matters should be discussed 'without reservation in the context of critical rationality' (and that must mean by scholars and students of any faith or none) really be sustained? Did I not dismiss too readily Torrance's insistence that reflection on these matters can only be a matter of faith seeking understanding (*fides quaerens intellectum* – to quote St Anselm's phrase[22])?

No one will want to deny that religious doctrines come out of communities of faith. The doctrines expressed in the Christian creeds are the result of centuries of reflection and debate by bishops and teachers committed to the Christian faith and schooled in the Hebrew and Christian scriptures. These doctrines were and indeed are the fruit of faith seeking understanding. But it does not follow that they are wholly unintelligible to those outside the circle of faith. They are not expressed in a purely private language. They put forward a whole worldview that claims to make better sense of the universe and of life than any other worldview; and they can be pondered and examined critically by anyone interested in questions of meaning and truth. Up to a point, at least, they can be considered hypothetically and their inner rationale explored.

After all, if the rationality of Christian belief – and that of any religious belief – were a purely internal matter, presupposing faith and commitment to the religious tradition and community in question, there could be no such thing as the comparative study of religions, the phenomenology of religion or the philosophy of religion. There could be no dialogue or communication between religions, or between believers and unbelievers. Yet all these things take place and make some progress. Human beings share a common nature and live in one world; they have developed, over time, standards of critical rationality that are being applied increasingly to all spheres of life and interest. Alasdair MacIntyre, in his book *Whose Justice, Which Rationality?*,[23] has certainly brought out the diversity of traditions, each with its own developing standards of rationality, but he exaggerates their incommensurablity, and even he allows that some succeed better than others at coping, both theoretically and practically, with life together in the world of today. This is obviously the case where science and technology are concerned; it is increasingly the case with politics; and the necessity of 'a global ethic for economics and politics worldwide'[24] is being forced upon our attention by the irreversible establishment of a global market. The religions, of all spheres of human life, tend to resist such globalization; but the idea that they must for ever remain incommunicable 'umbrellas of meaning',[25] each for its own devotees, is belied by what is actually achieved in the study of religion, in the philosophy of religion and in the dialogue of religions.

No doubt it helps to have some sympathetic interest in the world of religion, including the Christian creeds, if one is to attempt, from outside, to explore the meaning and plausibility, say, of the Christian doctrine of Creation. Dogmatic atheism is not an ideal starting point for critical reflection on the claims of any religion. But, then, dogmatic Christian fundamentalism is no more ideal as a starting point for serious philosophical theology. What is required is a combination of open-mindedness, genuine sympathy, and intellectual rigour. Given these qualities, there can surely be fruitful dialogue across the borders of belief and unbelief and across the borders of the different religions. Christian theologians have nothing to fear, and everything to gain, from allowing their subject matter to be discussed and scrutinized in such an open context.

For all that, it has to be acknowledged that the vast majority of authors and works surveyed in this book do come from within the Christian communities and do constitute examples of faith seeking understanding. The Society of Christian Philosophers in the United States is precisely that: a body of *Christian* philosophers dedicated to the philosophical investigation of specifically Christian themes. But just as the Society was, from the start, open to any who considered themselves both a Christian and a philosopher ('no questions asked on either score'[26]), so both the Society and its journal have taken the step of 'inviting honest, open dialogue with those who do not share our Christian commitment'[27]. The work under scrutiny in the chapters that follow, though written for the most part by Christian philosophers exploring the logic and the scope of their own traditions, is unquestionably offered for critical reflection by all. It is to be discussed, that is, to quote Pannenberg yet again, 'without reservation in the context of critical rationality'.

1.5 The Analytic Tradition

The question may well arise why attention is restricted, in this book, almost entirely to the analytic tradition of Anglo-American philosophy and the contribution it has made, and is making, to the critical study of Christian doctrine. In part this reflects my own interests and experience. I regard the Anglo-American analytic tradition as by far and away the most important strand in contemporary philosophy of religion. I admire it for its clarity and logical acumen and for the help it gives to anyone interested in pursuing, in depth but without obfuscation, the search for meaning and truth in the world of religion. It does not subordinate religion to philosophy, as do the traditions stemming from Kant, Hegel or Whitehead. The views of these philosophers on religion and on Christian theology are wide-ranging and profound, and time is well spent studying them. As mentioned at the beginning of this chapter, such study is part of the staple diet of the philosophy of religion. But the philosophical theologian, certainly if he or she is operating from within the Christian tradition, is likely to spend more time arguing with them than using them for clarification and progress. A good example of such argument is Alvin Plantinga's criticism of Kant in his *Warranted Christian Belief*[28]. An earlier example was Austin Farrer's criticism of Whitehead in his *Faith and Speculation*.[29]

Nor does the analytic tradition restrict its attention to the sphere of authentic human – or Christian – existence, as Kierkegaard and Bultmann did. Existentialism too is well worth study by Christian philosophers and theologians, as the work of John Macquarrie has shown.[30] But concentration on the human individual and on human authenticity fails to satisfy for long. Existentialism's inability to give an account of nature and history or even of human community, to say nothing of its obfuscatory style, at least in its twentieth-century philosophical forms (e.g. Heidegger and Sartre), renders it less than ideal as a vehicle for philosophical theology.

The continental tradition has itself moved on, through structuralism, into post-structuralism and postmodernism, schools whose bearing on philosophy of religion has been found curiously attractive to some, but of which I remain deeply suspicious. For one thing, such writing suffers from an even greater degree of wilful obscurity than was the case with Heidegger. This is bound to offend anyone schooled to think and to write clearly and precisely on important topics. For another, the post-structuralists and deconstructionists, as they are sometimes called, betray a tendency to impose wildly implausible generalizations on the history of ideas that make serious engagement with particular problems and issues raised by religion and theology very difficult to pursue. Let me cite a few examples. The first goes back to Heidegger, who proclaimed the death of metaphysics.[31] Metaphysics is the study of the ultimate nature of things, but, according to Heidegger, the whole western tradition of metaphysical thinking, from Plato to the twentieth century, is held to have run into the sand. Philosophy requires an entirely new start. Another example is the view of Michel Foucault that western thought invariably betrays a hidden agenda, the rationalization of interest and power.[32] Such generalizations become a kind of device for inhibiting serious reflection on the metaphysical implications of theism and of Christian doctrine, thus preventing us from learning anything from the philosophers and traditions so easily dismissed.

Or consider the question of postmodernism itself. What does this term really mean? To speak of postmodernism, we have to give the term 'modernity' a restricted range of meaning. Instead of using it in its natural sense of the relatively recent past, say, since the scientific revolution up to the present day, historians of ideas take 'modernity' to mean the eighteenth-century Enlightenment and its impact. This allows them to suggest that the Enlightenment project has run its course, broken down, even collapsed, leaving us in the condition known as postmodernism. What was 'the Enlightenment project'? What is it that is supposed to have broken down? Allegedly, it was a question of the human race having reached maturity and put its confidence in unaided human reason, and having achieved autonomy in all the spheres of life, ethics and religion included. What we are supposed to be witnessing in the twentieth, and now the twenty-first, century is the collapse of this universal idea, and the recognition of many different 'rationalities', incommensurable worldviews, different forms of life, different moralities, with no way of arbitrating between them. I have already mentioned Alasdair MacIntyre's version of this thesis. MacIntyre, unlike the continentals, writes lucidly and almost persuasively, as he paints a dark picture of the loss of a common framework within which moral disputes can be settled. But, as I say, he exaggerates and overgeneralizes, and fails to do justice to elements in the eighteenth-century Enlightenment, and in nineteenth-century liberalism, from which we can still learn.

I remain suspicious of the 'masters of suspicion' and their followers, who see a hidden, often political, agenda behind the clear, perspicuous, professional work of the analytic philosophers. All the latter are doing, I would claim, is critically examining (ideally in cooperation, not conflict, with the theologians) the central themes of Christian belief for their meaning, grounds and truth. And I hope that the quantity and quality of the work surveyed in this book will demonstrate the wisdom and benefit of staying with this main strand in philosophy of religion and philosophical theology today.

The vice of implausible and unjustified historical generalization has infected some theologians too, in both the continental and the Anglo-American traditions. It is sometimes urged[33] that modern atheism is a reaction not to the God of the classical Christian tradition, but to a post-eighteenth-century philosophical idol that has nothing to do with the true and living God. They even hijack the term 'theism' to refer to this construct or projection, and then suppose that they have warded off the atheistic critique. I hold that to be no way at all of arguing with atheism. Atheism means the rejection of any belief in God, ancient, medieval or modern.

Arguing with atheism is not the subject of this book, however. But the same point holds concerning the alleged irrelevance of 'the god of the philosophers' to which reference was made earlier on. In my view, there is no such thing as the god of the philosophers. Philosophers of religion in the analytic tradition are doing no more than singling out, for close scrutiny and analysis, aspects of, and implications of, the concept of God to be found in the great theistic traditions, some of these being common to all those traditions, others – the ones of special concern to us here – being peculiar to the Christian religion, shaped as it has been by the doctrines of the Incarnation and the Trinity.

One final word in defence of the analytic tradition – this time addressed to the modern theologians – is perhaps required, if further suspicions are to be allayed. I mentioned at the beginning of this chapter the legacy of logical positivism's aggressive rejection of all theology as meaningless. Theology was put on the defensive. Theologians retreated into their own shells, and ceased to think of philosophers as allies. This was quite understandable at the time; but it is a great mistake to tar the analytic tradition with the same brush as logical positivism. Sometimes theologians give the impression that Anglo-American analytic philosophy is simply an extension of logical positivism. Nothing could be further from the truth. Of course there are still many philosophers in this tradition who remain hostile to theology and metaphysics. One of the tasks of the philosophy of religion remains that of arguing with such folk. But there are also many philosophers, schooled in the techniques of philosophical logic and analysis, who, as we shall see, are now applying those techniques, in a thoroughly constructive fashion, to the clarification, articulation and defence of mainstream Christian doctrine. And if there are points at which they find themselves driven to challenge certain long-standing elements in classical theism, for example, over God's absolute timelessness, this is usually done in the interests again of constructive and helpful revision. So modern theologians have nothing to fear from these philosophers. Of course, there will be disagreements between philosophers and theologians, just as there are between different theologians and between different philosophers. We shall see many examples of such disagreements in the course of this book. But the scope for fruitful dialogue and mutual enrichment between philosophers and theologians is very great. No one should be afraid of reflection on Christian doctrine 'in the context of critical rationality'.

1.6   Faith and Reason

In order to illustrate the merits of such interaction, let us consider the eirenic example of Basil Mitchell, the philosopher of religion whose joint seminar in Oxford with Maurice Wiles on the relationship between philosophy and theology has already been mentioned. Mitchell contributed an essay on 'Philosophy and Theology' to the Festschrift for Frederick Copleston,[34] in which he argued that, whether he likes it or not, a theologian is bound to be, for much of the time, a philosopher. Granted that he requires his own specialist skills for the study of the Bible and the Christian tradition, nevertheless the task of interpreting that tradition for today, in respect of its meaning and import for contemporary life, is essentially a philosophical task, calling 'for familiarity with moral philosophy and the philosophy of mind' and, we may add, philosophical logic. For questions of coherence are at stake, as we shall repeatedly see in the present book.

Mitchell is equally clear that the theologically trained philosopher is not simply applying to the theological agenda philosophical methods that have worked well in other areas. The special problems of analogical discourse in talk of God have to be reckoned with. But the fact that the theologians use human language in ways that need careful scrutiny if they are to be understood in today's world, and the fact that religious language has meta-physical implications that have to be explicated and defended, show that the theologian is already something of a linguistic philosopher and something of a metaphysician. Philosophy can be overly critical, as with the logical positivists, and it can be overly imperialistic, as with the Hegelians, the Heideggerians and the Whiteheadians. But it can also help to make the issues clear and aid the process of resolving them.

In much of what follows we shall bear the work of Basil Mitchell very much in mind. Mitchell's own book, *Faith and Criticism*[35] contains an excellent defence of the interdependence of faith and criticism. 'Without faith in an established tradition', he writes, 'criticism has nothing to fasten on; without criticism the tradition ceases in the end to have any purchase on reality.'[36] This could be read in a purely 'internalist' way as a defence of the use of critical methods within a faith stance, seeking its own inner rationality. But that Mitchell is in fact appealing to standards of critical rationality intelligible to any careful enquirer is quite clear from his account of the discussion that he once had with a Hindu philosopher, who at one point remarked, 'I am surprised to hear you say that. I should have thought that from your point of view, you would have said something more like this . . . ' He then went on, so Mitchell tells us, to develop his, Mitchell's, position in directions that Mitchell had not thought of, but acknowledged to be right.

It is in this respect that Mitchell's approach is to be preferred to that of Diogenes Allen in his book, *Philosophy for Understanding Theology*.[37] In many ways, this is an extremely useful book. Allen shows how elements in all the schools of philosophy, from Plato to the present day, can be, and have been, used in order to appreciate more deeply the meaning of virtually every major Christian doctrine. But, for Allen, this is entirely a matter of faith seeking understanding. This is not just a question of the theological agenda controlling the selection and use of philosophical concepts. *Faith* is the precondition of the whole enterprise. One learns from philosophy, but only from a standpoint already adopted within the Christian religion and its theology. Much insight can certainly be achieved this way, as we shall see in the course of the present book. And Allen's very brief treatment of analytic philosophy in his concluding chapter contains some fascinating hints on the way in which the application to theology of the skills of linguistic philosophy can enable a religious object 'to emerge and to exhibit itself, so to speak'.[38] But Allen, apparently, does not agree with Mitchell's conviction that such insights can be shared across the borders of the different religions and across the borders of belief and unbelief.

1.7 Philosophers and Theologians

Most of the work considered in this book is by philosophers rather than by theologians. In the course of an interesting programmatic essay on the condition and prospects of Christian philosophy at the end of the twentieth century, Alvin Plantinga included a short section on philosophical theology, which he defined as 'a matter of thinking about the central doctrines of the Christian faith from a philosophical perspective; it is a matter of employing the resources of philosophy to deepen our grasp and understanding of them'. He drew attention to the excellent work that had been done in this area in recent years, but remarked that, unlike in the Middle Ages, theologians today 'don't seem to be doing the work in question'. 'I therefore hope I will not be accused of interdisciplinary chauvinism', he continued, 'if I point out that the best work in philosophical theology – in the English speaking world and over the last quarter of a century – has been done not by theologians but by philosophers.'[39]

Curiously, this is not so true of the German-speaking world in the period in question. One of the most encouraging aspects of post-Barthian theology in Germany has been the readiness of scholars such as Wolfhart Pannenberg,[40] Ingolf Dalferth[41] and Christoph Schwöbel[42] to show an interest in and to use Anglo-American philosophical analysis as well as their own continental resources. It is true that Pannenberg's work on the metaphysics of time, not least his retention of simultaneity in his attempt to articulate a more dynamic concept of eternity,[43] is open to serious philosophical criticism. But the possibilities of dialogue and debate and mutual illumination between theologians and philosophers are nevertheless evident from the work of these scholars. And from the English-speaking world, while Austin Farrer's paradigmatic contribution dates from the 1960s, the more recent work of the American Lutheran systematic theologian, Robert Jenson,[44] is also, in his case perhaps surprisingly, sympathetic to the philosophers. There is no hostility to philosophy on Jenson's part. He recognizes that theology entails metaphysics. It resists dependence on philosophy, of course, especially on a particular philosophical school. Rather, in conversation with philosophy, theology seeks the truth and coherence of the gospel. Two examples of the fruitfulness of this conversation may be given: Jenson's welcome stress on temporal infinity in talk of God (his criticism of Pannenberg is highly pertinent at this point[45]), and his wise retention, against both John of Damascus and Jean-Luc Marion, of suitably qualified talk of *being* where God is concerned.[46] However, this does not preserve Jenson from a certain lack of philosophical perception at other points. In a footnote in his second volume,[47] he accuses the present author of denying, in the course of treatment of the problem of evil, that God is both omniscient and omnipotent. Nothing could be further from the truth. The point – and this a point brought out by many contemporary philosophers of religion – is that the concepts of omniscience and omnipotence have to be reinterpreted in terms of what it is logically possible to know and of what is compossible (i.e. jointly possible) given the purposes of creation. Much more will be said about these matters in what follows.

To return to Alvin Plantinga: Plantinga himself has concentrated more on negative apologetics and on the epistemology of Christian belief than on the philosophical analysis of Christian doctrine,[48] although his work on the concept of God[49] is important and will be referred to from time to time here. But his advice to Christian philosophers,[50] to devote their attention and their energies to a specifically Christian agenda, has certainly borne fruit in much of the work I shall be surveying. A good example of this, and one that will provide much material for reflection in subsequent chapters, is the volume edited by R. J. Feenstra and Cornelius Plantinga Jr., *Trinity, Incarnation and Atonement*.[51] It is interesting to note that this volume was the fruit of cooperative work by philosophers trained in theology and theologians very much aware of contemporary Anglo-American philosophy. It was issued, the editors tell us in their introduction, 'in the hope that it will encourage cross-fertilization of ideas between analytic philosophers and theologians by displaying some of the fruit such efforts can yield'.[52] A similar hope informs the present book. Admittedly the work surveyed here comes more, as I say, from the philosophical than from the theological side. The theologians are respectfully invited to take note and to reciprocate.

CHAPTER TWO

Revelation

Before we embark on a survey of the contributions made by contemporary analytic philosophy to the study of the central doctrines of the Christian creeds, I have thought it wise to include a chapter on revelation. This is partly because the creeds themselves both presuppose and summarize a theology of revelation. And it is partly because there has been so much interesting work, in recent philosophy of religion, on the concept of revelation and on the logic of appeals to revelation.

2.1   Natural and Revealed Theology

One recent development, highly pertinent to the theme of this whole book, is the challenge that has been made to the traditional distinction between natural theology and revealed theology. This distinction, clearly exemplified by the approach of St Thomas Aquinas,[1] is the distinction between what can be known or rendered plausible by the use of human reason at any place and at any time, simply through reflection on the universally available data of our experience of the world, and what can be known on the basis of God's special acts of revelation at particular times and places, whether through some particular deeds done, or through some particular words spoken or written, or whatever. I say God's special acts of revelation, because it is quite in order to correlate natural theology with general revelation, and to suppose that there is a sense in which God reveals himself through just those universal data of experience available to unaided human reason everywhere.

Admittedly, Alvin Plantinga makes a strong case for taking general revelation, exemplified by the Psalmist's assertion that 'the heavens declare the glory of God',[2] to be a matter of immediate awareness rather than rational inference;[3] but the fact remains that such universally available data can be made the starting point for natural theology of the traditional kind all the same.

The distinction between natural and revealed theology, then, is the distinction between reflection on what is generally revealed and reflection on what is specially revealed. Of course, in using the shorthand phrase 'revealed theology', we do not mean that such *theology* is itself revealed. That would be a very extravagant claim. This shorthand phrase is used for human reflection, in the first place by Church theologians, on what has allegedly been specially revealed at particular times and in particular places in the course of history.

The distinction between what is held to be universally available and what is held to have been communicated through particular strands or individuals in history must surely be sustained. That distinction is undeniable. And, I suppose, it is not surprising that philosophers have tended in the past to disparage religious appeals to special revelation precisely because the alleged data are not universally available to human reason everywhere. For human reason is quite rightly held to be the sole proper tool for doing philosophy.[4] But it does not take much reflection to make one realize that this restriction is itself philosophically untenable. For reason can surely be put to work on any data, whether universally available or not. After all, the contemporary natural scientist is working on data that have only recently become available. And the alleged data of special divine revelation – say, the events to which the Christian scriptures bear witness – have, for a much longer time, been available for philosophical as well as theological reflection. And it is interesting to note that a number of philosophers of religion and theologians have recently been arguing that, if revelation claims, as well as 'the starry heavens above',[5] are equally available for rational scrutiny, then the distinction between natural and revealed theology, at least to that extent, breaks down.

An earlier proponent of this view was Herbert Farmer, who in his Gifford Lectures, *Revelation and Religion*,[6] suggested that a specifically Christian worldview, including both a theology of religion worldwide and a theology of incarnation and reconciliation, could be offered as an all-embracing hypothesis to be explored for its rationality and comprehensiveness and tested for its ability to make sense of things. It is no longer a matter simply of accepting revelation on authority. In this sense, revelation claims are being brought within the scope of natural theology.

I endorsed this approach in *The Problems of Theology*:

> [R]eason and revelation cannot be treated as different sources of knowledge. On the contrary revelation claims, despite being channelled through particular

historical traditions, are part of the data upon which reason has to operate. The fact that the philosopher pays less attention to the religious data than does the theologian is just unfortunate. It can no longer be a matter of principle.[7]

That book was published in 1980. Happily, as the present book will show, the last two decades of the twentieth century largely remedied the 'unfortunate' fact referred to. Philosophers are indeed paying attention now to specific revelation claims.

Further endorsement for the view that 'there is, ultimately, no important difference between natural and revealed theology after all' comes from the biblical theologian James Barr, in his Gifford Lectures, *Biblical Faith and Natural Theology*.[8] And Wolfhart Pannenberg's theology of revelation through history[9] – that is, of universal history, including the history of religions, culminating in the story of Jesus Christ and its effects – constitutes another example of the way in which a revelation-based worldview can be made available for discussion 'without reservation in the context of critical rationality'.

Of course, this assimilation of revealed theology to natural theology is in respect of its openness to rational scrutiny by anyone, not in respect of its particularity. The distinction between general data and special data remains. But it should be clear from this discussion that the philosopher's difficulties are, or should be, much more with appeals to authority and attempts to bypass reason than with any notion of special revelation. Particularity as such is no scandal. Philosophers have no right to dictate to God how and where he should act or speak. But they do have the right to examine the logic and the rationale of any such purported special acts of revelation. As Bishop Butler observed; 'reason . . . is, indeed the only faculty we have wherewith to judge concerning anything, even revelation itself'.[10]

I should stress at the end of this section on natural and revealed theology that the argument advanced here is controversial, even amongst philosophical theologians. We shall see plenty of examples in what follows of philosophers prepared to defend the rationality of appeals to authority. Nothing said here should blind us to the possibility of taking seriously the role of testimony in a rationally defensible worldview.

2.2 Does Christianity Need a Revelation?

This may seem an odd question to ask, given the fact that, apart from its first article on God the Creator, the Christian creed is entirely concerned with what has allegedly been revealed through God's special acts, namely the

Incarnation of his Son and the sending of his Spirit. But the question, 'Does Christianity need a revelation?' has been raised, notably in the exchange mentioned in chapter 1 between Maurice Wiles and Basil Mitchell.[11] Mitchell begins his contribution by noting the centrality of special revelation in Christianity and asks why theologians such as Wiles distrust it. He suggests three reasons for this: first, the conviction that the idea of divine intervention is incompatible with 'the modern worldview'; secondly, the fact that biblical criticism has inclined scholars towards naturalistic explanations of the contents of the Bible; and, thirdly, the crudity of some traditional views of inspiration.

These objections are not, on Mitchell's view, decisive. To hold that science can explain everything is not a scientific, but a metaphysical claim, open to philosophical challenge. Similarly, naturalistic explanations fail to do justice to key elements in the biblical tradition, such as God's active communication of his purposes to human beings. And, thirdly, crude views of inspiration can readily be replaced by less crude and more plausible ones, such as the teacher–pupil analogy, to be explored below.

The suggestion of theologians such as Gordon Kaufman and Maurice Wiles that God's creative act is universal, and that all particularity lies on the side of human response, fails to do justice, so Mitchell claims, to the notion of divine agency and communication. The process described by these theologians:

> is analogous *not* to the situation in which I come to know your character and intentions through what you tell me, but to the situation in which I conjecture your character and intentions from your non-verbal behaviour alone. And this is precisely *not* a situation in which it is appropriate to talk of your communicating with me.[12]

Wiles begins his response by noting widespread agreement on the need to reinterpret what was believed in the past. The idea of revelation as 'God's communication to men of truths they would not have discovered for themselves' demands such reinterpretation precisely for the reasons Mitchell summarizes; direct intervention is implausible in the light of science and criticism. And the teacher–pupil analogy is not the only way to capture the notion of inspiration. The Bible may well inspire discernment of religious truth, but as an integral part of the history of religions rather than as direct communication from God. This does not, *pace* Mitchell, require acceptance of the biblical writers' own understanding of themselves as special recipients of God's Word. The upshot of Wiles's reinterpretation, then, is that Christianity does not need a (special) revelation in order to convey divine truth.

Mitchell returns to the fray in his 1993 contribution to the *Festschrift* for Wiles.[13] His main argument remains that personal communication, in particular the making of promises and the pronouncement of forgiveness, requires particular words or deeds. God's revelation cannot be construed simply in terms of human discernment, as Wiles suggests. In this connection Mitchell develops the model of a teacher–pupil dialogue, allowing for active appropriation of the part of the pupil, but insisting on at least some novel input from the teacher. He grants that God's self-communication can be thought of too anthropomorphically. 'God does not literally speak.'[14] But, however God's personal communications are conveyed, the notion of divine initiative, of being actually addressed by God, is essential, so Mitchell claims, to any truly personal theism.

2.3   Revelation as Divine Discourse

Analytic philosophers who have contributed to the debate on divine reve-lation in recent decades would, nearly all of them, agree with Mitchell rather than with Wiles. The main disagreement among the philosophers has not been over whether Christianity needs a revelation, but rather over the primary *locus* of special revelation, whether this is best thought of in terms of verbal communication, or in terms of manifestation (either through histor-ical acts and events or through developing traditions), or through religious experience. I consider first those philosophers of religion who have stressed verbal communication and, in particular, the work of four scholars: George Mavrodes, Nicholas Wolterstorff, Alvin Plantinga and William J. Abraham.

In his little book, *Revelation in Religious Belief*,[15] Mavrodes distinguishes three models of divine revelation: the causation model, the manifestation model and the communication model. On the first model, the causation model, God is thought of as simply bringing about, by direct fiat, a desired effect, such as belief or faith. On the second model, the manifestation model, God is thought of as making himself known through some particular feeling, perception or non-verbal experience, such as those cited and classified in William James's seminal book, *The Varieties of Religious Experi-ence*.[16] On the third model, the communication model, God is thought of as conveying his call or his will in ways much more akin to speech. This is the model given special prominence by Mavrodes. Hence my citing him here under the heading of 'Revelation as Divine Discourse.'

Mavrodes, like Mitchell, does not suppose that God literally and directly 'speaks' to human beings (although he does note reports of 'auditions' in the Bible and in the lives of the saints). Normally, God's 'word' is held to be mediated by some human word, say the word of scripture or the word of preaching, or indeed by some striking human life or concatenation of events. But even in these latter cases, the believer will probably hold that God has *spoken* to him or her through the life or the events in question. Mavrodes presses the question of what distinguishes a human word or event through which God speaks from a word or event with no such divine instrumental import. He suggests a twofold answer: on the one hand, God himself is held to have been especially active in and through the revealing word or event. On the other hand, the believer understands himself or herself to have been actually addressed by God in some challenging or demanding way by the scripture reading, preached word or event in question. Since this last experiential claim is a necessary condition for acceptance of the claim that God has in fact spoken, such claims are not open to independent proof. Indeed, it is an implication of Mavrodes's analysis that revelation only occurs where it is in fact acknowledged by its recipient. We shall see reason to question this view, at least up to a point, in what follows.

The philosopher who has done most to substantiate the verbal communication model is Nicholas Wolterstorff, whose book *Divine Discourse* is given the sub-title 'Philosophical reflections on the claim that God speaks'.[17] But it should be noted straight away that Wolterstorff himself makes a sharp distinction between divine speech and divine revelation.[18] He writes interestingly about revelation, differentiating 'assertoric' revelation (where new information is asserted) from 'non-assertoric' revelation (where something new is manifested by some act or event); but he insists that divine speech is more a matter of promises and commands (what J. L. Austin would call 'illocutionary acts'[19] – that is, speech-acts through which something is actually done) than a matter of asserting things. Promises and commands, says Wolterstorff, are not revelations. The point does has some force, and certainly puts a question mark against Mitchell's reference to promising and forgiving as key factors requiring us to retain the idea of special revelation. But Wolterstorff surely exaggerates in concentrating his attention on such illocutionary acts. There are plenty of examples of divine speech in the Bible that do take the assertoric form: 'I am the Lord thy God who brought thee out of the land of Egypt' (Deuteronomy 5: 6); 'This is my beloved Son, on whom my favour rests' (Matthew 3: 17). And, in the Christian tradition, God is held to speak to men and women, not only in the modes of promise and command, but also in bringing home to them the great truths of the Gospel. Moreover, even where promising and commanding are concerned – and here we would be coming to Mitchell's defence – it could still be claimed that much is revealed about God through the promises he makes and the commands he gives. Admittedly Wolterstorff would want to classify these latter as cases of non–assertoric revelation. These truths are manifested through the illocutionary acts of promising and commanding. But, given the fact that these are not the only types of divine speech, we may not unreasonably consider Wolterstorff's remarks under the rubric of the verbal communication model of divine revelation.

Wolterstorff's book is the most sustained philosophical articulation and defence of the view that God speaks to us through the Bible. As is already becoming clear, the key issue for all the philosophers under scrutiny here is the question of the medium through which revelation occurs, or, in Wolterstorff's case, the medium through which God speaks. No more than Mitchell or Mavrodes does Wolterstorff suppose that God literally speaks. Nor does he suppose that God dictates the Bible. He is no fundamentalist. But the human words of the Bible do, he thinks, become the media of divine discourse to men and women down the ages and today. But it is interesting to note his lack of sympathy for Karl Barth's way of treating the Bible (and Christian preaching) as derivative forms of the Word of God. Barth, as is well known, distinguishes three forms of the Word of God.[20] The first, the primary *locus* of divine revelation and address, is Jesus Christ himself, the incarnate Word. The second is the word of scripture, which Barth takes to be the human witness to the primary revelation. The third is the word of preaching, as the preacher interprets scripture in such a way as to bring home to people today the import of the primary revelation. Barth insists that scripture and preaching are not in themselves revelation. Only as God actually brings home to people the truths of the Gospel, through the reading of scripture, and through hearing the sermon, do the latter become God's Word to men and women here and now. Wolterstorff's comment is that, despite all his talk of God's Word, Barth does not in fact suppose that God *speaks* to us through scripture and preaching. Rather, God brings it about that we appreciate the meaning of the primary revelation and acknowledge it for ourselves. In other words, Wolterstorff seems to be suggesting that Barth's work belongs to the causation model of divine revelation rather than the verbal communication model.

Once again, I find Wolterstorff's position a somewhat exaggerated one. Granted that Barth's 'actualism' means that scripture and preaching, in themselves, are merely human words and only become God's Word as God acts through them here and now. But it surely forces the distinction between speech and action to suggest that such action cannot be thought of as God's speech, God's address to people here and now. Again, the fact that great emphasis is placed on response, on acknowledgement of God's action through scripture and the preaching, does not prevent one from regarding a word heard and appropriated as in itself divine address, whether it takes the form of assertion, claim, promise or command.

In fact, Wolterstorff's own detailed analysis of mediated divine speech is very close to Barth's, despite his questioning Barth's status as the great theologian of the Word of God. He too stresses divine agency in and through the words of scripture and their reception. He has an interesting section on 'double agency discourse', showing how someone with authority can act through a representative or a deputy, and suggesting that God might be thought of as 'appropriating' the words of the prophet or apostle, or indeed the Psalmist, in order to speak to men and women today. Wolterstorff does not mention the name of the philosophical theologian most closely associated with the idea of 'double agency', Austin Farrer,[21] but clearly this idea is crucial for the understanding of mediated divine speech. We shall be returning to Farrer's work on 'double agency' in the final chapter of this book. Suffice it to say here that the problem with all the human parables of double agency offered by Wolterstorff and others in order to throw light on this key idea is that they, inevitably, tend to represent the divine agent acting through secondary agents as one agent among others operating at the same level. The great merit of Farrer's work was that he tried to do justice to the difference of level between divine action and human action, divine speech and human speech. It is because of the difference of level that there does not have to be any forcing or faking of the human story for it to become the vehicle of the divine address. But this point is not given sufficient prominence by Wolterstorff, or indeed, as we shall see, by many other philosophers working on theological topics today.

Be that as it may, Wolterstorff's analysis and defence of the way in which the discourse of the human authors of the Bible is appropriated by, and becomes the vehicle of, divine address has much to recommend it. We cannot go into all the details here, but some of his main points may be summarized. Wolterstorff brings out the way in which the Christian Church's regard for the Bible as God's Word requires serious consideration of the Bible as a whole, and commitment to principles of interpretation which enable the reader to appreciate the main point of a passage or text, to recognize, at times, its figurative nature and, above all, to let the Church's formed conviction of God's nature and purposes control specific interpretations. He also draws attention to the way in which more recent knowledge, say, scientific knowledge about the cosmos, and also changed and novel situations, are bound to affect the meaning found in particular biblical texts.

In Wolterstorff's hands, these remain principles by which the Christian continues to read the Bible as divine discourse. In other hands, as we shall see, traditions of interpretation themselves become the *locus* of divine address and revelation.

Remaining for the moment with revelation as divine discourse, I turn briefly to the treatment of revelation by Alvin Plantinga in his major study of religious epistemology, *Warranted Christian Belief*. In a footnote on p. 251, Plantinga explicitly endorses Wolterstorff's account of the way in which the Bible constitutes divine speech and divine communication (Plantinga, too, it seems, makes light of Wolterstorff's distinction between discourse and revelation). But he does so in the context of an epistemology of faith, taken over from Calvin, whereby it is the 'inward instigation of the Holy Spirit' which enables Christians to see the truth of what scripture says. When humans are functioning properly in accordance with God's design plan, this is how the great truths of the Gospel are revealed. Whether or not the Bible speaks to us, therefore, depends on whether or not we are receptive to this internal activity of God's Spirit. Wolterstorff himself stresses the importance of divine agency, of course, but Plantinga's more explicit emphasis raises the question whether the communication model preferred by Mavrodes can really be kept apart from the causation model. For are not all three philosophers committed to the view that faith in the truths of the Gospel is brought about by divine fiat? And despite what is said about the media or vehicles of divine discourse, does this not involve an over-literal, over-anthropomorphic view of divine agency as one cause among others? This may be deemed one of the principal difficulties with the communication model, as so far considered.

A more sensitive defence of both inspiration and revelation is to be found in the work of William J. Abraham. In the second of his two books on these topics,[22] Abraham certainly concentrates on divine revelation through God's acts in history. We shall consider this aspect in a later section. But Abraham argues strongly against the view that talk of divine acts can replace talk of divine speech in theologies of revelation. Without the idea of God's Word, spoken through prophets and apostles, Christians, he claims, would be reduced to guessing God's intentions from experiences, events and alleged acts of God. To reject the notion of divine speech (however mediated) is to 'whittle away the analogy on which the concept of divine revelation is built',[23] and to abandon revelation in the fully personal sense. Abraham is at pains to rescue the concept of propositional revelation from the fundamentalists and, like Wolterstorff, to deploy the performative theory of speech-acts in talk of divine revelation. Like Mitchell, but unlike Wolterstorff, Abraham includes God's speech-acts of forgiving, commanding and promising within the notion of special revelation.

This section will, among other things, have illustrated the way in which both theologians and philosophers have learned to be sensitive to issues of biblical interpretation ('hermeneutics', as this is called). As we saw in chapter 1, liberal theologians have been inclined to accuse philosophers of an over-literal conception of the Bible as the Word of God. But the philosophers considered in this section are perfectly well aware that God does not literally speak, or dictate the Bible. And, certainly, their analyses of the concept of divine discourse do not depend on any such literalism. The fact is that philosophers and theologians alike, for the most part, recognize scriptural hermeneutics to require serious consideration of the Bible as a whole, not the citation of isolated texts. This will become increasingly clear as we turn to other ways of thinking of special revelation and to further examples of philosophical theologians at work.

2.4   Revealed Truth

Just as committed to propositional revelation as the authors discussed in the previous section, but less concerned with divine discourse as such, is Richard Swinburne in his *Revelation*,[24] the second of four books by this author on central Christian doctrines, a tetralogy that may be seen as a major example of the way in which analytic philosophy of religion has turned its attention, in recent decades, to the problems of theology.[25] Swinburne's work deserves a section to itself precisely because of its concentration on what has allegedly been revealed rather than on God's alleged speech-acts through prophets and apostles. Certainly, for Swinburne, special revelation takes place through God's acts of Incarnation and Atonement, and through the verbal witness recorded in the scriptures. And of course the recorded words of Jesus, God incarnate, have a central role in this. But Swinburne's emphasis lies on the truths thereby revealed, truths expressed in the scriptures and creeds of the Church. This emphasis on objective truth means that, in a sense, revelation can, for Swinburne, be regarded and discussed apart from, and prior to, its acceptance by the believer. No longer is achieved communication internal to the very concept of divine revelation.

Swinburne's account of revelation may be summarized as follows: the prior probability that the God of developed theism would reveal truths of basic importance to human life is high. That such revelation reached its climax in the words and deeds of Jesus is authenticated first by his resurrection, and secondly by the Church's interpretation of the essence of that revelation. This came to be expressed in the Church's creeds, and in particular in the doctrines of the Trinity, the Incarnation and Atonement, doctrines whose rationale, in terms of their coherence, importance and power, is explored and defended by Swinburne in the first and third

books of his tetralogy, to be discussed in subsequent chapters here. Swinburne also argues, along similar lines to Wolterstorff, that the Church's Bible
may be regarded as the inspired witness to the events and words, whose
essential import is summed up in the Church's creeds. We note that
Swinburne's theory of meaning, to which he devotes the first part of his
book, allows him to distinguish figurative elements in the biblical witness
from the basic truths which they convey, and to extract the essential
revelation from its time-conditioned and less permanent forms of expression. So again there is no fundamentalism here.

There is some ambiguity in Swinburne's treatment of the *locus* of revelation, that is, the primary vehicle or medium of revelation. Given his
concern with propositional revelation, it is not surprising to find him
characterizing as 'the original revelation' the divine *teaching*, which culminated in the teaching of Jesus Christ. But we also find him speaking of
God's *dealings* with the Israelites and other nations, culminating in the
Incarnation. If that were the primary emphasis, we should have to place
Swinburne's work in the next section of this chapter, where we consider
revelation as God's acts in history. But we also find Swinburne speaking of
the creeds as expressing the essence of revelation and of Holy Scripture as its
primary vehicle. And, in the light of much sophisticated treatment of
inspiration, interpretation and development, Swinburne is even prepared
to conclude his book with the words: 'the revelation spoken by and the
deeds acted by Christ will be interpreted by human witnesses ... under the
guidance of the Spirit of God. The revelation goes on; it is their witness and
yet their witness to an original source which forms the revelation.'[26] If that
were the primary emphasis, we should have to place Swinburne in an even
later section of this chapter, where we consider revelation as tradition and
interpretation.

We have yet to explore, as I say, Swinburne's account of the rationale of
the *content* of revelation, the revealed truths expressed in the central doctrines of the creeds. But we should note that he does not restrict his apologetic to the rational defence of those doctrines. Swinburne, like Plantinga,
also defends the rationality of appeals to authority. But whereas Plantinga
puts the main emphasis on inspiration, the internal instigation of the Holy
Spirit, Swinburne puts the main emphasis here on external guarantees, in
particular, the Resurrection.

One other feature of Swinburne's account deserves comment. The issue
of other, indeed rival, revelation claims in other religious traditions than
the Judaeo-Christian one, is hardly faced in Swinburne's book. This is the
gravamen of Peter Byrne's long review article on Swinburne's book in the
journal *Religious Studies*.[27] Later in this chapter we shall consider two other

philosophical theologians, Keith Ward and John Hick, who explicitly address this aspect of the problem.

2.5   Revelation as God's Acts in History

One of the main alternatives to the idea of revelation as divine discourse is the view, espoused by many twentieth-century theologians,[28] that the *locus* of God's special revelation is the series of events in history which culminated in Christ's life, death and resurrection. In its strongest form, this is to claim that God reveals himself most specially to humankind through coming amongst us by incarnation, and acting out the divine love and forgiveness in person. Clearly this view would fall within Mavrodes's category of manifestation, though Abraham notes the surprising fact that there is no mention of the Incarnation in Mavrodes's book. Abraham himself, while stressing the importance of divine speech, as we have seen, gives the priority to God's acts in history and especially to the Incarnation. And, like Swinburne, he sees the Resurrection as God's guarantee that Christ's life and death, and Christ's teaching, do indeed have the exalted status claimed for them in the Christian tradition and its creeds.[29]

The most notable contemporary exponent of such a view is not a philosopher, but a theologian, the German systematician Wolfhart Pannenberg, who, as mentioned earlier, is one of the post-Barthian German theologians who pay serious attention to analytical philosophy as well as to the continental school stemming from Hegel. In his early, co-authored, book, *Revelation as History*,[30] Pannenberg argued that once positivism is rejected, attention to universal history requires us to consider the significance of the history of religions and, within the history of religions, the significance of Israel's history, including the eschatological horizon to her own understanding of world history. ('Eschatology', the doctrine of the last things, is the subject of chapter 7 below.) Within that context of Jewish faith and eschatology, the life, teaching and fate of Jesus, and its aftermath, suggest construal in revelatory terms. This thesis is developed at length by Pannenberg, here and in later works,[31] without special appeal to authority or inspiration. Of course, the theological conclusions drawn are expressed in terms of inspiration and incarnation, but these are the results not the presuppositions of the argument. Pannenberg's more recent work is admittedly more sensitive to the experiential elements involved both in the formation of the specific historical tradition, which provides the interpretative key to the meaning of universal history, and to the verbal witness, including scripture, proclamation and liturgical response, which the special acts of God in question evoke if rightly understood. But the fact that the revelatory events require mediation by words if their significance is to be grasped and communicated does not mean that the words, rather than the events, are the primary vehicles of revelation.

How are we to evaluate this preference for the model of special revelation by God's acts in and through a series of historical events over the model of special revelation by verbal communication? Certainly, it has the advantage of locating special revelation firmly in the public domain, in a particular life lived within a particular historical context, and in the specific effects of that sequence of events. All this is open to interpretation without appeal to authority other than to the moral and religious force of what emerged from that context. Further support may, of course, be given, and indeed is given by Pannenberg,[32] by appeal to the Resurrection as authenticating the inner authority of what is allegedly revealed, but the primary appeal is to the purely historical events themselves, within the horizon of universal history.

On this view, the scriptures may be regarded as sources for our knowledge of the revelatory events. And the subsequent creeds and theologies may be regarded as propositional expressions of the truths revealed in the events, life and consequences under review.

To locate special revelation primarily in act, event and presence, rather than in speech, is not to escape the problem of the all too human media of divine revelation. First century Jewish categories may have enabled the incarnate one to carry out his divine salvific role, but they too were embedded in the relativities of history and cannot be taken over without question after two thousand years of further history, including the rise of modern science. Philosophers and theologians have to explore the rationale of indirect communication, whether the media of revelation are held to be fallible or limited human words, or messy, ambiguous historical traditions and events. What is required is a plausible theory of special providence, an account of why God acts in and through fallible creaturely action to build up the context for his own incognito presence. This notion of indirect communication, and its rationale, were captured classically by Søren Kierkegaard in his parable of the king and the humble maiden.[33] To woo the maiden and win her love for himself and not for his kingly state, the king had to put on peasant's clothes and live the life of a peasant in the village.

Generalized, this idea of indirect communication brings us back to Farrer's conception of double agency.[34] This refers to God's action in special providence, incarnation and grace, as mediated by creatures with all their limitations and fallibilities. Whether the focus is on word or on event, a purely natural, purely human story can be told. But the puzzling, inadequate character of a purely naturalistic account is suggested, if not demonstrated, by the actual nature of the words or events in question and by their results, often when viewed in retrospect.

The idea of gradual, indirect, developing communication was already touched on with reference to Mitchell's use of the teacher–pupil analogy.[35] It will recur with greater force when we turn to David Brown's recent work on tradition and imagination. But it is clearly crucial to the idea of revelation being mediated by a providential sequence of historical events and developments, culminating in the life story of a first-century Jewish rabbi.

This is made crystal clear in an excellent and thorough study of revelation by a philosopher of religion whose name will feature frequently in these pages, Keith Ward. Ward's *Religion and Revelation*[36] is the first of four books on comparative theology in which central doctrines are explored in the context of the worldwide history of religions. I shall be considering the comparative religion aspect of Ward's treatment of revelation in the final section of this chapter. I mention the book here because, in its fourth part, entitled 'Christian Reflections: Revelation as Historical Self-Manifestation', Ward shows both sensitivity to the gradualness and historical conditionedness of the providential preparation for the Incarnation, and appreciation of the religious logic, if one can use such a phrase, of salvific revelation through incarnation. The revelation of God's love through incarnation to the point of crucifixion transforms the believer in a way no direct provision of information could possibly do. The distinctive Christian concept of revelation, Ward observes in his concluding chapter, is that of 'a historical self-disclosure with the power to effect liberating union with the Divine'.[37]

2.6   Revelation as Tradition and Interpretation

A key issue arising from what has been surveyed so far is whether special revelation is held to have occurred or reached a climax in the past, or whether, in Swinburne's words already quoted, 'the revelation goes on'. Any historically nuanced treatment will stress the gradual, mediated nature of special revelation, whether the stress falls on verbal communication or on manifestation through acts and events. The logic of indirect communication applies both to the developing tradition which yielded the Jewish and Christian scriptures and to the providential preparation for the Incarnation. But should the notion of special revelation be restricted to those past culminations of long historical processes?

When, in his Bampton Lectures, *The Glass of Vision*,[38] Austin Farrer set himself to explore the modality of divine action in special revelation, he restricted himself to the biblical images that constituted the vehicles of divine revelation in the minds of the prophets and in the thought and teaching of Jesus of Nazareth. According to Farrer, what enabled the prophets, and indeed Jesus, to be the bearers of special revelation was the inspired development of certain key images that came, for instance in the parables of Jesus, to open up some novel vision of the nature and will of God. What differentiates divine inspiration from poetic inspiration, and indicates its ultimate divine control, is not some special direct dictation or internal divine causation of such inspired teaching. The images have a history in the development of Israel's faith. They become vehicles of innovative disclosure through imaginative development and novel use. Just such human creativity and imagination in the context of a particular tradition of faith are held by Farrer to be the media of divine revelation. What suggests this interpretation are the quality and authority of what emerges from this process, namely, the prophetic and dominical teachings themselves. It is not the mediated process of inspiration that is to be construed as revelation. Rather, it is what results from it.

In a later essay on 'Revelation',[39] without going back on the idea that the inspired minds of prophets and apostles are indeed the vehicles of revealed truth, Farrer places the main emphasis on the Incarnation as 'the self-enacted parable of Godhead'.[40] This includes, of course, Christ's teaching, but the very heart of revelation is the life and saving deeds of God made man.

So, for Farrer, special revelation took place in the past in and through a particular strand of history that reached its climax in the Incarnation. Inspiration, of course, continues, as believers and the Church hear God's word and appropriate it in faith, but believers add nothing to the content of the faith. I endorsed this view when I wrote:

> By contrast with general revelation, providence, inspiration, and grace, special revelation took place once for all in the past – mediated, like those other forms of divine/human encounter or dialogue by fallible human words and deeds – but constituting an identifiable, public, event series, to which the Bible and the Church bear witness in ever developing, though equally fallible, interpretations.[41]

A strong challenge to this view has been made in recent work by David Brown. Already in his earlier writings, Brown was defending and developing the idea of indirect communication in ways that owed something to Farrer, but showed signs of extending the notion to allow for continuing and developing revelation. In his 1985 book, *The Divine Trinity*,[42] he put forward a view of revelation as a divine dialogue, in which God always respects the freedom and humanity of the recipients and the stage of development that they have reached. This accounts for the failures of moral insight that sometime occur, even in the Bible. Brown makes it clear that the rationale behind this conception of gradual revelation in and through fallible human recipients is akin to the free will defence in respect of the problem of evil.

In a subsequent paper,[43] Brown develops his dialogue model with the help of the teacher–pupil analogy, which we have already encountered in Mitchell's writings. The good teacher adapts and accommodates his instruction to the pupil's level and capacities, and gradually, through dialogue, raises the level of insight and understanding. Brown takes up, at this point, Farrer's notion of inspired images as vehicles of revelation, and extends it in a very interesting way to the creative transformation of certain natural symbols present in the unconscious. He stresses the point that such transformations are experienced in religious contexts not just as new insights but as encounters and interactions with their divine source.

This extension of Farrer's view from biblical images to natural symbols suggests a move from a theology of special revelation to a theology of general revelation; but, while Brown's later work does indeed involve a much wider conception of the media of revelation, it is clear that his two major books, *Tradition and Imagination* and *Discipleship and Imagination*,[44] still belong within the sphere of reflection on special revelation. These two books constitute by far the most detailed and thought-provoking defence of the idea of continuing revelation that has yet appeared from the pen of a philosophical theologian. Brown's thesis, in brief, is that, since God takes seriously each particular environment and setting, the process of revelation has to continue beyond scripture. Its vehicles are the various trajectories of tradition, developing and correcting what went before, drawing on the insights of other traditions, and using all the resources of human imagination, including art, to clarify God's purposes and the meaning of his acts. Brown, no less than Farrer, sees the Incarnation as pivotal. But, unlike Farrer, Brown holds, to quote Swinburne again, that the revelation goes on.

Given Brown's conviction of the historical relativity and fallibility of all the vehicles of continuing revelation, the question of the criteria of revealed truth becomes paramount. The final chapter of the second of these books is devoted to this question. Brown lists nine types of criteria by which the Church might judge authentic from inauthentic developments of the tradition as a vehicle of continuing revelation: historical criteria, empirical criteria, conceptual criteria, moral criteria, criteria of continuity, christological criteria, degree of imaginative engagement, effectiveness of analogical construct and ecclesial criteria. The reader is referred to *Discipleship and Imagination* for the details. But there is no doubt that we have here a most impressive analysis of revelation in terms of tradition and interpretation.

2.7   Revelation as Religious Experience

I have cited Mavrodes's manifestation model of divine revelation as including manifestation through act and event, but Mavrodes himself concentrates, under this heading, on manifestation through religious experience. We turn then, finally, to the idea that divine revelation is conveyed primarily through religious experience. It should be noted at once that this idea is strongly contested in much Christian theology, including philosophical theology. Two German theologians, mentioned in chapter 1 as being, like Pannenberg, equally at home in analytic and continental philosophy, namely Ingolf Dalferth and Christoph Schwöbel, treat theology of revelation and theology of experience as two quite different, even opposed, categories, the one reflecting on God's initiative, the other reflecting on human reception.[45] Similarly, William Alston, in his major study of the epistemology of religious experience, *Perceiving God*,[46] treats appeals to revelation as something other than, although in his case complementary to, appeals to religious experience.

But there is another strand in contemporary philosophy of religion, exemplified most clearly in the work of John Hick, that sees divine revelation precisely in the moments of intense religious awareness, whether of mystical union or devotional ecstasy. Hick has expounded this notion particularly in connection with his philosophy of religious pluralism, as we shall see. But already, in his first book *Faith and Knowledge*,[47] long before his interest in comparative religion, Hick was arguing against what he called the Thomist-Catholic propositional view of revelation as 'the divine communication to man of the truths, belief in which comprises faith'. At that stage, Hick did not locate revelation wholly in religious experience. Rather, he saw it taking place where people experience certain key events, those of salvation history, as revelatory. The way he put the matter in this early book has a particular interest for us in the light of what was said about natural and revealed theology at the beginning of this chapter. 'According to this view', wrote Hick, 'the two objects of "natural" and "revealed" theology, God's existence and God's revelation merge into one. The divine being and the divine self-communication are known in a single apprehension which is the awareness of God as acting self-revealingly towards us.'[48] But Hick's increasing involvement in issues of religious pluralism, as he tries to make sense of the many revelation claims in the world's religions, including the non-theistic religions like early Buddhism, has led him more and more to define revelation purely in experiential terms. Thus in a much later book, *The Fifth Dimension*,[49] writing of the great spiritual figures behind the rise of world religions, Hick remarks that 'they were men . . . who were exceptionally open to the Transcendent, experiencing it with extraordinary vividness in ways made possible by their existing religious contexts. Such immensely powerful moments of God-consciousness, or of Transcendence consciousness, are what we mean by revelation.'[50]

At a certain mid-point of his development, Hick was more conscious of the break with traditional views of revelation which this latest definition involves. In an exchange in the journal, *Theology*, in 1983,[51] Hick concedes to Philip Almond that the term 'revelation' is more at home in the theistic than the non-theistic religions. 'I have tried to use it, however', he goes on, 'in a wider sense which does not entail divinely disclosed propositions or miraculous interventions in the course of human history, but in which all authentic religious awareness is a response to the circumambient presence and prevenient pressure of the divine Reality.'[52] That this much wider sense of revelation is at home in the religions of the east is clear from K. Satchidananda Murty's book, *Revelation and Reason in Advaita Vedanta*: 'All discovery of God, experience of God and knowledge of God "must" be God's disclosure of himself to us; for God is spirit, and can only be known in spiritual encounter.'[53] This is expressed in theistic terms, but, as is well known, the ancient Hindu scriptures, known as 'sruti', a word translated as 'revelation', are not always interpreted as revelations given by the gods. These ancient texts expressed, rather, spiritual insights achieved by the sages through mystical penetration into ultimate reality. This is a very different sense of 'revelation' from that which has dominated the Christian philosophical theology surveyed in the present book.

And yet the comparative religion issue cannot be ignored. The merit of Keith Ward's tetralogy,[54] by contrast with Swinburne's,[55] lies in Ward's resolute attempt to produce an 'open' theology, relating specifically Christian revelation claims to those of other religions. We shall see an example of the way in which Ward does this in the next chapter on Creation. Where revelation is concerned, Ward holds that 'the rational course is to commit oneself to a tradition of revelation', while accepting that 'the Supreme Reality has not been silent in the other religions of the world'.[56] This involves setting out the logic of, say, Christian incarnational belief, but at the same time looking for the common and complementary features in revelation claims elsewhere. Whether or not the central doctrines of the Christian creeds are susceptible to such treatment is one of the key issues in philosophical theology today. It has to be said that most of the philosophers mentioned in the current chapter remain sceptical about the possibility of going very far down the road towards Hick's extreme religious pluralism. As we have seen, the model of revelation as religious experience is the model most open to treatment in these terms. The model of revelation as tradition and interpretation allows for much learning from, and reinterpretation in the light of, other traditions, but, at least in the hands of scholars such as Brown, it remains more of an internal discipline, exploring the continuing, developing, stream of specifically Christian revelation. The model of revelation as God's acts in history is even less open to treatment in pluralistic terms, given its stress on the specificity of the event series culminating in the Incarnation; although there is no reason a priori why the God made known through incarnation could not have acted salvifically elsewhere as well. Similarly the model of revelation as divine discourse does not require the Christian hearer of God's Word to deny that the God of the whole earth has spoken and speaks at other times, in other places and through other cultural traditions. Much will depend on the commonalities, compatiblities and complementarities that are actually discovered to obtain. This problem will not be pursued in depth in the present book. Here we survey work done on the logic of specifically Christian belief. But it is a clear implication of conviction of the rationality of revealed theology that such comparative work is required and can be done.

CHAPTER THREE

Creation

_____

The first major doctrine of the Christian creeds is the doctrine of Creation. It is a basic tenet of both natural and revealed theology that the universe exists with a derived reality, created out of nothing by the infinite, eternal God. And the first, most straightforward answer to the question 'Who or what is God?' is that God is the maker of the world. In this chapter we shall be looking at some of the contributions made by philosophers of religion to the analysis of what it means both to think of God as Creator and also to think of the universe as created.

3.1 The Creator God

3.1.1 Maximal greatness

That there is an absolute distinction between Creator and creation, between God and the world, is fundamental to Judaism, Christianity, Islam and many other religions too. The classical expression and defence of this doctrine may be found in the writings of Thomas Aquinas in the thirteenth century, in particular in Books I and II of his *Summa Contra Gentiles*.[1] These have been explored in detail by Norman Kretzmann in *The Metaphysics of Theism* and *The Metaphysics of Creation*.[2] These are not only fine studies of natural theology in its classical form but also fine examples of how natural theology can be practised today. Kretzmann's discussion of the kind of objections to natural theology associated with the name of Alvin Plantinga is required reading for anyone interested in the question of the relation between natural and revealed theology. The first of Kretzmann's books traces the way in which Aquinas, after arguing that the world requires a first cause or ultimate explanation, then goes on, by a process of elimination, to show the characteristics which this first cause must have, if it is to fulfil its explanatory role and not be just part of what cries out for explanation. These largely negative arguments, although with far from negative conclusions, show that the first cause must be 'the transcendent, personal, omniscient, omnipotent, perfectly good creator and governor of the universe'.[3] Kretzmann puts great emphasis on arguments from perfection. It is from God's perfection that we are to infer his infinity, his intellect, his will (agent causality yielding the best explanation of the world's existence) and his personhood. And in the final chapter Kretzmann shows how Aquinas infers joy, love and liberality in God from all that has gone before. Two features of the Aquinas–Kretzmann metaphysics of theism that have given rise to much debate and disagreement among contemporary philosophical theologians are the arguments for divine simplicity and for the necessity of some creation or other. To these controversial themes we shall be returning later in this chapter.

Another version of the argument from perfection is to be found in the work of T. V. Morris.[4] Morris gives the name 'Anselmian theism' to the approach in philosophical theology that seeks to spell out the implications of 'maximal greatness'. The idea goes back to Anselm's famous definition of God as 'that than which nothing greater can be conceived'.[5] It is important not to interpret this as the greatest conceivable being, since our human powers of conception are weak, and Anselm is certainly pointing beyond anything *we* can conceive. 'Maximal greatness' is a much more objective, as well as positive, way of putting the idea. Morris expands on this notion with an intriguing definition of God, which will govern much of what follows in this book: 'God is to be thought of as exemplifying necessarily a maximally perfect set of compossible great-making properties.[6] The properties comprising maximal greatness must, of course, be 'compossible' (possible together) if we are to have a coherent idea of God. We cannot ascribe to God two or more properties, however exalted, if they are contradictory or incompatible.

It is this criterion of maximal greatness that pushes the idea of God beyond the reach of the child's question, 'Who made God?', which often occurs to the child when told that the world was made by God. As with Aquinas, developed theism is driven to insist on God's necessity as opposed to the world's contingency, God's infinity as opposed to the world's finitude, God's self-explanatoriness as opposed to the world's being of such a nature as to call for explanation. All these considerations exemplify the metaphysical pressures that drive the theist to insist on the distinction between God and the world, Creator and creation.

Let us contrast this idea of the Creator God's maximal greatness with Plato's cosmogonic myth in the *Timaeus*.[7] There the divine architect or 'demiurge' is pictured as shaping up pre-existent matter in accordance with the eternal Forms. So, in Plato's scenario, there are three unexplained ultimates: (a) the demiurge himself – a somewhat anthropomorphic myth-ical figure, (b) pre-existent matter, which is just there, waiting to be formed up, and (c) the eternal Forms, or paradigms, or ideal essences of all the kinds of thing that come to be when matter gets shaped up in accordance with these Forms. Even if the three ultimates – Forms, matter and demiurge – are eternal, in the sense of being without beginning or end, they are still unexplained. The picture may not be quite as crude as the Indian story of accounting for what holds up the Earth by saying that it rests on the back of a cosmic elephant, and accounting for what holds the elephant up by saying that it rests on the back of a cosmic turtle, and then just stopping. But the lack of ultimate explanation is equally clear. Plato does, in the *Republic*,[8] introduce a more ultimate, metaphysical, first principle, the Form of the Good, to account for everything, Forms as well as particulars. And the Form of the Good, he says, rather obscurely, is itself 'beyond being, surpassing it in dignity and power'.[9] But it is not surprising that Christian Platonists saw in Plato's analogy between the Good and the Sun a philosophical intimation of developed theism.

The greatest difference between Plato and the Christians was not only the doctrine of Incarnation, which Augustine singled out,[10] but precisely the doctrine of Creation with which we are at present concerned. For Christian Platonists, the Forms became ideas in the mind of God, and not just matter but the whole finite world came to be thought of as created out of nothing and sustained in being by the continuous activity of God. So, in place of three ultimates, Forms, matter and demiurge, we get a world crying out for explanation, and explained by reference to the creativity of an absolute, necessary, infinite, self-explanatory ground, best conceived of by analogy with Spirit, if justice is to be done to the intellect, will and agency held to constitute the best explanation for the whole world process.

We are not so much concerned here with the arguments in natural theology, by which Aquinas, Kretzmann and Morris seek to establish the reality of God. We are concerned more with the coherence of the doctrine of the Creator God that emerges from these arguments, or indeed with the coherence of the doctrine of God developed and handed down in allegedly revealed theology. Not that the two sources of the doctrine are unrelated. The philosophy or natural theology needs to be complemented by the revealed theology, and the revealed theology needs to be refined and tested by the philosophy. But our prime concern is with the coherence of the idea that this evolving universe in which we find ourselves depends for its very being, for its nature and for its destiny upon the creative will and intention of an absolute, infinite, self-existent Spirit, who is both transcendent to this finite world and immanent within it, and who is known in the great theistic religions of the world as God.

3.1.2   Creatio ex nihilo

This notion of the world's ontological dependence on the creative act of a God conceived of in terms of maximal greatness is summed up in the traditional doctrine of *creatio ex nihilo*. It is one of God's basic great making properties to be able to posit in being a whole universe 'out of nothing'. Reviewers of George Gamow's book, *The Creation of the World*,[11] complained that the author totally ignored absolute creation in this sense. The book was entirely concerned with previous states of the universe and how its present state had emerged. Gamow replied that he was using the word 'creation' in the sense in which Paris dress-designers talk of their 'new creations' – that is, new states or forms of the fabric. This idea is quite different from the theistic doctrine, for which there is no pre-existent stuff out of which the world was made. It was, or is, simply actualized by God in an act of pure and absolute creation. And it is a fundamental error to regard 'nothing' as a shadowy sort of something – 'meontic' being (from the Greek for non-being) – as in some Neoplatonist theories of emanation.

The contrast between creation and emanation is sensitively explored by Keith Ward in his *Rational Theology and the Creativity of God*,[12] in terms of the very different views of Aquinas and Hegel. For Aquinas, the universe is posited in being and held in being by simple divine fiat. Its origin is God's creative act, but it is not made out of anything. For Hegel, by contrast, the developing world of nature and finite Spirit is an unfolding of Absolute Spirit itself.[13] Put crudely, the world is not made out of nothing. It is formed out of God's own substance in a process of self-expression. There is a sense in which, for Hegel and the Hegelians, God and the world are one reality, not two. For Aquinas, there remains an ultimate dualism between God and the world. It is not that the world has no origin or source. Its source is God. But it is not made out of the divine substance any more than out of any other substance.

The difficulties of this notion of pure creation out of nothing will be addressed in later sections of this chapter. But one particular question can be tackled at once. Does the *creatio ex nihilo* doctrine entail that the world had an absolute beginning in time? It is well known that, for Aquinas, reason could not prove this to be the case.[14] For him, *creatio ex nihilo* meant sheer ontological dependence, whether or not the world had a temporal beginning. But T. V. Morris's discussion of 'Creation ex Nihilo' in his *Anselmian Explorations* takes the doctrine to entail a temporal beginning, say in the Big Bang, some fifteen to twenty billion years ago. Certainly, Morris succeeds in showing the intelligibility of this notion, by contrast with Bertrand Russell's fanciful suggestion that there is no way of telling whether or not the world was created five minutes ago, with all the apparent signs of a long history built into it.[15] (Actually, Russell's suggestion is not just fanciful; it is illogical. A human being, for example, could not – logically could not – be posited in being fully grown, with apparently developed character traits and apparent memories. One would not be a person at all, let alone the actual person that one is, without a real-life story of interpersonal relations.) But it is odd to find Morris, at least in this article, failing to recognize that *creatio ex nihilo* applies equally to a temporally unbounded ontological dependence.

One philosopher of religion who explicitly rejects the *creatio ex nihilo* doctrine is Richard Creel.[16] Creel does not suggest that God requires some stuff or medium out of which to create a world. But he does argue that creation presupposes the existence of a realm of unactualized possibilities – he calls it 'the plenum' – between which God freely chooses in actualizing a world. For Creel, therefore, the Absolute is not equated with God *simpliciter*, rather with God and the plenum. (We are reminded, once again, of Plato's independently existing eternal Forms.) This view is rejected by most philosophical theologians and, in a later section on 'Other Necessities', we shall survey alternative ways of accounting for abstract ideas, numbers and possibilities.

3.1.3 Continuous creation

A further implication of the view that, in creation, God actualizes a world out of nothing is that creation is a continuous affair. The world is not only posited in being, but is sustained in being at every moment by God's creative act. On this view, divine creation and divine conservation are virtually equated. The view is ably defended against, and contrasted with, the deistic view that, once posited in being, the world is self-sustaining by Jonathan Kvanvig and Hugh McCann, in their essay, 'Divine Conservation and the Persistence of the World'.[17] The argument rests partly on the incoherence of the idea of created things sustaining themselves, and partly on the incoherence of the idea of the Creator God releasing his creation from the scope of his act and power. Maximal greatness requires both transcendence and immanence where the God–world relation is concerned.

These arguments apply whether or not it is held that the world had a beginning in time. But clearly the constant ontological dependence of creation on Creator is more obviously required if there was no temporal beginning.

The problem that now arises is whether the virtual equation of creation and conservation leaves any room for the relative independence of what Aquinas called secondary causation. If the sustaining hand of God is necessary to the continuing existence of the world and all that it contains, can we maintain that creatures possess their own causal powers, and in particular that humans have free will? These issues will be considered further when we turn to the nature of the created order itself, but some attention must be paid here to the divine side of the God–world relation. So convinced have some theists been of the universality of God's creative power that they have seen it operative not only in the continuing existence of the world, but in every change and every instance of causal efficacy in the world process. This doctrine is known as 'occasionalism', and is particularly associated with the seventeenth-century French philosopher-theologian Nicolas Malebranche (1638–1715).[18] This, however, is an extreme view and not an inevitable implication of the equation of creation and conservation, as is ably argued by Philip Quinn in his essay 'Divine Conservation, Secondary Causes, and Occasionalism'.[19] Put briefly, and in terms of the maximal greatness criterion, it is greater to be able to create and sustain in both being and potency creatures with their own God-given causal powers, including freedom, than for God to have to do everything as well as make and sustain everything himself.

3.1.4   Analogies for creation

The idea of God creating the world out of nothing remains a difficult idea for the human mind to grasp. Believers have explored a range of analogies for such absolute creation, in order to try to throw some light on this idea. Philosophers are quick to point out the limitations of the biblical analogy with a potter fashioning a pot out of his clay.[20] There may be some features of the analogy that can be retained: the potter's purpose governing the process, and his control over the whole process and its end product. But it is a simplistic analogy, and it succeeds no better than Gamow's dress-designer analogy in capturing the unique idea of the positing in being of a whole finite world.

So the theist looks for alternative analogies to express this notion of the sheer creation of a material universe with all its capacities for evolution and novelty. The analogy with human creativity in great art presents itself. Something absolutely new appears on the scene as a result of the creative powers of the human mind and imagination: a great symphony, for example. (Such a musical analogy was used very powerfully by J. J. R. Tolkien at the beginning of *The Silmarillion*.[21]) One of the most suggestive analogies is Austin Farrer's 'author' analogy, thrown out in the course of a treatment of divine providence:

> The Creator of the world is not to be compared with those bad novelists who make up the plot of their story first and force the characters to carry it out, all against the grain of their natures. He is like the good novelist who has the wit to get a satisfying story out of the natural behaviour of the characters he conceives. And how does he do it? By identifying himself with them and living them from within?[22]

According to Farrer, this is true at every level of nature and history. God 'thinks all the natural processes at any level into being themselves and into running themselves true to type. And yet without faking the story or defying probability at any point he pulls the history together into the patterns we observe.'

A similar analogy is suggested by the Swiss Roman Catholic theologian, Hans Urs von Balthasar, this time from the composition of an opera.[23] He notes the unimaginable creative freedom with which Mozart could produce a consummate work of art like *The Magic Flute*. We shall return to this analogy in a later section of this chapter.

These are very illuminating analogies, but they, too, clearly have their limitations. There is no real parallel between thinking up a symphony, a novel or an opera and thinking up and actualizing a substantial universe. Not only is the creation of the whole world's *being* not really captured by such analogies. Unlike the characters in a play or an opera, however subtle and 'natural' the characterization and the plot, God's human creatures have a life of their own and the power freely to interact, as they make or mar their own world history.

3.1.5 Is creation necessary for God?

The question, 'Why does God create a world?' and 'Is creation necessary to God?' are clearly linked, since if the answer to the second question is 'yes', the first does not arise. Traditionally, most Christian theists have held that creation is not necessary to God. Rather, creation is a matter of free grace.

Certainly, both the ability to create and creativity as such are part of God's nature. That is undeniable. But the dominant intuition, in maximal greatness theology, has been the view that free creativity is greater than any compulsion, even inner compulsion, to create.

A number of philosophical theologians, however, have recently urged that, while it is up to God's free choice which world to create, God is bound by his own nature to create some world or other. I have already mentioned that this was Kretzmann's view.[24] And Keith Ward, in *Religion and Creation*,[25] admits that, while he used to think creation a free act on God's part, he now believes that God's essential nature as love compels him to create an object for his love, namely a world of finite persons. The reasoning behind this move calls for much reflection. Ward seems now to think that God's perfection – his maximal greatness – can only take the form of love if there are created persons to be loved. And since maximal greatness must include love, it must include some creation or other, provided that creation comes up with creatures capable of entering into loving relations with God. In other words, there would be a major great-making property lacking in God were he not to create.

But this argument is premised on the analogy between God and an isolated individual. As we shall see in chapter 5 on the Trinity, contemporary trinitarian theology attempts to articulate a differentiated, relational concept of God, in which love given, love received and love shared still more are held to belong to the very essence of maximal greatness – that is, to God as such. In which case the theist can hold that creation is not necessary to God, if God is love. Rather, God's own nature as love is simply expressed and reflected in the free creation of yet more centres of love and communion.

If creation is not necessary to God, the question 'Why does God create a world?' does indeed arise. This question gets its traditional answer in terms of the sheer goodness of free creativity, as the perfection of God's inner trinitarian love finds further expression in the gratuitous creation of finite realms of personal and interpersonal being, where God's creatures can come to know and love each other and their maker in perfected communities which reflect God's glory and God's love. As we shall see in chapter 7, the process of creation, on a theistic worldview, is seen as heading, under God's providence, for just such a future and final consummation.

3.1.6   *Must God create the best?*

God's freedom in creation is also challenged by the supposition, put forward most notably by Leibniz,[26] that this must be the best of all possible worlds, since God, being absolutely perfect, must, if he is to create, create the best.

This too seems to rule out choice. Only the best of all possible worlds can be actualized by maximal greatness. Voltaire mocked the Leibnizians for this doctrine in his *Candide*,[27] not least in face of the Lisbon earthquake of 1755, which killed thousands of people, many of them worshippers in churches on All Saints Day. Objections based on the problem of evil will be considered briefly in the final section of this chapter. Here we address the threat to God's freedom.

One response has been to say that the notion of the best of all possible worlds makes no sense, any more than the notion of the largest possible number. Possible worlds simply cannot be ranked in a single scale, with a lowest and a highest member. As Richard Swinburne argues,[28] any world could always be improved by the addition of one more valuable state of affairs. Another response is to say, with Robert Adams,[29] that God is under no obligation to create the best, since no one is wronged by not being created. One could perhaps supplement the point by repeating our earlier remark that free creativity is better than having no choice, so maximal greatness will include the former rather than the latter.

A particularly interesting discussion of this whole issue is to be found in T. V. Morris's article, 'Perfection and Creation'.[30] To those who argue that the possibility of the creation of a better world entails the possibility of a more perfect Creator, Morris replies that is makes no sense to try to correlate degrees of goodness in creation with degrees of goodness in the Creator. Maximal greatness theism means that God's perfection is absolute. That perfection is simply expressed in the creation of any one of innumerable possible good worlds, irrespective of their degrees of goodness.

Another response is to try to block the idea of degrees of goodness in creation. I mentioned Balthasar's analogy from Mozart's composition of *The Magic Flute*. He deploys this explicitly against Leibniz in a footnote well worth quoting:

> Does it make any sense to ask of this work whether it might not have been even more perfect? Obviously the question can be put in the abstract, but it is impossible to come up with any meaningful concrete suggestion as to the direction in which the improvement might be made. On the other hand, the work of art radiates so much freedom that it would be just as mistaken to label it 'best' once and for all, in such a way that, had Mozart lived longer, he would have been unable to write a more perfect opera.[31]

Balthasar concludes his footnote with the obvious point that God's goodness will ensure that whatever he creates is good (on this, see below), but this does not dictate a single option.

3.1.7 Does creation increase the total quantity of goodness?

Another problem raised by critics of the traditional doctrine of Creation is that, if the Creator is defined in terms of maximal greatness, there seems to be no room for further good states of affairs, such as the perfected consummation of the whole creative process. Maximal greatness presumably includes maximal goodness. Yet it would appear that the goodness of the Creator God plus the goodness of the perfected creation would be greater than the goodness of God alone. This problem, too, is well handled by T. V. Morris in the chapter on creation in his book, *Our Idea of God*.[32] He points out that one cannot treat God and the world as if together they comprised a single individual, whose combined goodness would be greater than God's goodness alone. God and the world do not constitute an individual. The world's created goodness is indeed something other than God's infinite, necessary goodness. But God's goodness is expressed in, not increased by (or for that matter diminished by) the world's goodness. There is little more that need be said about the resolution of this problem.

3.1.8 Is creation a timeless act?

A much more complex and controversial difficulty concerns the relation between eternity and time. Much classical theism has thought of God as eternal in the very strong sense of absolute timelessness. In contradistinction to the developing, changing, space-time structure of the created world process, God is wholly outside time. God's maximal greatness must exclude temporality. God is absolutely simple, pure actuality, in every way immutable. On this view, creation has to be thought of as a timeless act on God's part, the whole story of the created universe, past, present and future, being posited in being in a single atemporal creative act. All change is on the creature's side of the God–world relation only.

This view has come to seem very problematic to many philosophical theologians today. For one thing, such an understanding of God contrasts very sharply with the living, interacting God of the Bible and religion. It is held to reflect more the influence of Plato, for whom time was 'the moving image of eternity'.[33] But Plato's Forms, even the Form of the Good, were impersonal ideal essences, hard to equate with a God of love. Classical theism, it is true, was moved by a very proper unwillingness to bring the Creator down to the level of creation. For, in our world, our time is a matter of beginnings and endings, of dissolution, loss and decay. None of that can possibly be attributed, even analogically, to the eternal, transcendent Creator.

Certainly the infinite, necessary God, Creator and Lord of all, must be without beginning or end. But does that mean that God is utterly atemporal? Of course God cannot just be part of our space-time world. But maybe loss and decay are not aspects of the temporal as such, but only of a spatio-temporal universe like ours. And if God is creating a genuinely temporally structured, open-futured world, does he not have to relate to it in a manner appropriate to the actual nature of what he is doing, namely in a temporal manner, involving real relation and reciprocal interaction with the world process? The Christian doctrine of the Incarnation, which we shall be considering in the next chapter, is very hard to square with the classical view of timeless eternity. But so is the notion of a timeless *act* of creation. For an act is surely a novel realization of a prior intention, an actualization of a potentiality.

To theists brought up on the classical (Aristotelian-Thomist) view of God's pure actuality excluding all potentiality, this may take some swallowing. But philosophers of religion such as Richard Swinburne[34] and Keith Ward[35] have made a very good case for it, along the lines sketched here. Indeed, Ward has shown how in four major theistic contexts – Jewish, Christian, Muslim and Hindu – leading thinkers have been qualifying the traditional static, timeless conception of deity in favour of a much more dynamic, freely interacting and creative God, able to relate personally to his creatures as he fashions a world in which genuinely free creatures make their own responses, and either cooperate with the divine Spirit or not. Such a view, including the ascription of analogous, primordial temporality to God, was already being adumbrated by Austin Farrer in the 1960s[36] in the interests of safeguarding personal language in talk of God.

To revert to the concept of maximal greatness: the issue at stake here is whether it is greater to possess the capacity – the potentiality – freely to create, and interact with, an open-futured world than to actualize, atemporally and immutably, a whole world story. Paul Helm has dubbed the latter view the 'no-risk' view of creation and providence, by contrast with the 'risk' view, whereby God's creative work is seen as genuinely open and undecided in the manner of its outworking.[37] We shall return to this distinction in a later section of this chapter and in chapter 8. But clearly the arguments of Farrer, Swinburne and Ward (and Morris[38]) favour the temporal, dynamic, reciprocal nature of God's creative work as itself constitutive of maximal greatness. Their case is all the stronger, of course, if the 'no-risk', atemporal view of the Creator God can be shown to lack coherence.

These questions are hotly debated in contemporary philosophy of religion. Helm himself defends the 'no-risk' view of creation and, with it, the traditional notion of divine timelessness.[39] Unlike the Thomists, however, he admits that these ideas entail the impossibility of genuine freedom in creatures. We might well take this as an argument for the other side of the debate. The cognate ideas of divine immutability and divine simplicity also find defenders, notably among those nurtured in the Thomist tradition.[40] But the weight of current opinion goes the other way. On immutability, Richard Swinburne argues that, while God cannot change in character and power, creation and incarnation both require continual and reciprocal interaction with a changing and developing world.[41] And on divine simplicity (the traditional view that there are no distinct attributes, no complexity of any kind, in God) Morris argues that Anselmian theism does not require this. All that is required is the permanent stability of the core defining attributes of God.[42]

One question that does not arise if the idea of creation as a timeless act is maintained, but which does arise on the dynamic, temporal view of the divine nature, is why God did not create the world at an earlier, or later, stage in God's time. To this, Morris replies, first, that in infinite time there can be no reason or advantage in earlier or later creation. Maximal greatness simply includes the power freely to create at some time or other. Secondly, he hazards the suggestion that maybe God has other creative enterprises anyway, unconnected with this universe, at other times.[43]

3.1.9   Process theology and the prior actuality of God

Space prevents more than a brief look at a powerful school of philosophical theology, more influential in North America than in Britain, that has pushed the kind of arguments just surveyed even further in the interests of a whole metaphysic of 'becoming', namely 'process theology'. The fountainhead of this school was the philosopher A. N. Whitehead, who collaborated with Bertrand Russell on *Principia Mathematica*, then later went to the United States, where, much to Russell's astonishment and disgust, he developed a whole new philosophy, sometimes known as 'the philosophy of organism', in which the fundamental categories were not 'being' and 'substance', but 'becoming' and 'event'.[44] Whitehead's ideas were taken up by Charles Hartshorne, David Griffin, Norman Pittenger[45] and a number of theologians who came to constitute a notable strand in twentieth-century Protestant theology in America. For these 'process theologians', God and the world are not wholly distinct, but mutually involved in a single process. God is the chief exemplification of the basic categories of process, giving all other entities their initial aim, inspiring their creative advance and accepting their achievements into the eternal divine memory. God is thought of more as *anima mundi*, the soul of the world, surpassing himself and growing in knowledge as the world process continues. On this view, the world, or at least a world, is necessary to God as the sphere and object of God's love.

The strengths of process theology lie in the way in which it provides a philosophical underpinning of the biblical idea of God, one which reckons, much more than classical theism does, with the activity and involvement of God, and with the fundamental idea of the interactive, suffering love of God.

But, despite some affinities with the arguments of Farrer, Swinburne, Ward and Morris in favour of a more dynamic, interactive concept of God, process theology is judged by all these writers to have gone too far. It blurs the distinction between Creator and creation, and tends to bring God down to the level of worldly categories, albeit as their supreme exemplar, making the world necessary to God and limiting God to his relations with the world. Farrer is particularly interesting in this connection. In his last book,[46] and in a lecture on 'The Prior Actuality of God',[47] Farrer mounted a strong attack on process theology, while at the same time, as I have indicated, recognizing the need to modify classical theism in the direction of admitting temporality, change, real relatedness to the world and suffering in God.

For Farrer, there are two main reasons why God cannot be thought of as the soul of the world. On the one hand we cannot compare the world to a single organism that could be thought of as informed by a purely immanent soul. The world is, rather, a vast system of interacting energies and sub-systems, each going their own way, yet combining, through cosmic and biological evolution, into a theatre of life and the many forms of life. And, on the other hand, for God truly to be the Creator of the whole process, God must transcend the world and have, as it were, a life of his own prior to the world, not necessarily temporally prior, but logically and metaphysically above and beyond his creative work. Farrer spells out this 'prior actuality of God' with reference to the Christian doctrine of the Holy Trinity. Prior to creation, God exists in the fullness of interpersonal relation and love. Recent work on the logic of trinitarian belief will be surveyed in chapter 5.

3.2 The Created Universe

3.2.1 *The contingency of the World*

A world created out of nothing and sustained in being by the activity of God is clearly a contingent, not a necessary, state of affairs. But what exactly do we mean by contingency? There is a temptation, in theistic metaphysics, to define the world's contingency in terms of ontological dependence. The worldview under consideration sees the universe as wholly dependent on God for being here and for being what it is. Matter or energy, the world stuff, as one might crudely call it, exists, all the time, with a derived reality. And its fundamental nature and laws, together with its capacities and potentialities, also derive from, and are sustained by, an infinite, self-existent creative will.

But to define contingency in terms of ontological dependence is to deprive oneself of a premise for theistic argument. You cannot argue from contingency to necessity if you have defined contingency as dependence on a necessary ground. This may not matter, if, like T. F. Torrance[48] or even Wolfhart Pannenberg,[49] you are simply articulating a theology of nature, setting out what form a theistic metaphysic might take, and trying to show its coherence. But it is worth asking whether there is not a more restricted way of understanding contingency that does not build the conclusion of, say, a cosmological argument into the main premise from which one starts, and which therefore does provide a genuine premise for theistic argument.

The contingent, on this view, is simply the non-necessary or non-self-explanatory. Contingency of being means the fact that something — say, the world — exists, when, as far as one can see, it might not have done. And contingency of nature means the fact that things have the properties and powers they have, when, as far as one can see, these might, indeed might well, have been otherwise. This latter point, especially when spelled out in terms of the universe's manifest capacity to evolve life and mind, could then provide the starting point for a teleological or design argument.

There is an interesting discussion of the cosmological argument, the argument from contingency to necessity, in Peter Geach's long article on Aquinas.[50] In commenting on Thomas Aquinas's 'third way', Geach takes its starting point, not from some 'I know not what "sense" or "experience" of contingency, but from the plain fact that some things are perishable'. For Aquinas, the whole world cannot have been like that for ever. Otherwise, sooner or later, it would have perished, like apples and people and planets and stars eventually do. To reply that a world of perishable things may consist of imperishable matter under different and changing forms is not to refute Aquinas. It is to go along with the first stage of his proof. Aquinas might well agree that imperishable matter provides the necessary basis of a world of contingent, i.e. perishable, things. But the second stage of his proof is to argue that imperishable matter does not possess its relative necessity from itself. In another sense, matter too is contingent, in that it is not self-explanatory. If so, it can only derive its being and character from something absolutely necessary, something, that is, that does not derive its necessity, or imperishable character, from something else. It is this second stage that points in the direction of God as the absolutely necessary ground of the world's being, even if the 'stuff of the world' is imperishable. The danger here is once again that of *defining* 'contingency' in this second sense as dependence or derivedness, thus building the conclusion of the argument into the premise of its second stage. But the starting point of this stage of the argument is simply no more than that even the imperishable matter or energy that constitutes the stuff of the world is not self-explanatory. It exists with a certain total magnitude, it possesses certain basic properties and powers, and it operates under very specific, mathematically expressible laws. But its existence and its nature, as far as we can see, are not absolutely necessary. The question why it exists and is just so, when presumably it might not have existed or might have been different, still arises. This is the point of the cosmological argument and indeed of the design argument when the actual capacities of the universe are reckoned with.

It is interesting to note that secular philosophers, such as Bertrand Russell[51] and A. J. Ayer,[52] try to block this argument sometimes by saying that the universe is just a brute fact and that 'why?' questions get no purchase hold at this level, and sometimes by saying that the universe is itself absolutely necessary, in the sense of underived imperishableness. These are very different responses. The first seems quite arbitrary, the second highly implausible. The human mind cannot be prevented from pressing 'why?' questions, and it is not difficult to think of other possible worlds.

The contingency of the universe, therefore, 'consists in its being just so and not otherwise, when for all we can tell, it might have been otherwise'.[53] And that goes for the bare existence of just such a world (the cosmological point) and for the specific character of just such a world, its capacity for evolving persons (the teleological point). A theistic metaphysic will, of course, explain this contingency in terms of creation: such a world depends for its being, its nature, its purpose and its destiny on the will and action of God. And in theistic religion, the world's contingency *is* often sensed or experienced, as by mystics such as Julian of Norwich. Geach has no business disparaging this.

3.2.2 The finitude of the World

Theistic metaphysics also employs the contrast between finite and infinite. The created universe is finite, that is, it is limited or bounded in some way, by contrast with its infinite, unlimited, unbounded creative source and

ground. The notions of finitude and contingency are clearly linked, especially when we think in terms of metaphysical finitude, that is, the ontological dependence of the created world on its Creator for its very existence
and persistence in being.

But, again, it is important to note that the finitude of the universe is not
necessarily a matter of its temporal or spatial finitude – its having a beginning in time, or having a limited spatial extent or a specific total mass. We
shall touch on the scientific treatment of these issues in the next section. In
philosophy, the finitude of the universe is more a matter of existential and
metaphysical analysis. A common starting point is to dwell on our own
finitude. Martin Heidegger, for example, in his account of human temporality, of our 'throwness' into the world, of our 'being towards death',
stressed just this fundamental experience of our finitude.[54] And the leitmotif
of Heidegger's whole philosophy was that our own finitude reflects the
finitude of all modes of being in the world.

In a very different, more Aristotelian, mode of philosophy (a mode of
philosophy more akin to that of the analytic tradition), Austin Farrer's first
book, *Finite and Infinite*, also moved from an exploration of the finite self, its
unity and its nature, expressed through its willing acts in a given world, to
an analogous exploration of the nature of finite substance in general. The
coexistence of the elements in finite substance, Farrer suggests, is intelligible
only on the supposition of God's existence as the ground of such finite
coexistence.[55]

3.2.3   Science and Creation

Questions of the world's temporal and spatial finitude cannot be considered
without reference to the work of contemporary physicists and cosmologists
who have offered some intriguing, if not readily intelligible, speculations on
these matters.

Stephen Hawking's lecture, 'The Origin of the Universe',[56] attempted to
show the non-specialist that 'Big Bang' cosmology need not necessarily
involve a temporal beginning to the universe. We have already seen how
some philosophers, such as Morris, interpret the singularity to which cosmologists press back in their speculations about the early history of the
universe as suggestive of creation out of nothing.[57] A similar inference is
drawn by William Lane Craig in his debate with Quentin Smith in their
book, *Theism, Atheism and Big Bang Cosmology*.[58] But Hawking, together
with his colleague Jim Hartle, put forward the intriguing hypothesis of a
finite, multidimensional, but unbounded universe, operating under the laws

of quantum gravity, in which any singularity to which we are driven back in real time ceases to entail an absolute beginning from the perspective of imaginary time. The philosopher may well wonder if this makes sense, especially the bit about imaginary time. But it is worth noting the difference between the way in which Hawking ends this lecture and the way in which he ends the comparable chapter in his best-selling book, *A Brief History of Time*.[59] In the lecture, he concludes: 'Although science may solve the problem of how the universe began, it cannot answer the question, Why does the universe bother to exist? I don't know the answer to that.' In the book, he concludes: 'If the universe is really completely self-contained, having no boundary or edge, it would have neither beginning nor end: it would simply be. What place, then, for a creator?'

John Polkinghorne gives this last question a straight answer: 'Every place – as the sustainer of the self-contained spacetime egg and as the ordainer of its quantum laws.'[60] And Keith Ward, at rather more length, shows how, even if self-contained, the fundamental structures of the universe – the quantum fields and the laws of physics – still need explaining.[61] The upshot of this discussion is clear: Hawking was nearer the mark in his lecture than in his book. And the need to postulate a Creator does not depend on a temporal beginning to the universe. But, as we have seen, that was already clear to Aquinas.

Another way of eliminating a temporal beginning is the multiple universe theory. (Here, 'universe' cannot mean *everything* there is. It means rather our whole space–time cosmic system and any other such systems there may be.) The theory may take the more straightforward form of suggesting an endless succession of expansions and contractions or the more esoteric form (not unrelated to Hawking's theory) of simultaneous, but unrelated, unbounded space–time systems. These extravagant and, one has to say, unverifiable and therefore metaphysical hypotheses are advanced not only in order to evade the relatively unimportant question of a temporal beginning, but also to avoid the teleological or design implications of the so-called 'anthropic' principle.

For, if our space–time cosmic system constitutes the one and only entire universe, there is no doubt that the 'fine-tuning' of the initial conditions in and immediately following the Big Bang does suggest design. There are a number of factors: the total mass of the universe, its density, the rate of expansion, the degree of inhomogeneity of radiation, etc., etc., all of which had to obtain within a very narrow range of possibilities, if galaxies and planetary systems were to evolve with conditions under which life could appear. The 'anthropic principle' argument for design, based on this fine-tuning, is most readily to be found in the Appendix B, added by Richard

Swinburne to the second edition of his *The Existence of God*.[62] More detailed treatments of the anthropic principle may be found in Barrow and Tipler's *The Anthropic Cosmological Principle*,[63] Gribbin and Rees's *The Stuff of the Universe*[64] and Leslie's *Universes*.[65] The last of these, in particular, considers the alternative 'multiple universes' hypothesis extensively.

My own view is that the alternatives are pretty fanciful, and that there is a strong case for design on the basis of this fine-tuning. But it also needs to be stressed that, if the multiple universes alternative is adopted, thus rendering the cosmic coincidences less implausible, given innumerable, perhaps infinitely many, throws of the dice, there is still a case for design, given the capacity of the world stuff to evolve life and mind and personality at all. Objections to this argument from the problem of evil will be considered later.

3.2.4   *Other necessities: abstract ideas, possibilities, numbers*

We turn now from the contingencies evident in the created universe, the factors that, as far as we can tell, could have been otherwise, to those aspects of this and any possible world which possess a kind of necessity, the factors, that is, that could not have been otherwise. There is a sense in which this is true of all abstract ideas. There may or may not be such entities as cats. Cats are wholly contingent beings. But catness – what it is to be a cat – is necessarily what it is in any possible world. If a world contains cats, this is what they will be like. That is not to say that it is necessary that there should be the idea of catness. Rather, any world containing cats will necessarily have these features.

The same goes for possibilities. The range of possibilities is necessarily what it is. An even more obvious case, as Platonists down the ages have urged, can be made for the necessity of mathematical objects, such as numbers. In any possible world, two plus two will equal four. Moreover, while the stuff of the world and the fundamental laws of nature might have been different, the fact that its basic structure is mathematically expressible, perhaps by a single equation, shows that there are necessary, rational constraints on the kind of world there can be.

How is theistic metaphysics to make sense of all this? I have already mentioned Creel's implausible view that the range of possibilities, the plenum, as he calls it, between which God chooses in actualizing a world, exists independently of the Creator.[66] The contrary view – namely, that all these necessities are to be construed as dependent necessities, dependent, that is, on the nature and mind of God – is powerfully argued by T. V. Morris and Christopher Menzel in their joint essay, 'Absolute Creation',[67] and by Menzel in his article, 'Theism, Platonism and the Metaphysics of Mathematics'.[68]

Morris and Menzel call the abstract necessities, to which any contingent world has to conform, 'the framework of reality', and ask the key question whether the Creator has to be thought of as responsible, not only for the contingent created world as it actually is, but also for the necessary framework itself. They argue for the view that the God of 'maximal greatness' theism must indeed be the absolute Creator of necessary as well as contingent reality. What are we to make of this?

Well, we can surely go along with this view as far as abstract ideas and possibilities are concerned. They can be seen as creative ideas in the mind of God. But mathematical equations and the laws of logic have a different kind of dependent necessity. Morris and Menzel quite rightly reject Descartes's notorious opinion[69] that the laws of logic were chosen by God, and could have been otherwise. But the inner necessity of the laws of logic is surely more a matter of their necessarily reflecting the consistency and rationality of the divine nature than a matter of internally necessary divine causation. My conclusion would be that, while some dependent necessities are indeed God's creative ideas, others depend on and reflect God's nature.

3.2.5   The world's openness to the future

At several points in our discussion of the nature of the created universe I have suggested that maximal greatness theology will be inclined to prefer an understanding of God's creative enterprise that sees the world as open to the future, containing many possibilities of free action and response, with God's personal creatures given the opportunity to make or mar their own futures, and thus the world's future, in cooperation with, or against, God's non-coercive grace and inspiration. This, it will be recalled, entailed a 'risk' view of creation and providence rather than Helm's 'no-risk' view.[70] Such a theology is defended by Keith Ward in chapter 11 of his *Religion and Creation*.[71] He contrasts it with the 'block-time' model of the universe favoured by many mathematical physicists, and raises the key question whether 'the mathematical point of view gives insight into the real structure of reality, or whether it is an abstraction, useful for purposes of calculation, but misleading if taken as a model of reality'.[72]

It is certainly much easier nowadays to accept a non-deterministic view of the world than it was in Newton's day. Both quantum theory and chaos theory have revealed a fuzziness or flexibility at the heart of the world's constituent energy that may well be the necessary condition for the evolution of free creatures, as has been argued in their different ways by Anscombe[73] and by Polkinghorne.[74] A non-deterministic, developing world is open to the future, in the sense of containing more and more open possibilities for realization through the free choices and creative innovations of beings such as ourselves. The nature of such a world and the nature of time as the matrix of free personal life and interaction has been explored in detail by the Oxford philosopher John Lucas, in a series of books from *The Freedom of the Will*[75] to *The Future*,[76] in which he also spells out the theological implications of all this. He concludes the last of these books with the following words:

> If God created man in His own image, He must have created him capable of new initiatives and new insights which cannot be precisely or infallibly foreknown, but which give to the future a perpetual freshness as the inexhaustible variety of possible thoughts and actions, on the part of His children as well as Himself, crystallizes into actuality.[77]

The limitations which this entails for God's omniscience have been much debated in recent philosophical theology.[78] Certainly we have to suppose that the infinite, eternal God knows all that can be known, all past and present facts and the future in so far as it is determined. But where freedom, creativity and open possibilities are concerned, even God cannot know precisely what we will do. This is one of the risks that an open-futured creation involves. Not that the Creation can get wholly out of the Creator's control. God knows what to do whatever we do, and how to bring our tortuous human history into a perfected harmony in the end. But the precise route of that interactive journey cannot be foretold even by omniscience. We may even be forced to put a question mark against the view that omniscience entails knowledge of every possibility. Knowledge of possibilities may, necessarily, be restricted to the kinds of thing there may be and the kinds of thing that may be done. Even God cannot know in advance all the possible people there may be, or all the possible operas that may be written. Possible people – the individuals there might have been or may one day be – cannot be known in advance of their formation through particular life histories. Possible operas cannot be known in advance of their actual creative composition. *The Magic Flute* was Mozart's creation, not the copying of a divine blueprint. The greatness of the Creator's work consists, among other things, in the creation of a world that can come up with a Mozart who can come up with *The Magic Flute*.

One way in which some philosophers think that these limitations on divine foreknowledge can be avoided is by adopting the late medieval theory known as 'middle knowledge' (scientia media),[79] whereby God, in his omniscience, is supposed to be aware of all contingencies, including future contingents and all 'counterfactuals of freedom', for example, what each of us would have done, had things turned out differently, and what each of us would do in whatever future circumstances come to pass. But are we seriously to suppose that God knows precisely what President Kennedy would have done in 1967 had he not been assassinated in 1963, or what I would do next year if I were to go to Australia (which I will not)? The incoherence of middle knowledge has been ably argued by William Hasker in God, Time and Knowledge,[80] and several issues of Faith and Philosophy contain discussions of this widely ramifying issue in philosophical theology.[81]

3.2.6   The goodness of the world

Even if the notion of the best of all possible worlds is rejected (see section 3.1.6), it follows from God's perfection that anything he creates will be good. Maximal greatness theology is bound to echo the Genesis affirmation that 'God saw what he had made and behold it was very good'.[82] It follows that matter or energy, the fundamental stuff of the world, is good, and that all its products, all natural kinds, including life, mind, spirit and persons in relation, are in essence good. Creation as a whole, including, of course, its intended consummation in the end, has to be affirmed as very good. I will mention in this connection just two books: Robert Adams's Finite and Infinite Goods[83] and Mark Wynn's God and Goodness.[84] Admittedly the former is primarily concerned with ethics and the latter with natural theology, but readers will find much illuminating reflection on the nature of created goods in their pages.

What, then, is to be said about evil? The problem of evil is undoubtedly the greatest threat to the credibility of theism and of the view of creation sketched in this chapter. There is a huge literature on this subject,[85] and only the briefest of treatments can be offered here.

The first thing to be said is that evil is not a substance. No created substance is, in and of itself, evil. Evil states of affairs consist in deprivations or frustrations brought about either by unintended clashes and accidents or by the perversion and abuse of the human will. This is the import of the Augustinian analysis of evil as privatio boni (deprivation of good).[86] This does not mean that evil is simply a negative phenomenon, an absence of good.

The clashes and perversions can indeed take very positive and appalling forms. But they cannot be regarded as part of the actual stuff of the world.

But why are such terrible states of affairs and perversions permitted to occur in God's creation? The only credible answer is that they are part of the 'risk' God takes in fashioning an environment capable of producing, forming and sustaining finite personal and interpersonal life. One aspect of this can readily be seen. We know from experience that human free will is always open to abuse. Human beings are not robots or computers. The point of human life would be lost if we were simply programmed always to act well. But the reason why our freedom is so much at risk to temptation and abuse is that we humans are rooted in and drawn out of an impersonal natural world that can always frustrate and annul our highest aspirations. Sometimes, as I say, this is a matter of our succumbing to temptation; sometimes it is a matter of accident or disaster. These risks in the creative process can only be understood if we can come to see that human life *has* to be built up from below, fashioned indirectly in and through a regularly structured environment that, as well as producing and sustaining us, can also do us so much harm. Once formed in this way, we acquire the capacity for transformation, by the Creator, into the perfected conditions of eternity. But the created world, with all its glories and risks, is the *necessary* condition of our coming to be. Heaven cannot be posited in being directly, any more than a mature, wise artist or saint can be posited in being directly.

So, the goods of creation, including the great good of its perfected state in the end, can be held to justify the risks involved only if those risks are necessary conditions of the realisation of those goods.

CHAPTER FOUR

Incarnation

The second, and longest, main section of the Christian creeds is devoted to Jesus Christ. In it are affirmed his identity: the incarnate Son of God, and the purpose of his coming: the salvation and judgement of the human race. This doctrine of the Incarnation, from early days, came to form the heart of traditional Christianity. With it, there emerged the doctrine of the Trinity; since belief in the divinity of Christ was held to entail a revised understanding of the God of Jewish faith. We shall consider the doctrine of the Trinity in the next chapter. Here we examine what Anglo-American analytical philosophers of religion have contributed to the criticism, clarification and defence of the doctrine of the Incarnation.

4.1   The Doctrine of the Incarnation

But what precisely is the doctrine of the Incarnation? It is well known that its classical formulations in the creeds and confessions of the Christian Church were the result of centuries of contested debate, and that they remain subject to very different interpretations, not least in contemporary Christian theology. Readers who wish to scrutinize the relevant New Testament texts, and the first agreed summaries in the Chalcedonian Definition and the Athanasian Creed, will find them cited in the very useful article on 'Incarnation and Christology' by Peter van Inwagen in the *Routledge Encyclopedia of Philosophy*,[1] together with interesting reflections on the metaphysics and the logic of incarnational belief. I will offer my own summary statement as a starting point for our survey and discussion here.

The doctrine of the Incarnation sums up mainstream Christian belief that the first-century Jewish rabbi, Jesus of Nazareth, was more than a prophet, more than just a normal, even extraordinary and highly influential, human being. Partly as a result of the impact of his life, teaching and fate, partly as a result of their post-Easter experiences – not only the Resurrection appearances but also their experience of him as a living presence in their hearts and in their worship – the early Christians came to think of Jesus as having come to them from the side of God, indeed as God made man. They came to see the history and faith of Israel as culminating in God's personal presence here on earth in and as the man Jesus, bringing salvation, in the sense of both forgiveness and, eventually, eternal union with God, for all humankind. Centuries of debate and controversy led to the classical formulations, whereby Jesus Christ was held to be both God and man. Without ceasing to be the God he ever was and is, God, in one of the modes or centres or 'Persons' of his eternal being, had taken our nature upon him, lived out a human life and died a human death, and, by his Resurrection, taken humanity into God for ever. The risen Christ, they held, remains the human face of God for all eternity, and remains the focus and the fulcrum of our eternal destiny. As I say, the trinitarian implications of the doctrine of the Incarnation will be examined in the next chapter, but it needs to be stressed here that, according to Christian belief, Jesus was and is not God made man *simpliciter*, but the divine Word or Son incarnate. As we shall see, some such differentiation or distinction in the theology of God was necessary if sense was to be made of the conviction that God himself had come amongst us in and as a man who prayed to God.

4.2   Myth, Metaphor or Truth?

Classical Christian belief in the divinity of Christ was challenged by the Quakers and the Unitarians in the early modern period, by the liberal Protestant critique of the history of dogma in the nineteenth century and at the Girton Conference of the Modern Churchmen's Union in 1920.[2] The much discussed volume, *The Myth of God Incarnate*,[3] which appeared in 1977, summed up the difficulties found by many modern Christian theologians with the credal affirmations. That book's editor, the distinguished philosopher of religion John Hick, will be taken here as the clearest and most challenging exponent of a non-incarnational version of Christianity.

In his own contribution to *The Myth of God Incarnate*, Hick stressed the problems for Christian incarnational belief posed by the other world faiths, whose status as vehicles of liberation and salvation for millions of people worldwide and down the ages would, Hick thought, be bound to be depreciated if Jesus Christ and Jesus Christ alone were 'literally' God incarnate. This difficulty is one of the three main objections to the doctrine of the Incarnation put forward in *The Myth of God Incarnate*. The other two were the problem of evidence (what historical evidence could possibly establish so extravagant a doctrine?) and the problem of coherence (surely it is a straight contradiction to affirm both humanity and divinity of the same individual). Hick himself developed this third objection in subsequent writings, in his Gifford Lectures,[4] and in *The Metaphor of God Incarnate*.[5] We shall consider the first two objections – the problem of other religions and the problem of evidence – in later sections of this chapter. But our main concern in philosophical theology is with the logical question of whether the Christian doctrine of the Incarnation is coherent.

If the doctrine is incoherent, it cannot possibly be true. At worst it is a nonsense; at best it is really (I do not say only) a myth or a metaphor. But this contrast between truth on the one hand, and myth or metaphor on the other, is not nearly as perspicuous as might appear at first sight. So, before we examine the logic and metaphysics of God incarnate, that is, the case for thinking the doctrine of the Incarnation to be both coherent and true, it will be well worth while spending a little time on what is meant by calling it mythical or metaphorical rather than true.

A statement, belief or doctrine is true if things are in reality what it says they are. The doctrine of the Incarnation is true if Jesus was indeed God made man, if he was indeed both human and divine. Such talk of the divinity of Christ is mythical or metaphorical, if the doctrine is not literally true, but rather expresses, figuratively and indirectly, some other fact or attitude. Myths and metaphors are not lies or falsehoods, nor are they meaningless nonsenses. On the contrary, they often themselves express deep truths, truths hard to convey in straight prose, deep truths, underlying the surface meaning of the myth or metaphor. The difference between myths and metaphors is this: a myth is an extended story, illustrating or conveying some underlying meaning or truth; a metaphor is a figure of speech suggestive of some underlying meaning or truth. Often it is claimed that the underlying meaning or truth can only be hinted at indirectly and figuratively by means of myth or metaphor. But we can always try to articulate more directly what is conveyed by the myth or metaphor.

Here are some examples, first, of myth: the creation myths at the beginning of Genesis are not literally true. Creation, for example, did not take place in six days. But they convey very powerfully, in story form, the absolute dependence of the universe on the creative will and act of God for being in being at all. (In other words, what we were doing in the last chapter was articulating and exploring the deep truths underlying the creation myths of Genesis.) And here is an example of metaphor: when we sing the hymn,

'Rock of Ages, cleft for me', we are using the metaphor 'rock' to signify, figuratively, the enduring steadfastness of almighty God.

Of course, the language used in articulating the doctrine is itself stretched and extended from normal everyday use. Thomas Aquinas taught the way of *analogy* as characterizing our talk of God and God's action.[6] Mere humans cannot comprehend the ineffable divine. But we can speak of God on the basis of the attributes and acts of those creatures made in God's image. Examples of such analogies are 'Creator', 'wise', 'love', 'will'. Analogies are not metaphors. There is a real relation of resemblance between human love and divine love. One way of distinguishing between metaphors and analogies is to ask, 'But is A really x?'. God is not really a rock. That is a metaphor. But you cannot say 'God is not really love'. That shows that 'love' is not a metaphor. The word is being used analogically.

Not all talk of God is analogical. 'Divine' itself is a literal, 'univocal' term, as are several other specially coined theological terms. But it is important to remember that Aquinas included the analogical under the heading of the literal or 'proper' in his analysis of talk of God.[7] So we need have no compunction in pressing the question whether or not some doctrine is literally true.

To return to the Incarnation: the dispute between the authors of *The Myth of God Incarnate* and the authors of the immediate reply, *The Truth of God Incarnate*,[8] was over whether talk of the divinity of Christ was literally true, or whether, in fact, it was either a figurative way of expressing some more general truth, such as 'that which makes possible a profound inner union of the divine and the human in the experience of grace in the life of the believer now and more broadly in the life of the church as a whole' (thus Maurice Wiles[9]), or else 'a story which . . . invites a particular attitude in its hearers. . . . In the case of Jesus it gives definitive expression to his efficacy as saviour from sin and ignorance and as giver of new life; it offers a way of declaring his significance to the world' (thus John Hick[10]). In his later book, Hick prefers to speak of the metaphor of divine incarnation: 'Just as Winston Churchill "incarnated" the British will to resist Hitler, so Jesus "incarnated" God's will and love for humankind as well as the ideal of human life lived in response to God.'[11] Hick's main reason for denying literal truth to the classical Christian doctrine of the Incarnation, in both texts, is that a literal incarnation makes no sense. Just as there cannot, logically cannot, be a square circle, so the notion of one who is both God and man is a contradiction in terms.

It is interesting to note that the majority of the Anglo-Saxon analytic philosophers of religion who have addressed this issue have not been persuaded that there is a straight contradiction here. But clearly this is the key issue for philosophers. And it is to work on this issue that we must now turn.

4.3   The Logic and Metaphysics of God Incarnate

I had already provided an immediate response to the charge of logical contradiction prior to the publication of *The Myth of God Incarnate*:

> What is the basis for comparing talk of one who is both God and man to talk of a square circle? Certainly a square circle is a contradiction in terms. The terms 'square' and 'circle' are precisely defined terms, and their logical incompatibility is obvious from the definition. But 'God' and 'man' are far from being such tightly defined concepts. It is difficult enough to suppose that we have a full and adequate grasp of the divine nature. Who are we to say that the essence of God is such as to rule out the possibility of his making himself present in the created world as a human being, while in no way ceasing to be the God he ever is?[12]

Such a response does not, of course, get us very far. The point surely holds; but it does no more than reject the comparison with a square circle. And its appeal to ignorance, while consonant with the time-honoured doctrine of divine incomprehensibility, does nothing to substantiate the positive content of incarnational Christology. What is needed is some positive account and defence of the metaphysics of God incarnate, together with an argued rebuttal of all accusations of incoherence. Such a defence is highly likely to involve analogy, as is the case with most of our talk of God. But, as explained in the previous section, this does not take us outside the sphere of literal truth-claims.

I will concentrate here on the work of five philosophers who have made important contributions to the clarification of the logic and metaphysics of God incarnate, namely David Brown, Thomas V. Morris, Richard Swinburne, Alfred J. Freddoso and Peter van Inwagen.

David Brown's book, *The Divine Trinity*,[13] was cited in chapter 2 for its treatment of divine revelation on the analogy of a teacher–pupil dialogue, and it will, of course, be discussed in the next chapter on the Trinity. But it also contains sustained reflection on the Incarnation and especially on the coherence of the doctrine. Brown considers six 'models' for incarnation, rejecting four of them on grounds of incoherence, and defending the coherence of the other two, as offering different, but equally tenable, ways of thinking of Christ as both human and divine. It should be noted that Brown operates with a somewhat loose sense of the word 'model' in speaking of models for incarnation. He seems to mean little more than 'ways of understanding' the doctrine.

The four rejected ways of understanding incarnation are:

1   Apollinarianism: the denial of a human soul to Christ, the human soul being replaced by the divine Logos. This yields an incoherent account of Christ's humanity.
2   Nestorianism: the supposition that there are two persons, human and divine, in Christ. This yields an incoherent account of Christ's identity.
3   The model of grace: the suggestion that a perfectly grace-filled human life is a sufficient way of understanding Christ. This yields an incoherent account of Christ's divinity.
4   The mythological model: the kind of account typified by *The Myth of God Incarnate*. This (as we saw above) yields no serious account of incarnation at all.

The two models explored in detail and defended by Brown are the 'two-natures Christology' and the 'kenotic model' (the word 'kenosis' means 'emptying' and is used to denote the restriction or limitation of the divine attributes allegedly involved in incarnation). The first of these models (basically, the view formulated at the Council of Chalcedon in 451) affirms that in Christ, and in Christ alone, we have to do with a single person who possessed, at one and the same time, both a fully human and a fully divine nature; the second, that, in the Incarnation, the divine Son, by an act of self-limitation, put his divine attributes in abeyance, and lived, for a time, a human life on earth, expressing the divine love in purely human form. In attempting to show the coherence of each of these models, Brown first considers analogies, such as Aquinas's human nature cum animal nature analogy for the first, and the more common reincarnation analogy for the second. He then shows how divine and human attributes may, on the two-natures model, be ascribed to Christ qua God and to Christ qua man respectively, and may, on the kenotic model, be ascribed to the divine Son prior to, and during, incarnation successively. Brown sees no problem in ascribing fallibility to the human Christ on either view. Most importantly, he considers the key question of identity. How, on the two-natures view, is Christ's personal identity secured? And how, on the kenotic view, is continuity of identity maintained throughout the process of self-emptying? With regard to the two-natures view, further analogies from split personality and from our conscious and subconscious selves are explored. Brown is prepared to speak of two centres of consciousness in the incarnate one, but the extent of the two-way flow between them is held to rule out talk of 'inspiration' or 'possession' and to require personal unity and identity. With regard to the kenotic view, continuity of character and memory (even if the latter were temporally suspended) suffice to sustain personal identity throughout the successive stages.

Brown's reflections constitute a fine example of how such a central theological topic as incarnation can be explored and analysed philosophically. As is the case with all rational reflection, the treatment is not beyond criticism. I will mention three objections to Brown's conclusion that the two favoured models present equally coherent and tenable, but alternative, views. First, it may be doubted whether Brown has taken the measure of a 'two-consciousnesses' view of the Incarnation. Indeed, at one point (p. 233) he accuses it of incoherence in attributing a split personality in the *divine* nature (my emphasis), while at another (p. 261f.) he uses split personality as an analogy for ascribing two centres of consciousness to the one divine-human person. Secondly, as Swinburne pointed out in a review of Brown's book,[14] Brown's concept of personal identity as being constituted by the causal connections of character and memory does not do justice to the ultimacy of what it is to be an individual person. And thirdly, one may question whether Brown's two favoured models really are alternatives. Is there not a case for recognizing the kenotic element in Christ's human nature and experience within an overall two-natures view that does justice to the full divinity of the one who takes human nature into himself, by channelling the divine life through a fully human life without ceasing to be the God he ever was and is?

Before developing these thoughts, I turn to consider the contributions of Morris, Swinburne, Freddoso and van Inwagen to our theme.

Morris's book, *The Logic of God Incarnate*,[15] and a subsequent essay in the Feenstra/Plantinga volume,[16] present us with a robust defence of the 'two-consciousnesses' or 'two-minds' view of the Incarnation. Morris is not happy with kenotic Christology.[17] The idea of abandoning or putting in abeyance the divine properties of omnipotence, omniscience, etc. is held not to do justice to the full divinity of the incarnate one. Morris prefers to think in terms of the second Person of the Trinity taking on a human body and a human mind and living a human life on earth, 'without relinquishing the proper resources of divinity'.[18] On this view, the incarnate one was fully human without being merely human. His human mind was not, as is the case with all other humans, the ultimate, metaphysical, ontological subject of his life and action. Christ's human mind was 'contained' by his divine mind. This was not just a matter of an 'asymmetrical accessing relation' between the divine mind of God the Son and the human mind of Jesus.

Such a relation holds between God's mind and all human minds. In the case of Jesus alone, we are to suppose that 'the personal cognitive and causal powers' of his earthly mind, and indeed life, were those of the divine mind and life of God the Son.[19] It is this ultimate and unique metaphysical ownership that characterizes the Incarnation and makes the incarnate Son of God one Person, despite his unique possession of two natures.

John Hick, in *The Metaphor of God Incarnate*,[20] criticizes Morris for concentrating on the mind of Jesus rather than his whole life, and also for failing to do justice to Christ's freedom. The second of these criticisms is a serious one and will be considered in a separate section of this chapter. But the first can easily be countered. Concentration on the mind of the incarnate one is surely justified, since what is at stake is the ultimate metaphysical subject of Jesus' life and action. But Morris is quite clear that what we are talking about is a human life lived out from a centre in God.

As was the case with Brown, critics may well have some reservations over the analogies which Morris deploys in defence of his 'two-minds' view. Human instances of multiple mentality, in dreams, split personality, and hypnosis are cited as partial analogies for the two-minds view. But these fall foul of Swinburne's objection to Brown. Indeed the more Morris goes along with a many-levelled view of the human mind, the less he does justice to the ultimacy of subjectivity. And we may further object to the way in which such analogies tend to treat the divine mind on the same level as the human mind. It is a theological point that must be respected in philosophical theology, that it is only the infinite otherness of God the Creator that allows a creaturely life to be the vehicle and medium of the divine life. Morris's metaphysics retains greater plausibility the less we pursue these dubious analogies. We still use analogical language of course, in talk of the divine life and mind. But we refrain from pressing the human side of these analogies too far.

Richard Swinburne's *The Christian God*[21] is another book to which we shall be returning in the next chapter on the Trinity. But its treatment of the Incarnation must be considered here. In his ninth chapter, 'The Possibility of Incarnation', Swinburne defends the coherence of Chalcedon, taking it to mean that, by incarnation, God the Son, without abandoning his divine properties, acquired a human nature, that is, a human body and, with it, a human way of experiencing, thinking, willing and acting. Swinburne uses the divided mind analogy to illustrate and explain this way of understanding the Incarnation; but it is clear that he is in fact operating with much the same 'two-minds' view as Morris. But we have to recall Swinburne's own point, against Brown, about the ultimacy of personal identity. This means that the human mind of Christ, God incarnate, does not constitute an individual person, as it does with the rest of us. The ultimate subject of the incarnate life is, uniquely, God the Son. Christ is the divine Son incarnate, and cannot be thought of, even theoretically, as an independent human individual, assumed by God the Son. Swinburne is quite prepared to accept Christ's human limitations, qua man, and he rejects the Lutheran insistence on the total interpenetration of divine and human attributes. These are not to be confused. But Christ's being the incarnate Son, while allowing his susceptibility to temptation, rules out the possibility of his doing wrong or even being inclined to do wrong. We shall return to this point in the section of Christ's freedom.

In insisting that Christ's human nature cannot be 'hypostasized', i.e. regarded as a theoretically independent human soul, Swinburne draws attention to and expresses gratitude for an article in *Faith and Philosophy* by Alfred J. Freddoso, entitled 'Human Nature, Potency, and the Incarnation'.[22] This debt is fully justified. Freddoso's article is one of the most powerful philosophical investigations of the metaphysics and logic of incarnation. And in some ways it is even more persuasive than Swinburne's chapter. For it shows more clearly that the impossibility of Christ's individual human nature being only contingently united to a divine Person need not prevent us from speaking of Christ's humanity as that of an individual composed of a body and an intellective soul. The crucial point is that Christ's human soul and personality are, necessarily and uniquely, the earthly, incarnate, vehicle of the divine Person.

Difficulties are caused, in incarnational Christology, by uncertainty over which term to use for the ultimate personal subject of Christ's life. The tradition has reserved the term 'person' for this and allowed talk of two wills and two minds, but not two persons. Swinburne, perhaps confusingly, reserves the term 'soul' for this ultimate metaphysical subject. Freddoso is perhaps wiser to allow talk of Christ's human soul. One could move the other way and allow talk of Jesus Christ as a human person, but not an independent human person, a person, that is, existing in personal relation to the second Person of the Trinity. For the tradition holds that the human person Jesus *is* the incarnate Son, just as his human mind and will *are* the divine mind and will operative under human conditions. What permits talk of two minds and two wills – and, on this extended view, two persons – is recognition of the fact that the divine retains its divinity while operating under those conditions. Perhaps it would be better to respect tradition and avoid talk of two persons. But the last thing the tradition wanted was to deny full humanity to the incarnate one.

Swinburne happily distinguishes between what can be said of Jesus Christ qua divine and what can be said of him qua human, but his use of this mode

of speech is somewhat undermined by his commitment, which he shares
with Morris, to a Leibnizian theory of absolute identity. (The philosopher
G. W. Leibniz, is well known for his theory of the identity of indiscernibles,
the view that, if a and b are identical, then they have all their attributes in
common.) He may be right about this. I have myself insisted that the human
being Jesus just *is* the incarnate Son of God. But it is worth considering how
the more flexible theory of *relative* identity might be used in explicating the
doctrine of the Incarnation.

This is where we turn to the work of Peter van Inwagen. In articles
reprinted in his book, *God, Knowledge and Mystery*,[23] and in the encyclopaedia article referred to at the beginning of this chapter,[24] van Inwagen has
used the notion of relative identity to show how one and the same subject
can have incompatible properties, provided they are relative to different
conditions. Thus the Son of God incarnate, qua divine, was and is omnipotent, omniscient and omnipresent; but the Son of God incarnate, qua
human – that is, qua the man Jesus of Nazareth – was weak and helpless
(as a child), ignorant of many things and located specifically in first-century
Palestine. The supposition of incarnational Christology is that one and the
same divine Person, without ceasing to be God, could and did live out a
truly human life, under truly human conditions, here on earth. The concept
of relative identity allows us to give 'yes' and 'no' answers to key questions
about this doctrine. Was Jesus Christ a creature? Yes, qua the man Jesus; no,
qua God the Son. Did God die on the cross? Yes, qua God incarnate; no, qua
God the Son.

Van Inwagen himself does not go very far into the ontology of incarnation. Reflecting further on this matter, we would have to stress the
godness of God in becoming incarnate. Only a divine Person could live
out a human life as the vehicle and expression of the divine love in human
form. Here the asymmetry that Morris speaks of is more than cognitive. It
has to be spelled out, metaphysically, in terms of that human life being the
life of God the Son in human form, not the other way round. But the
advantage of relative identity theory is, in the first place, that we can avoid
having to ascribe, e.g., eternity to the human being, Jesus (Morris is driven,
implausibly, to suggest that having a temporal beginning is not of the
essence of humanity[25]) and, secondly, that we can take full advantage of
the moral force of kenotic Christology when speaking of God incarnate.
God really does subject himself, in human form, to the limitations of our
existence and to betrayal and a cruel death. Another advantage of embracing
kenoticism within a two-natures understanding of the Incarnation is that it
make more sense of the idea, essential to Christian soteriology (its doctrine
of salvation), that humanity is taken into God for ever. Indeed, through

personal union with the risen Christ we too, so Christians hold, are taken into God, not, of course, as yet more incarnations (that makes no sense at all, as we shall see) but, in biblical language, as 'fellow heirs with Christ by adoption'.[26] These matters will be treated more fully in chapter 6 on Salvation.

4.4 Is the Incarnation a Miracle?

I have said nothing, in this examination of the metaphysics of God incarnate, about the tradition, already embedded in some later books of the New Testament,[27] that Jesus of Nazareth had no human father. The aspect of this tradition that most concerns philosophical theologians is the question whether the Virgin Birth, or, more accurately, the virginal conception of Jesus, is essential to the metaphysics of incarnation. Now the birth of a male child from a virgin, involving, as it would have to do, the special creation of Y-chromosomes, would certainly be a miracle. Such a miracle might well be an appropriate sign of the unique nature and significance of Jesus. But it is usually agreed by theologians such as Karl Barth,[28] as well as by philosophical theologians, that the Incarnation, as such, need not necessarily have involved a virginal conception. Admittedly, David Brown suggests that a virgin birth would be required by a *kenotic* Christology considered as an alternative to a two-natures Christology.[29] But his arguments for this do not carry conviction. And, in any case, it is Brown's view that a two-natures Christology does not require such a miracle. Swinburne states categorically that a virgin birth 'is not necessary for God to become man'.[30] It is interesting to see how Keith Ward, while still inclined, like Brown and Swinburne, to accept that Jesus had no human father, is quite clear that 'the virgin birth does not seem essential to the truth of the claim that Jesus is the incarnation of the cosmic Christ'.[31] The credal reference to 'born of the Virgin Mary' could, he says, be interpreted in a symbolic sense.

This consensus rests partly on recognition that the infancy narratives in Matthew and Luke contain much legendary material expressive of the significance of the birth of Jesus, their role, vis-à-vis the Incarnation being comparable to that of the Genesis creation myths vis-à-vis the Creation, and partly on recognition that God's particular presence in the world in human form no more requires the breaking of the natural fabric of creation than does God's action in the world in general. The fabric of creation, on a theistic view, is flexible and open to divine providence in many ways, and, as we shall see in the final chapter, providential intervention does not necessarily mean miraculous intervention. The possibility of miraculous intervention is not denied. J. Houston has shown how Hume's famous arguments against belief in miracles are totally beside the point.[32] Our experience of what normally goes on has nothing whatever to do with whether or not, for good reasons, God specially intervenes. But there are good theological reasons, if we are theists, and especially if we are Christian theists, for us to suppose that God respects the structures of creation, and works providentially within them, unless, as is the case with the Resurrection, there is no alternative to miraculous intervention. Those theological reasons have much to do with theodicy in respect of the problem of evil, but much too to do with a conception of the God–world relation that does not treat divine action as one causal factor among others, operating at the same level. So, if the Incarnation can be construed as the climax of God's providential ordering of things, it may be best to take it that way, and treat the Virgin Birth as legendary picture language, expressive of the conviction that Jesus came to us from the side of God.

4.5 Christ's Freedom

Traditionally, it has been held that Christ's humanity, the humanity of the incarnate Son of God, was like ours in all respects save that of sin. Christ was certainly subject to temptation. But, being who he was, he could not possibly have succumbed. For God is necessarily good and if Christ was God incarnate, then it follows not only that he did not sin, but that he could not have sinned. Sinlessness was, and is, a necessary property of the incarnate one.

The view that it belongs to the very essence of being human to be a sinner is not too difficult to refute. Someone who did no wrong would not thereby be disqualified from belonging to the human race. But impeccability, not being able to sin, does appear to deprive a human being of significant freedom. And being significantly free surely does belong to the essence of humanity. The question of Christ's freedom is therefore one of the most crucial issues in debates over the coherence of incarnational Christology. John Hick regards the inability of a 'two-minds' view of the Incarnation to accord significant freedom to the man Jesus as a decisive objection to all attempts to revive and defend Chalcedonian orthodoxy.[33]

Let us consider the ways in which Christian philosophers have attempted to face up to this problem. T. V. Morris argues that being tempted is an epistemic matter.[34] It does not, as such, entail the real possibility of acting wrongly. It is enough, humanly speaking, for the incarnate one to have felt the power of temptation, even if, being who he was, he could not have done otherwise than what God willed. Morris is less persuasive in calling upon Harry Frankfurt's much discussed examples of how genuinely free actions do not necessarily entail that one could have done otherwise.[35] Those examples showed how an act would still be freely one's own, even if all alternatives, unbeknownst to one, were causally blocked off. For the causal factors that blocked off the alternatives would have played no role at all in the actual decision and act in question. But, as Swinburne points out,[36] the agent in this case could have *tried* to act otherwise. And that, for someone tempted to do wrong, would itself be a sin.

Swinburne's own solution, however, also fails to convince.[37] He suggests that God incarnate, being who he was, could do no wrong, but that he was genuinely free to act in a variety of good ways, not only in the sense of duties but also in the sense of supererogatory acts (i.e. beyond the call of duty). So far we may concur with Swinburne. But, implausibly, he goes on to suggest that felt temptation to do wrong would be illusory temptation. Real temptation must involve desire to take another path. On Swinburne's view, Christ's temptations could only have been temptations to take some other good path than that of the supererogatory call to tread the way of the cross. But, as Thomas Flint points out,[38] the temptation not to do his Father's will would, on this analysis, still involve a real inclination towards sin.

Flint's own solution relies on acceptance of the Molinist doctrine of middle knowledge, the view that God, in his omniscience, knows what any possible creature would freely do in any situation in which that creature were placed. Equipped with middle knowledge, God can actualize a scenario in which Christ will freely, and contingently, do his Father's will. Only so, claims Flint, can the divine Son's necessary impeccability be reconciled with the man Jesus' significant freedom.

In the previous chapter I questioned this doctrine of middle knowledge (see chapter 3, section 3.2.5), and in the final chapter I shall argue again that it must be rejected on grounds of incoherence, and hence that it can play no role in a doctrine of divine providence. But where does this leave the issue of Christ's freedom? Unless we go along with Hick's rejection of incarnational Christology, all we can do is try to hold together the more plausible aspects of Morris's and Swinburne's analyses, while dismissing the implausible ones. We are left with the following picture.

If, as Morris holds, the personal cognitive and causal powers of Jesus' life and mind were those of God the Son in incarnate form, then divine impeccability necessarily carries over into the incarnate life. Being who he was, Jesus Christ, necessarily, could do no wrong. This makes Morris's use of Frankfurt-style examples quite irrelevant, as Swinburne says. But

Swinburne's analysis of temptation will not do. Felt temptation is not illusory, even if it was bound to be overcome. It still cost agony and bloody sweat. And a desire overcome is not a sin.

Significant freedom is not always a matter of choice between good and evil. God's freedom is not like that, nor is the freedom of the blessed in heaven who have passed beyond the sphere of temptation. Christ's freedom to act in ways that were always good is to that extent like the freedom of the blessed in heaven. But, unlike theirs, it was exercised on earth and thereby subject to temptation to go astray. Where the rest of us are concerned, there is no guarantee that temptation will always be resisted. (We do not have to go so far as to entertain the logical possibility of 'transworld depravity', the view that sooner or later every possible human creature *will* do wrong, as Plantinga does, curiously just because of his acceptance of middle knowledge vis-à-vis the problem of evil.[39]) But Christ's being who he was, the incarnate Son of God, did guarantee that temptation, however acute, would be resisted. But that did not make him less than human, any more than the absence of temptation makes the blessed in heaven less than human. To suppose that incarnation involves the real possibility of succumbing to temptation is no more theologically plausible than to suppose that sin belongs to the essence of being human.

4.6   The Purpose of the Incarnation

Anselm's question, *Cur Deus Homo?*, Why did God become man?, will be discussed more fully in chapter 6 on salvation. For the primary purpose of the Incarnation, according to the Christian creeds, was 'for us and for our salvation'. However, philosophically minded theologians have given some thought to the wider implications of that 'for us'. One way of doing so is to ask, as Austin Farrer did, whether Christ would have come even if the human race had never sinned. Farrer's answer was a categorical yes:

> Christ would still have come to transform human hope, and to bring men into a more privileged association with their Creator than they could otherwise enjoy. For it is by the descent of God into man that the life of God takes on a form with which we have a direct sympathy and personal union.[40]

(Farrer is here siding with the Franciscans against the Dominicans in a well-known medieval dispute.) Swinburne expresses some doubt as to whether there are strong arguments allowing us 'to say what God would have done under certain unrealized circumstances',[41] but he does consider a number of reasons, over and above the soteriological ones, why God might well become incarnate. Incarnation would manifest divine solidarity with God's creatures; it would demonstrate the dignity of human nature; it would reveal the nature and extent of God's love for his personal creatures; it would exemplify an ideal human life; and it would provide uniquely authoritative teaching. A sixth reason, based on God's willingness to subject himself to suffering and evil, spells out the themes of solidarity and love, and will, of course, play an important role in soteriology, as we shall see in chapter 6.

I have endeavoured to make similar points myself by asking what would be lost from Christian faith if incarnational Christology were abandoned in the way suggested by the authors of *The Myth of God Incarnate*.[42] In summary, the elements that would be lost include experience of God's presence and love in person; revelation of the trinitarian implications of the divine love as it is in itself in the inner life of God, experience in prayer and sacrament of Christ as living Lord, recognition of Christ's cross as God's cross in our world and the eschatological hope of Christ as the human face of God with whom we are to be united for all eternity.

All these factors are, of course, moral and religious considerations rather than philosophical ones, but they are pertinent to philosophical theology, insofar as they reinforce the case for taking incarnational Christology seriously. They contribute to spelling out the inner rationale of the doctrine of the Incarnation and provide reasons, as Swinburne puts it, for the theist to expect an incarnation.[43] The relevance of such a notion vis-à-vis assessment of evidence for the Incarnation will be discussed in the next section.

4.7   Evidence for the Incarnation

It will be recalled that one of the three main difficulties which the authors *of The Myth of God Incarnate* found with classical Christology was the paucity of historical evidence for so extravagant a doctrine. Applying the methods of historical criticism to the Christian scriptures, the only substantial records available, New Testament scholars have often been led to the conclusion that ascriptions of divinity to Jesus Christ are few and late, and intelligible in terms that fall far short of credal orthodoxy. But the question arises whether this issue can properly be settled by purely historical enquiry. The main contribution of philosophers of religion to discussion of this problem has been to show, in the first place, how much one's assessment of the historical evidence is affected by the system of beliefs one brings to its scrutiny, and, in the second place, the inevitable limits to the scope of purely historical investigation, where incarnational Christology is in question.

Thus Michael Dummett argues: 'Estimates of probability depend crucially on background assumptions. Without some background beliefs, no judgement of probability can be made.'[44] Similarly, Alvin Plantinga argues that the presuppositions about the uniformity of history (to be found especially in the writings of Ernst Troeltsch) represent no threat to Christianity with its quite different framework of basic beliefs.[45] David Brown, with much greater sensitivity to historical development than we get from either Dummett or Plantinga, shows how the divinity of Christ was a conclusion which the Church, with its convictions about God, was bound to draw from what was implicit in the story of Jesus and its aftermath and in the Christian community's experience of worship.[46] Swinburne, more than any other philosopher of religion, has shown how assessments of probability differ in relation to background evidence. How one weighs historical evidence depends crucially on what one's background beliefs lead one to expect.[47]

Purely empirical considerations do play a role in the matter of evidence. There are historical truth conditions of the truth of Christianity, both negative and positive. If it were proved that Jesus never existed or was himself a malefactor, Christian doctrine would be falsified. Also, the character and life of Jesus had to be of such manifest goodness as to suggest and support the doctrines that emerged. Other purely historical factors to which justice has to be done include the transformation of the disciples from disillusioned men into preachers of a new age, their conviction of Christ's resurrection and their claimed experience of his presence in their worshipping communities. All this constitutes relevant evidence. But its interpretation depends on background beliefs and expectations, and, one has to add, on experiential confirmation through participation in Christian life and worship today.

This latter factor is not easy to handle in relation to the cumulative case for Christian incarnational belief. But among the many contributions to philosophical theology by Austin Farrer, this matter of 'experiential verification' was given a key role in his apologetic, both in its own right and in relation to the spelling out of the inner rationale of Christian doctrine.[48]

Returning to the public case for incarnational belief, we now have to reckon with the role of the Resurrection in substantiating conviction of the divinity of Christ. Evidence for the Resurrection is closely bound up with evidence for the Incarnation, as both Brown and Swinburne make clear.[49] For one of the factors that gave rise to high Christologies was conviction that God had raised Jesus from the dead. Appeal to the Resurrection, like appeal to Christ's sacramental presence and saving power is a trans-historical appeal, but it includes empirical components: the empty tomb tradition and the claimed Resurrection appearances. How one evaluates these again depends on one's prior beliefs and prior expectations. Considered purely historically, one may get no further than the historian E. P. Sanders's frank conclusion: 'That Jesus' followers had resurrection experiences is, in my judgement, a fact. What the reality was that gave rise to the experiences I do not know.'[50] Philosophers will observe that that agnosticism reflects an agnostic perspective. A theistic perspective, and a fortiori an incarnational perspective, will contain different expectations, and thus different evaluations of the evidence.

4.8 The Uniqueness of the Incarnation

The other main reason for demythologizing incarnational belief was a moral argument in favour of religious pluralism. According to John Hick, a global perspective requires us to give equal revelatory and salvific significance to all the great world religions.[51] From this perspective, the Christian doctrine of the Incarnation constitutes a major stumbling block. For if the Word became flesh in Jesus alone, the revelatory and salvific importance of this event is bound to exceed that of all other faiths, however positive and life-enhancing they may be as channels of the Spirit's commerce with humanity. Hick's religious epistemology, and his assumption that no one religion could be closer to the truth than others, are sharply criticized by Plantinga in *Warranted Christian Belief*.[52] And indeed, if the arguments surveyed above concerning the coherence of the Incarnation, together with its purpose and its evidence, carry weight, then the assumption of equal status cannot stand.

Swinburne's point about theistic expectation of an incarnation would lead one to suppose that the idea of a divine incarnation or indeed of divine incarnations would have occurred elsewhere in the history of theistic religions. And, of course, it has, most notably, though not exclusively, in the avatar doctrine of Vaishnavite Hinduism, the most striking feature of which is the alleged fact of many incarnations, animal as well as human, of the god, Vishnu. The data are surveyed most accessibly in Geoffrey Parrinder's *Avatar and Incarnation*.[53] Ninian Smart goes so far as to speak of the incarnation strand in the history of religions.[54] Most Christian philosophers, however, have tended to stress the difference between the Christian doctrine of the Incarnation and Hindu avatar beliefs. Thus Keith Ward writes: 'The avatars of Vishnu do not suffer the limitations of having a real human nature.'[55] They are appearances, manifestations of the supreme reality. The same point is made by Julius Lipner, a specialist in the philosophy of Indian religions. After a detailed comparative study of the Hindu and Christian doctrines, he concludes that, for the Hindus, avatara are not fully human, conditioned by previous karma (the law of consequence) like the rest of us. They are appearances of the divine in human (or other) guise.[56] H. H. Farmer, too, contrasts the notion 'of a divine being who merely drops into the human scene in an embodied form, unheralded, unprepared for, without roots in anything that has gone before in history and without any creative relationship to the unfolding of events in what comes after',[57] with the embeddedness of the story of Jesus in the history of the covenant, old and new.

The Christian tradition has certainly held that only once did the divine Son come amongst us in incarnate form. Indeed, as Farmer says, it has seen the whole of human history as pivoted around that unique turning point. It was long prepared, within the history of religions, by the history and developing faith of Israel, and the whole future of humanity is determined for all eternity by the universal salvific efficacy of the Christ event (on this see chapter 6). But a number of Christian philosophers, such as Ward and Morris, are prepared to follow Thomas Aquinas in thinking that, while the Incarnation was in fact unique, more than one incarnation of the divine Son was possible, either here on Earth in human form or in some other world among extra-terrestrials.[58]

Against this view, I have argued for the impossibility of multiple incarnations,[59] chiefly on the grounds that if we take seriously the point insisted on by Morris himself that the ultimate subject of Jesus' life is God the Son, then any other purported incarnation, here or elsewhere, would have the same ultimate subject and thus be the same person. In the context of Resurrection belief, this would entail the presence, in the eschaton, of a number of finite personal vehicles of the divine life, all of them coexistent and theoretically capable of interpersonal relation. This makes no sense. 'One individual subject cannot, without contradiction, be thought capable of becoming a series of individuals, or, *a fortiori*, a coexistent community of persons.'[60]

If this is right, and multiple incarnations are indeed impossible, then the uniqueness of the Christ event – the so-called 'scandal of particularity' – is seen to be less offensive. For, in the nature of the case, God's revelatory and salvific purposes could only have been achieved through a necessarily unique incarnation.

CHAPTER FIVE

Trinity

The Christian concept of God has already come under scrutiny in chapter 3 on Creation. A leading theme of that chapter was the basic distinction between the finite, contingent universe and the infinite, necessary, all-powerful, all-knowing mind and will that underlies, and accounts for, the very being, as well as the nature, of the whole evolving world. But Christianity has come to understand the one Creator God in a very different way from other monotheistic faiths. God is understood by Christians in all the mainstream churches – Orthodox, Roman Catholic, Anglican and Protestant – as the Holy and Blessed Trinity, three Persons in one God, Father, Son and Holy Spirit. This doctrine shapes the classic Christian creeds, and together with the doctrine of the Incarnation, which we considered in the last chapter, constitutes the distinctiveness of Christianity, at least in terms of its belief system.

On any reckoning, the doctrine of the Trinity is difficult to understand. Many people, lay people and philosophers, regard it as a nonsense. How can the eternal Creator God possibly be both one and three? Theologians themselves have often tried to explain the doctrine away. It is not many years since the Regius Professors of Divinity at the universities of both Oxford and Cambridge were, to all intents and purposes, unitarians.[1] But, more recently, there has been a remarkable revival of trinitarian theology, building on, but also challenging, the work of the mid-twentieth-century masters, Karl Barth, Karl Rahner and Bernard Lonergan.[2] In Roman Catholic theology, we may cite the name of Walter Kasper,[3] and in Protestant theology those of Wolfhart Pannenberg, Jürgen Moltmann, Robert Jenson and T. F. Torrance.[4] Eastern Orthodox theology has always been resolutely trinitarian.[5]

Anglo-Saxon philosophers of religion have also turned their attention to the analysis, clarification and, surprisingly often, defence of the doctrine of the Trinity. In this chapter we will survey and discuss a selection of their work. The main questions that have been addressed concern the reasons for affirming God's triunity, the intelligibility of the doctrine, and, above all, whether social trinitarianism, modelling God's identity on a society of three, inevitably entails tritheism, that is to say, belief in three Gods.

But, first, let us consider the prior question whether the triune nature of God is susceptible of rational and metaphysical enquiry.

5.1   Is the Doctrine of the Trinity Rationally Accessible?

There are, of course, limits to what can be said about God. In its time-honoured doctrine of divine incomprehensibility the Christian Church has recognized, and taught us to respect, the mystery of God and the incapacity of the created human mind fully to comprehend the divine essence.[6] But, as was argued and illustrated in our first two chapters, that does not mean we can say nothing positive and true about God. As already pointed out, the way of analogy[7] permits a degree of understanding of the divine nature. And what is said about God can be reflected on rationally and probed for its intelligibility and coherence. This is obviously the case with natural the-ology, but, as was shown in chapter 2, revealed theology is just as open to discussion 'in the context of critical rationality'.[8]

That this was indeed Thomas Aquinas's position is convincingly shown by Norman Kretzmann in his essay, 'Trinity and Transcendentals'.[9] Kretz-mann shows that, while Aquinas thought the Trinity to be a revealed doctrine – i.e., not inferable from the existence and nature of the world – he certainly believed the doctrine to be open to rational scrutiny, and indeed exemplified such scrutiny at length. At the end of his essay, Kretzmann makes the further convincing point that philosophical theology cannot, and should not, start from scratch in the enterprise of critical reflection. It must use and build on the work of its predecessors in the long dialogue between theology and philosophy down the ages of the Christian tradition.

Kretzmann's own attempt to apply the scholastic metaphysics of the 'transcendentals' ('being', 'one', 'true' and 'good') to the theology of the Trinity is unlikely to carry conviction, however. The transcendentals are the most general terms, transcending all categories for classifying things. They can indeed be used in the theology of God. But the case for 'appro-priating' the terms 'one', 'true' and 'good' to the three Persons of the Trinity who constitute the being or essence of God is not made out. These terms, it is more plausible to suggest, apply to God as such, who is the Supreme Being, and necessarily one, true and good. Not that all these terms should be thought of as expressing attributes of God. Being or substance (the 'nuclear realization of being qua being', as Aristotle defines it[10]) is not an attribute. It is what, in each case, God included, possesses its essential and, for that matter, non-essential attributes. Unity, as Peter Geach, following Frege, makes clear,[11] is not an attribute. To affirm that God is one is to affirm that the infinite is indivisible and that nothing else can possess the core attributes of God with comparable absoluteness and necessity. Truth is indeed the attribute of beliefs and propositions when they correspond with how things really are. But to speak of God as the supreme Truth is not simply to speak of God's knowledge. It is also to speak of God as the source of everything being what it is and what it will be.[12] Goodness, alone of the transcendentals (unless we add beauty to the list[13]), is a core attribute of God. But again, to call God supremely good is not to classify him as the highest in the class of good things (or perhaps one should say good persons, since personal goodness is the relevant kind of goodness at issue here). It is to speak of God's goodness as transcending all forms of human goodness as their perfect source and exemplar.

The relevance of the transcendentals to trinitarian theology has much more to do with the oneness of God than with God's triunity. All the same, the Christian tradition insists that the three Persons of the Trinity are one in substance or being with one another, and are all supremely good, beautiful and true. So, in this respect, these terms are as central to trinitarian theism as they are to any other form of monotheism.

That the metaphysics of substance is indeed an appropriate tool for the philosophical investigation of trinitarian theology, in respect of God's being and unity, is argued powerfully by William Alston in his contribution to an interdisciplinary symposium on the Trinity held at Dunwoodie in 1998.[14] Alston shows that substance metaphysics need not be saddled with the static features of immutability, timelessness, impassibility and lack of real relations to the world, to which its critics often object. We have already considered the case for thinking of the Creator God in more dynamic open-futured terms.[15] But that did not involve abandoning talk of the divine substance. The same is true of trinitarian theology. What is at issue here, as in the chapter on Creation, is the nature of the divine substance.

Another philosopher unwilling to abandon substance metaphysics in talk of the triune God was Donald MacKinnon. In an essay in the Festschrift for T. F. Torrance,[16] an essay to which we shall be returning in a moment, MacKinnon wrote of the 'openness of texture' in the notion of substance, whereby the Christian tradition has tried to articulate the ontological implications of the doctrines of the Incarnation and the Trinity. He refers here to the way in which the doctrine of the Trinity involves a blurring of the frontiers between substance and relation, and to the way in which the doctrine of the Incarnation involves a rethinking of the relation between eternity and time.

The matter is complicated by divergences between the western and eastern Christian traditions over the term 'substance' itself. Richard Cross, in an important article, to which we shall also be returning,[17] suggests that, once one realizes that, for the West, 'substance' is equated with 'being' or 'essence', while, for the East, 'substance' is equated with 'hypostasis' or 'person', it becomes clear that the underlying metaphysics of western and eastern trinitarian theism is not all that different. Cross's article exemplifies finely both the possibility and the fruitfulness of substance metaphysics in the analysis of trinitarian God-talk.

Before pursuing these matters, we must consider the reasons for affirming God's triunity in the first place. Clearly, for MacKinnon, this was a matter of trying to make sense of the Incarnation and the coming of the Holy Spirit. But it is worth asking whether there are not prior, indeed a priori, grounds for affirming personal relation in God.

5.2   A Priori Arguments for Trinitarian Theism

The chief a priori argument for affirming a plurality of Persons in God is the one already mentioned in the chapter on Creation. If God is thought of by analogy with an isolated individual, some creation or other appears to be necessary for God to have an object of his love. It follows that the supreme goodness of interpersonal relation cannot be predicated of God as such. But the only alternative to making some created object necessary to God, if God is love, is to postulate the relation of love given and love received in God. This argument is really an aspect of maximal greatness theology. As was pointed out in chapter 3, the perfection of love cannot be thought of as lacking in that than which no greater can be conceived. Aquinas himself, as Norman Kretzmann shows,[18] was persuaded that reason could demonstrate that God is love. Admittedly, for Aquinas, this entailed no more than speaking of the love God has of himself. But, as C. J. F. Williams insists, in an essay of great importance for philosophical reflection on this particular doctrine,[19] talk of self-love cannot capture the nature of what love is: 'real love, love in the literal sense, requires more than one person'.[20]

Williams refers to the treatment of his topic by Peter Geach, in the book mentioned above.[21] Christians need not worry about the possibility of love in a solitary person, says Geach; for Christians understand the divine life as a life of mutual love between the divine Persons.[22] And Geach will have nothing to do with the suggestion that 'person' in trinitarian theology means something quite different from its normal use. Trinitarian theology supposes that there is mutual address in God: 'In the Scriptures "I" and "you" are used for the discourse of the divine Persons to one another.'[23] So the analogy of at least two different subjects of personal relation in the one God cannot be avoided.

A corollary of this argument, to which we shall return later in this chapter, is that, when thinking of the personal, we have to think of persons in relation, not individuals, as basic. The individual is something of an abstraction. Maximal greatness cannot be modelled on such abstraction. It must include, essentially, interpersonal relation.

So far, this a priori argument for a plurality of Persons in God goes no further than the affirmation of love given and love received within the Supreme Being as such, the affirmation, that is to say, of at least two subjects or personal centres in the divine. There is, however, another a priori argument that purports to show that maximal greatness must include not two, but three such subjects. This argument is to be found, amongst a number of much less plausible arguments, it has to be admitted, in Swinburne's chapter on 'The Trinity' in his book, *The Christian God*.[24] Swinburne accepts the argument, already sketched, that God's love must, necessarily, involve a mutuality of giving and receiving, but goes on to point out that cooperation in sharing is a further essential element in the perfection of love that cannot be thought absent from the divine. Just as the model of a single isolated individual fails to capture the nature of love, so the model of two subjects related only to each other fails to capture the excellence of cooperation in sharing with a third.

Swinburne refers to an early version of this argument in the medieval theologian Richard of St Victor,[25] who argued that supreme charity or love must include not only 'dilection' (love for another) but also 'condilection' (mutual love for a third). This too cannot be lacking in the supreme and all-perfect good. This entails a Trinity of persons in the divine.

In some ways Richard of St Victor's argument is to be preferred to that of Richard Swinburne, who, more than somewhat implausibly, writes in terms of reasons for a first divine individual to bring about a second and a third. Richard of St Victor, by contrast, simply argues that there must be, in God, a Trinity of persons between whom both dilection and condilection everlastingly occur. We shall return to this question of the derivedness or equal underivedness of the second and third Persons of the Trinity later in this chapter.

The two Richards – Swinburne and St Victor – are agreed that no further case exists for postulating more than three personal subjects of love given and received and shared still more in the divine. To put the matter, again, in maximal greatness terms, there is no further excellence in the nature of love, beyond sharing and cooperation in sharing, that would require there to be four or more such subjects in the supreme analogate of love.

So much for a priori arguments for trinitarian theism. It will be recalled that they are premised upon the incoherence of making some creation or other necessary to God, if God is love, and the consequent inadequacy of any concept of God modelled on an isolated individual. These premises, it may be observed, gain some support from a telling remark by Thomas Aquinas. In reply to the objection that, since God is with the angels and the souls of the blessed, God cannot be said to be alone, Thomas says: 'Although angels and the souls of the blessed are always with God, nevertheless it would follow that God was alone or solitary if there were not several divine persons. For the company of something of quite a different nature does not end solitude, and so we say that a man is alone in a garden although there are in it many plants and animals.'[26]

5.3   Revelation–based Arguments for the Trinity

As a matter of historical fact, the doctrine of the Trinity was not developed on the basis of a priori reasoning, but rather as a response to what Christians believed to be divine revelation. The heart of that alleged revelation was the Incarnation. Growing conviction of the divinity of Christ led, over centuries – although its beginnings are there in the New Testament (cf. the Prologue to the fourth Gospel) – to profound and often tortuous reflection on what this meant for the doctrine of God that Christians had inherited from the faith of Israel. Sense had to be made of the fact that the one believed to be God incarnate prayed to God, calling him Father and existing in a relation of love – love given and love received – with the God of Abraham, Isaac and Jacob. By itself, of course, this source would have led to no more than binitarian theism, premised on the relation between the divine Father and the divine Son.

Similarly, the gift of the Holy Spirit, 'another Advocate' (John 14: 16), as experienced by the early Christians and described by Paul (the indwelling Spirit, writes Paul, 'intercedes with sighs too deep for words': Romans 8: 26), came to be thought of as revelatory of another interpersonal relation within the one God, leading to doctrinal expression in trinitarian rather than binitarian terms.

In holding that trinitarian theism arose within Christianity as a response to revelation, philosophical theology is confronted once again with the debates over the *locus* of revelation which were discussed in chapter 2. Stephen Davis[27] and to a certain extent Richard Swinburne[28] see the Christian scriptures as the main vehicle of divine revelation and therefore the main sources for the development of trinitarian theology. If, as was suggested in chapter 2, it is rather the Incarnation itself and experience of the risen Christ and of the indwelling Spirit, to which the scriptures bear witness, that are the primary vehicles of revelation, then the sources of trinitarian theology are best thought of as being these historical, and more than historical, events, requiring, as they did, a radical rethinking of the doctrine of God.

Either way, to argue for trinitarian theism on the basis of revelation is not to forsake the domain of critical rationality. As was shown in chapter 2, appeals to revelation are not just appeals to authority. They are appeals to new data, just as susceptible of rational scrutiny as any more generally available data or indeed as any a priori considerations. Moreover, the tentative a priori considerations, sketched in the previous section, 'become enormously more probable if backed up by revelation', as Swinburne observes.[29] And the same is true the other way round. Revelation-based arguments find support, even confirmation, in the a priori arguments.

That it was indeed the Incarnation and the gift of the Spirit that led to, and indeed required, the development and articulation of the doctrine of the Trinity is argued by a number of philosophical theologians, including Donald MacKinnon and David Brown. MacKinnon, in his aforementioned article,[30] concentrates on the Incarnation. It is the story of the Son's 'descent from heaven' that makes a reconstruction of the doctrine of God in trinitarian terms unavoidable. Only so can this 'descent' be seen as 'supremely, indeed paradigmatically, declaratory' of what God is in himself. And only if there is already in the eternal, transcendent God both gift and receptivity can the incarnate Son's life on earth be interpreted as the 'painfully realized transcription into the conditions of our existence of the receptivity . . . that constitutes his person'.[31]

David Brown's rehearsal of the argument from history for the divinity of Christ has already been discussed in the chapter on Incarnation. But the context of that argument was his book *The Divine Trinity*, and the argument represents the first stage of his presentation of the case for trinitarian theism. The second stage forms chapter 4 of Brown's book, entitled 'Holy Spirit: The Argument from History'.[32] Brown agrees that the problem here is not so much the divinity of the Holy Spirit but rather whether the Spirit is to be thought of as a third Person in the one God. After giving the case against such a view, Brown proceeds to set out four considerations that cumulatively suggest that we are bound to regard the Holy Spirit as a distinct personal subject in the divine.

The first involves an explanation, in terms of the incarnational Christ-ology set out in his (and our) previous chapter, of why the incarnate one did not himself say much about the Spirit. This negative point is then comple-mented by three positive considerations: first, the powerful 'Pentecost' experience of the earliest Christians, who clearly felt themselves over-whelmed and empowered by the gift of the Spirit from on high. Moreover the early Christians explicitly differentiated this inspiration from the pres-ence, now withdrawn, of the risen Christ. The second positive consider-ation involves reflection on the further New Testament evidence, in Acts and Paul, concerning the witnessing, interceding, life-giving, indwelling character of the divine Spirit in their hearts and in their midst. (I ignore some rather curious remarks, on Brown's part, about why Paul partly misconstrued all this. Brown fails to bring out the force of Romans 8.) In the third place, Brown claims, St John's talk of the Paraclete, the Advocate or Comforter, to be sent by Christ from God the Father, reinforces the personal and distinct nature of this divine presence. Brown's final point concerns non-biblical experience. Here he notes the way in which a number of the great mystics describe their experience not simply in terms of union with God *simpliciter*, but in terms of participation in love given and love received within the Godhead. Interestingly, Brown cites not only the Christian mystics, but non-Christian mystics too, as giving expression to a comparable sense of union with God in relation to God, in other words, of being caught up into an internally differentiated, relational divine life.

Brown's whole approach to the analysis and defence of trinitarian theism was sharply criticized at the time of its publication by Nicholas Lash[33] and Kenneth Surin[34] for its alleged failure to respect the 'grammar' of Christian theology. Brown's reply[35] is a masterly refutation of the way in which some followers of Wittgenstein have attempted to rule out of court the whole approach to philosophical theology that constitutes the subject matter of this present book. I commend it, therefore, as an invaluable supplement to my own first chapter here. Of particular interest in this article is Brown's section on 'The Trinity and the Priority of the Social'.[36] Here Brown himself appeals to Wittgenstein in order to question 'the modern stress on an irreducibly ultimate individualism' as an appropriate basis for analogical talk of God's unity. Taking full account of the context in which trinitarian theism first arose and of the forms of interpersonal relation, human and divine, to which it gives expression, Brown goes on to defend the social rather than the psychological analogy for the articulation of a Christian doctrine of the triune God.

5.4   Arguments in Favour of the Social Analogy

Of the writers considered so far in this chapter, Williams, Geach, Swin-burne, MacKinnon and Brown all favour the social analogy over the psychological analogy for very obvious reasons. The psychological analogy, despite its venerable pedigree in Augustine and much western theology, contains a fundamental weakness. It seeks a model or image of the triune life of the God of the Christians in the distinctions and relations between, say, memory, understanding and will in an individual human mind. But this does not begin to make sense of the interpersonal relations within God of love given, love received and love shared still more that are revealed through the Incarnation and the gift of the Spirit, and required by maximal greatness theology, if God is not to lack the specific excellencies of love. As T. V. Morris puts the matter, in a brief exposition of trinitarian theism,[37] it is difficult to see how 'singularity theories', as he calls those employing the psychological analogy, can do justice to 'the full data of biblical revelation and Christian experience'. 'And it is hard to see how any such theory will suffice to block what we have called the problem of the lonely God.'[38] These considerations, he concludes, lead the Christian theist to embrace some form of social theory of the divine.

Swinburne clearly holds a form of social trinitarianism. The a posteriori arguments from revelation and the a priori arguments from the nature of love require us to understand the divine essence as consisting in three related, but logically inseparable, divine individuals. As pointed out above, Swinburne thinks it necessary to suppose that this involves eternal depend-ence relations of ultimate derivation where the second and third 'Persons' of the Trinity are concerned. Only so can their necessary, everlasting harmony of will be secured. Swinburne is more careful in his book than in the article in which he first put forward his arguments for trinitarian theism[39] to reserve the term 'God' as such for the Trinity, and to speak of the Trinity as three divine individuals, inseparably interrelated. But, as Peter van Inwa-gen points out in an article in the *Routledge Encyclopedia of Philosophy*, the suspicion of tritheism remains, and it is far from clear that the Christian tradition has to maintain so stark a form of 'subordination', where the relations of the Son and the Spirit to the Father are concerned.[40] We shall return to these points later in this chapter.

David Brown's much more extended discussion[41] concludes that the factors that led to acknowledgement of the divinity of Christ and of the Spirit's work in taking us into the life of God can only be made sense of in terms of 'three distinct centres of consciousness, each with its own distinctive mental content'.[42] The crucial question on such a view, of course, concerns the divine unity or identity. Brown rejects numerical identity. This would mean that the Father was the same as the Son. He also rejects relative identity. 'God' and 'Person' are not the same thing under different descriptions. He also rejects a 'constitutive' analysis. 'God' is not a term like 'gold' that can be shared by three distinct ingots. (There is a delightful scene in Graham Greene's novel, *Monsignor Quixote*,[43] where the Monsignor explains the doctrine of the Trinity to the Communist ex-mayor by pointing to the three bottles of wine they have just consumed: one and the same wine, three bottles. But 'God' is not a sortal term like 'wine'.) According to Brown, the identity of the three Persons as one God is rather a generic identity, each one instantiating the core attributes of deity. Their unity consists not only in their essential harmony of will and action, but also in the way in which an inseparable loving union of Persons itself transcends individuality. To this last point, undeveloped by Brown in his book, we shall have to return.

Peter van Inwagen is more sympathetic to the theory of relative identity than either Brown or Swinburne. We have already considered his use of it in respect of the doctrine of the Incarnation in the previous chapter (see section 4.3). He attempts to defend its application to the doctrine of the Trinity in another essay in *God, Knowledge and Mystery*[44] and, later, in the above-mentioned encyclopaedia article. On this analysis, one can differentiate what one wants to say about God qua Father, God qua Son and God qua Holy Spirit, in particular about the relations between them, without denying that God remains one in substance, essence or being. In other words, it does not follow from 'the Father is the same being as the Son' that 'the Father is the same Person as the Son'.

We have here, in Brown's generic identity theory and van Inwagen's relative identity theory, two examples of the kind of argument for the coherence of social trinitarianism which philosophical theology must provide, if the strong case for the social analogy outlined above is to be sustained.

An encouraging aspect of Richard Cross's article already mentioned[45] is that, while he restricts himself to an examination of the underlying metaphysics of trinitarian theism, he is nevertheless prepared to say that 'Eastern and Western views of the divine essence are both consistent with social accounts of the Trinity'.[46] Moreover, he ends his article by suggesting that the greater the list of properties, chiefly relational properties, that distinguish the Persons of the Trinity, the greater the case for some sort of social trinitarianism.[47]

The a priori and a posteriori arguments surveyed in this section, and in the two previous sections of this chapter, indicate precisely what these relational properties are: namely, love given, love received and love shared still more.

5.5   Arguments Against the Social Analogy

It is time we looked at the objections that have been raised against social trinitarianism. Three scholars, Keith Ward, Sarah Coakley and Brian Leftow, will serve to illustrate the other side of the argument.

We have already encountered Ward's views in chapter 3 on Creation. Ward frankly accepts the consequences of his critique of social trinitarianism in holding that some creation or other is necessary to God, if God's goodness is to have the form of love. But what precisely are his reasons for rejecting 'the idea of a social Trinity'? They are spelled out in the section given that title in his book, *Religion and Creation*.[48] First, he accuses Brown of virtual polytheism, an accusation to which we shall have to return in the final section of this chapter. The chief difficulty is held to be the apparent need to postulate a principle of necessary unity that is superior to the Persons of the Trinity themselves. But this criticism fails to do justice to the ways in which accusations of tritheism are actually met by social trinitarians, as we shall see. Ward's critique of Swinburne's solution, whereby the Father is deemed the source of the Son's and the Spirit's being and unity, is much more telling. We have already questioned its evident subordinationism. Pannenberg's solution,[49] whereby the divine essence is thought of as consisting in the mutual loving relations of the trinitarian Persons, is unfairly criticized by Ward as treating love 'as a force superior to the persons in which it is actualised'.[50] There is no reason why love should be thought of in those terms. Ward's only alternative is to assert that 'God is love, not as three loving individuals, but as a unity of three coinherent modes of action of one supreme Being'.[51] The 'modalism' of this view is manifest, as is that of Karl Rahner, whom Ward quotes: 'Within the Trinity there is no reciprocal Thou.'[52] The basis of Ward's criticism then emerges when he writes: 'A model of love within the Trinity must be in the end simply the love of God for the divine self, and not the love of another.'[53] The dominance of the isolated individual in Ward's thinking could hardly be more blatantly expressed.

Sarah Coakley's contribution to the Dunwoodie symposium,[54] while directed specifically against the contributions of van Inwagen, Brown and Swinburne, is primarily historical in character. She shows, convincingly, that Gregory of Nyssa is not so readily to be cited as a source for social trinitarianism of the kind defended by the analytic philosophers of religion just named, for whom talk of three Persons is modelled on that of a society of three human individuals. That Gregory did not use the term 'hypostasis' in the sense of distinct consciousnesses or self-consciousnesses may well be the case. Many other images, often 'impersonal' like the colours of the rainbow, were used by Gregory, all of them subject to control by a fundamental 'apophaticism', that is, an insistence on the unknown mystery of God. Now we have already come across a comparable assimilation of the eastern (Cappadocian) tradition to the western (Augustinian) tradition in Richard Cross's article, discussed in the last section. But Cross, as we saw, allows for the development of this common theistic metaphysic in the direction of social trinitarianism, if there are good reasons for such a development. And the most notable aspect of Coakley's critique is her failure to consider the reasons why, irrespective of reference to Gregory and the other Cappadocians, the analytic philosophers with whom she takes issue have pursued the path of social trinitarianism and insisted, as we saw Geach doing, on the word 'person' bearing something like its modern sense. Those reasons were primarily, in the first place, the need to make sense of the Incarnation of God in and as a man who prayed to God and, in the second place, the need to see in God as such the prime analogate of the relational properties of love given, love received and love shared still more. Hence Geach's insistence on the concept of persons involved in I–Thou relations. Hence too the implausibility of Rahner's denial of any reciprocal 'Thou' in God. Gregory's use of images like that of white light refracted and reflected in the colours of the rainbow is no help at all in this connection.

One of the most detailed and sustained critiques of social trinitarianism is Brian Leftow's essay in the same volume.[55] With relentless logic and great clarity, Leftow attacks the 'three centres of consciousness' model for its inability to avoid either tritheism or Arianism, that is, the postulation of lesser or created 'deities'. His arguments on the latter score are entirely convincing. Swinburne's 'subordinationism', the view that the second and third Persons of the Trinity are brought about by God the Father, in order to instantiate, at the highest level, the excellencies of love, is sharply criticized for the inequalities between the Persons which it inevitably entails. But the accusation of tritheism against a view like that of C. J. F. Williams is not so plausibly made out. Social trinitarianism of a non-subordinationist kind holds that the one God simply *is* tripersonal. When Christians speak of God they are either referring to God the Father (as, so Christians hold, are Jews and Muslims) or to God the Son, as they do when they pray to the risen Christ, or to God the Holy Spirit, as they do when they invoke the indwelling Comforter, or to God the Holy and Blessed Trinity, as they do when referring to God as such, who is none other than these three Persons in relation. Leftow makes things much too easy for himself by treating social trinitarianism as belief in three divine substances, three individual cases of deity.[56] Christian theology has always (except where 'substance' was equated with 'hypostasis') seen the divine as one, infinite and necessary substance. The trinitarian distinctions and relations are internal to the Ultimate. There are not, and could not be, three ultimates, externally related. This enables us to pinpoint one of the basic flaws in Leftow's approach. All the models and analogies which he attacks are from limited, finite minds, externally related. He nowhere ponders the difference made by the fact that theology is concerned with the necessarily unique, because infinite, substance that underlies all finite, created being. The question at issue is whether sense can be made of the supposition that the one infinite is best thought of as internally differentiated and interrelated in three mutually loving and interpenetrating subjectivities.

Leftow fails utterly to do justice to the grounds for supposing this to be the case. Like Coakley, he gives no consideration at all to the revelatory factors, that is, to what is revealed through the Incarnation and the indwelling Spirit, which have been stressed in this present chapter. He does refer to the a priori grounds from maximal greatness theology, as set out by Swinburne. But he quickly gets diverted on to the 'inequality' problem, which is a problem with Swinburne's version, not, e.g., Williams's, and he does little more than mock the basic argument from love's excellencies ('dilection' and 'condilection' in Richard of St Victor's terms) by citing many other facets of love in the all-too-human finite scene of family and social life. There is no serious exploration of the minimum requirements for analogical predication of the virtue of love in talking of the divine as such.

5.6   The Social Trinity and Tritheism

The accusation of tritheism is strongly resisted by defenders of social trinitarianism. We have already noted Brown's reference to the way in which an inseparable loving union of Persons transcends individuality. It is this insight that invites reflection and expansion in this final section of our chapter on the Trinity. Brown himself develops the point in an essay in the Feenstra/Plantinga volume.[57] In it, he acknowledges the wide and changing range of meanings of the word 'person', but suggests that 'so far from defenders of the social model being firmly trapped by modern understanding of the person, it is their detractors who are trapped'.[58] To focus attention too literally on the finite, human aspects of the social model – three separate, externally related, finite individuals, such as those portrayed in the Rublev ikon – is to fail to do justice to the way in which separate, autonomous, self-conscious persons are already something of an abstraction, even in the human world, let alone where the infinite paradigm of personality and relationality is concerned. Even in the human world, it can be shown that communion is more basic than the individual, and that persons in relation, not least in intense loving and mystical communion, glimpse or achieve a unity that transcends their separateness. Brown endeavours to substantiate his case by distinguishing first between individualism and individuality, the latter, but not the former, being ascribed to the Persons of the Trinity, and, secondly, between consciousness and self-consciousness, the former being ascribed to the Persons severally (how else could they be in 'I–Thou' relations?) and the latter only to God *tout court*.

It might be thought that this second distinction, between consciousness and self-consciousness, is a little forced. It trades on the somewhat pejorative conception of individual self-consciousness as self-absorption. But Brown is quite right to stress the way in which commitment to a task or to another person is at its most exalted where one 'loses' oneself in the project or the relation. There is perhaps a hint here of the way in which the unity of the tripersonal God involves the highest degree of mutual interpenetration (*perichoresis* in the Greek terminology, *circumincessio* in the Latin). But what Brown fails to give sufficient attention to, either in his book or in this later essay, is the fact that, unlike finite persons in relation, the infinite simply cannot be thought of as consisting of separate, externally related, personal beings. But, again it has to be emphasized that to see the infinite as internally differentiated and interrelated in mutual loving relations is not a matter of modelling the Godhead on human *self*-love. For that, too, would be to give the priority to the isolated individual. Brown's essay constitutes a bold attempt to break with that paradigm.

Cornelius Plantinga's essay, 'Social Trinity and Tritheism', in the same volume as Brown's,[59] is the work of a systematic theologian, not a philosopher; but it provides, for philosophical reflection, an admirably clear example of social trinitarianism. First, Plantinga spells out the biblical sources for trinitarian theism. He then attempts a statement of a social theory, in terms of 'a divine society of three fully personal and fully divine entities', each possessing the divine essence and together constituting the one God. There is some tendency in Plantinga to characterize the trinitarian relations as involving derivation as well as mutual love and common action, but it would be easy to amend his statement and present it in a non-subordinationist form. Plantinga claims that each member of the Trinity 'is a person, but scarcely an *individual*, or *separate* or *independent* person' (his italics). They 'are "members one of another" to a superlative and exemplary

degree'.[60] Social trinitarianism, thus defined, is then declared, against modalism (God being just *one* person, with different operations) and against
Arianism (ontologically graded distinctions between God the Father and
God the Son) to be the mainstream Christian tradition, both western and
eastern. But is this social trinitarianism tritheistic? No, says Plantinga. Only if
the three Persons were finite and potentially opposed would the Trinity
amount to three gods. And then, of course, they would not be God. The
Persons of the Trinity are not, even theoretically, independent. 'Each is
essentially the fellow of the other two. And such interdependency is a vice
only to egoists and individualists.'[61] Again we note the suggestion that it is
the opponents of social trinitarianism who are working with the model of
persons as isolated individuals.

Very reasonably, Plantinga goes on to suggest that classical Christian
trinitarian theism is not necessarily committed to the strong (Neoplatonic)
doctrine of divine simplicity, whereby each Person is identical with the
divine essence. That would mean they were identical with each other.
Rather, each possesses the generic essence of divinity, and each possesses
his own essence, defined primarily by the relations which each bears to the
others within the one infinite Godhead.

The doctrine found in Thomas Aquinas,[62] that the Persons of the Trinity
are best thought of as 'subsistent relations' within the one Godhead, is
perceptively discussed by C. J. F. Williams in the essay mentioned
above.[63] Williams confesses that at first he thought it utter nonsense; for a
relation exists *between* things or subjects. But, with some help from Aristotle,
Williams came to realize that Thomas was speaking of relational *properties*
without which the subjects in questions – the Persons of the Trinity –
would not be what they are. The Father subsists eternally as the Father of
the Son, the Son as the Son of the Father, and the Spirit as the Spirit of the
Father and the Son. Admittedly, Aquinas himself interprets these relations as
those of self-love, and I have already mentioned Williams's (and Geach's)
categorical rejection of this as failing to capture the nature of love as a matter
of interpersonal relations.

Williams concludes his essay with some very illuminating reflections of
the unity of the tripersonal God. The interpenetration of the divine Persons,
of which the Christian tradition speaks, is glimpsed, albeit faintly, in the
poetry of love and in the literature of mysticism, east as well as west. Both in
will and in act, the persons of the Trinity are eternally and necessarily at one.
Williams makes the all-important point that 'the reasons that we have for
affirming the existence of a God at all are reasons for affirming that there
cannot be many Gods'. 'It is precisely as Creator, as the source of all
contingent being, that God must be one. How could this unity be more

gloriously manifested than in the love of the utterly distinct and uncon-
founded Persons who together constitute the Holy and undivided
Trinity?'[64]

The contribution of analytic philosophers of religion to the case for and
against the coherence of social trinitarianism may be further studied in a
number of articles in *Faith and Philosophy*. C. Stephen Layman's defence of
the social analogy[65] is interesting, but suffers from his unwillingness to
pursue the question of the ontology of infinite substance. Similarly, the
purely logical arguments for and against the coherence of the doctrine,
contributed by John Macnamara, Marie La Palme Reyes and Gonzalo E.
Reyes in a joint article,[66] and by E. Feser in reply,[67] while they certainly
show that the question remains an open one (unlike the arguments of
Richard Cartwright, who claims to have decisively refuted the social
theory[68]), fail to do justice to the potentialities of the doctrine of relative
identity vis-à-vis the unique case of the infinite. Of particular interest is
T. W. Bartel's attempt to show the coherence of ascribing the property of
sovereignty to the three distinct divine 'individuals' comprising the Trinity.[69] But even here, as with Swinburne's reflections on the property of
omnipotence,[70] the treatment is marred by concentration on the finite
analogies rather than on the infinite *analogatum*.

CHAPTER SIX

Salvation

According to all the Christian creeds, the purpose of Christ's coming was 'for us and for our salvation'. It is a central tenet of Christian belief that what God did through Jesus Christ was, and is, the reconciliation of the world to God. That this is so is agreed by all Christians. But precisely how this was, and is, achieved is the subject of much uncertainty in popular belief and theology alike. It has to be pointed out, of course, that the doctrine of the Atonement, as it is called, is not, as such, set out in the creeds. But it remains one of the most contested areas of Christian understanding. In this chapter we survey the contributions of Anglo-American philosophers of religion to reflection on this doctrine.

6.1 Subjective and Objective Theories of the Atonement

In the history of the Christian Church the spectrum of views on this topic extends from subjective or 'exemplarist' theories of the Atonement, such as those associated with Peter Abelard in the early twelfth century[1] and Hastings Rashdall in the early twentieth century,[2] to objective views, such as those associated with Anselm of Canterbury in the late eleventh century[3] and Gustav Aulen in the mid-twentieth century.[4] As we shall see, there is more to 'subjective' views than just the provision of an example, in the life and death of Jesus Christ, of costly love in action, for us to be won over by, and for us to follow. But the emphasis is on the change in us actually inspired by the Gospel story. Objective views, by contrast, stress a change in our state achieved by what God did in Christ, prior to and irrespective of our own reactions; although, of course, much is also said about the consequent transformative effects in us of what God did. In particular, by his death on the cross, Christ is held to have defeated the powers of evil, or purchased our liberation, or endured in our place the penalty of sin, or offered a sacrifice sufficient to expiate or 'atone' for our guilt. This last suggestion makes one aware of the twofold meaning of the word 'atonement'. In its etymological sense, it simply means 'at-one-ment' and is virtually synonymous with 'reconciliation'. As such it can be used, without difficulty, in connection with subjective or exemplarist theories. But it also has a narrower use in connection with theories of sacrifice, whereby propitiation or expiation is made for guilt incurred by wrongdoing, as in the sacrificial cult of ancient Israel.

Philosophers of religion, reflecting on this doctrine, will, as always, be concerned to examine these theories for their intelligibility and coherence; but they will also be concerned to probe their moral tenability. Moral philosophy has, of course, been a guiding element in our enquiries in previous chapters, not least in connection with the goodness of God and the goodness of Creation. But theories of the Atonement give rise to moral questions in an even more insistent way. This is not just a matter of facing up to moral objections from secular ethicists. Such objections have to be listened to and responded to. But, for Christian philosophy, it is more a question of Christian ethical criticism, and of probing the moral sense of the doctrine in the context of a developed Christian theology of the love of God.

These issues are raised and explored in a dense and searching essay by Donald MacKinnon: 'Subjective and Objective Conceptions of Atonement', in the Festschrift for H. H. Farmer.[5] MacKinnon's dissatisfaction with exemplarist theories stems from his recognition that the deepest contradictions of human life require more than just enlightenment or inspiration, if justice is to be done to them and they are to be overcome. There is a risk of trivializing the work of Christ if we fail to capture the sense of the lengths to which God in Christ was prepared to go in order to redeem the world. The meaning of the cry of dereliction on the cross ('my God, my God, why hast thou forsaken me?') cannot be grasped simply in terms of an example of costly, self-sacrificial love. We have to be made to face up to the truth about ourselves, and we have to be enabled to change. MacKinnon shows how, in the fourth Evangelist's depiction of Christ's Passion, these themes of judgement, truth and atonement are inextricably woven together. By his own identification with human suffering and evil, with the effects of betrayal, cruelty and judicial murder, God in Christ at once shows us the truth about ourselves, reveals the nature and the cost of the divine forgiveness and draws us into union with the triune God. To this theme of identification we shall be returning later in this chapter.

MacKinnon himself was aware of the moral objections that have been raised against objective theories of the Atonement. He implies that the primary focus of these objections is the use made of categories 'borrowed from the history of the religious institution of sacrifice, from types of redemption-mythology, from the contractual order of feudalism, from the conceptions of retributive justice embodied in traditional penal systems';[6] and the purport of his essay is to delve more deeply into the moral requirements that remain despite these questionable categories. Other defenders of an objective view are equally critical of some of the aforementioned theories. Thus Richard Swinburne, in his *Responsibility and Atonement*,[7] (of which much more will be said below), rejects the notion of Christ's death as a victory over the powers of evil on the grounds that it makes no sense. It does not explain either how our guilt is removed or why the powers of evil could not have been defeated more directly. Swinburne also rejects the view that Christ's suffering and death constitute a ransom paid to the devil. Quite apart from the question whether belief in a personal devil makes any sense, this view fails to explain why such a ransom was required in the first place. Similarly, the penal substitution theory is rejected by Swinburne for its lack of moral intelligibility. For God to punish himself, in the Person of his Son, in place of us is compatible with neither love nor justice. To Swinburne's preferred sacrificial theory we shall return.

These objections are endorsed, and pressed further, by J. R. Lucas in his chapter in the Swinburne Festschrift.[8] 'The hypothesis of a personal Devil with rights sits uneasily with the sovereignty of God', he observes. Equally dubious is the element of trickery involved in the depiction of God's dealings with the Evil One such as is found in C. S. Lewis's well-known children's book, *The Lion, the Witch and the Wardrobe*.[9] Lucas refers to Charles Taliaferro's defence of this view in his essay, 'A Narnian Theory of the Atonement'.[10] But a reading of Taliaferro's essay fails to convince. Neither the case against literal belief in the Devil nor the above-mentioned points about divine sovereignty or divine trickery are seriously considered by Taliaferro. The penal substitution theory is also rejected categorically by Lucas: 'That all too easily portrays God the Father as a wrathful power demanding the death of Jesus because other people deserve punishment.'[11] Quite apart from this point, the penal theory presupposes an implausible hard-line retributivism in the ethics of punishment. We shall return to this aspect of the matter shortly, as we shall to Lucas's criticism of Swinburne's sacrificial view and to his own preferred 'identification' theory.

The most trenchant objection to objective views is expressed by John Hick in his contribution to the Swinburne Festschrift.[12] It is that all these views leave no room for divine forgiveness. Hick points out that there is no hint in Jesus' words about forgiveness (in the parable of the Prodigal Son, for example[13]) that God's forgiveness depends on an atoning death. We shall have reason to appreciate the force of this point in the course of the present chapter; but it should also be noted that it is his non-incarnational Christ-ology (discussed, above, in chapter 4) that leaves Hick with no alternative but to embrace a purely exemplarist view.

Before we consider Swinburne's sacrificial view and Lucas's identification view, some attention must be given to philosophical reflection on the themes of sin, judgement and forgiveness, which provide the context for the doctrine of the Atonement in all its forms.

6.2   Sin, Judgement and Forgiveness

The word 'sin' is a religious or theological term. It is not simply to be equated with wrongdoing or alienation, although it can be used in that more general sense. Indeed, Austin Farrer, defined 'to sin' as 'to do the wrong thing in relation to some person'.[14] But, for our purposes here, sin is to be understood as wrongdoing or alienation vis-à-vis God. Swinburne defines it as 'failure in a duty to God'.[15] That definition has to be expanded to include the state of alienation from God brought about by such failure and by participation in the consequences of many such failures. This is the state from which, according to the Christian gospel, we are rescued, saved and liberated by what God did in Christ. Swinburne goes on to differentiate between objective and subjective sin, the former being some wrong deed or state in which we are involved unwittingly, the latter something for which we are knowingly responsible and guilty.

The most contentious aspect of the Christian understanding of sin con-cerns 'original sin', the ancient doctrine, derived from St Paul and de-veloped by, among others, Augustine, Luther and Calvin, whereby the whole human race is held to have inherited the consequences, even the guilt, of Adam's primal sin. We are all, unwittingly or wittingly, 'fallen' creatures, alienated from God, just by being born and brought up in a fallen world. Philosophers have attempted to make some sense of this doctrine, but, generally speaking, have balked at the idea of inherited guilt. Swin-burne rejects the notion of original guilt, but accepts that the circumstances of our evolutionary origin make us inevitably prone to sin.[16] We may point also to the social and cultural pressures that surround us from childhood. In a fascinating essay defending the doctrine of original sin, with some help from the eighteenth-century American Calvinist philosopher Jonathan Edwards,

William Wainwright argues that, while 'there is a sense in which the guilt of the communities to which I belong is mine, it is mine only in the same sense in which the histories of those communities are part of my history'.[17] In the end, Wainwright, too, insists that I cannot literally be guilty of the offences of my ancestors.

This distinction between original sin and original guilt is clearly set out by Michael Langford in the course of a discussion of the sinlessness of Christ.[18] The conclusion of his brief exegetical and historical survey is that 'no one is born with original guilt, but original sin is simply part of the human condition, a condition that does not absolutely necessitate that we sin, but which – given the fact that we are relational beings – encourages us to do so, and entails that nearly all do'. Again, with regard to the doctrine of the fall, he writes: 'The human race is indeed "fallen", in the sense that there is a *collective* problem of human frailty and sin which nearly always drags both individuals and institutions downwards.'[19]

Langford's defence of the propriety, indeed the necessity, of subjecting Christian doctrine to rational scrutiny might be thought to fall foul of Merold Westphal's insistence, in an article on sin as an epistemological category, on the corruption of the intellect as well as the will as inherent in the 'total depravity' of the human condition.[20] But Westphal's appeal to St Paul's attack on 'the wise' fails to take the measure of, for example, Paul Gooch's demonstration that Paul's target is not reason as such but rather the arrogant conceit of the worldly wise.[21] And for a Christian philosopher to appeal to Marx, Freud and Foucault in the course of castigating his fellow Christian philosophers, Plantinga and Wolterstorff, for their use of critical rationality in theological investigation does not inspire much confidence in Westphal's judgement. Much to be preferred is Swinburne's view that there is 'every reason internal to Christian theology for resisting the Calvinist position' on total depravity.[22] Human sin and alienation from God are serious enough problems without the morally implausible magnification accorded them by some Calvinists.

We turn now to the questions of judgement and punishment. It goes without saying that wrongdoing has consequences, not only for its victims, but also for its perpetrators themselves. The consequences for its perpetrators include guilt and, at least on the human scene, some form of condemnation and reckoning. Before things can be put right, there has to be not only repentance and apology, but in many cases redress, where that is possible, and, in serious cases, as determined by law, punishment. Forgiveness is another matter. Even in human terms, it is not obvious that forgiveness is only possible where repentance, apology and redress, let alone punishment, have taken place.

There is not space here to consider the vast literature on theories of punishment. The reader is referred to the chapters on this subject in Swinburne's book[23] and in J. R. Lucas's *Responsibility*.[24] In his light-hearted Appendix 2, '*The* Which? *Guide to Theories of Punishment*', Lucas shows how, while deterrent and reformative theories of punishment have a clear utilitarian logic, only retributive theories succeed in matching punishment to guilt and vindicating both the law itself and the victims of wrongdoing. Above all, as both Swinburne and Lucas insist, only retributive theories leave room for mercy. Swinburne, indeed, goes further than this: 'Mercy can only be meritorious if retribution is right. Mercy goes beyond justice.'[25] It is important to note the difference between such a 'vindicative' interpretation of retribution, and a 'vindictive' interpretation. Philosophers are agreed that the latter, while reflecting a natural emotion, makes no moral sense at all.

Before we ask how far these understandings of punishment apply to God's dealings with the sinner, we need to reflect further on the subject of mercy and forgiveness. We have already noted that, on the purely human scene, it is quite possible for people to forgive even the most appalling evil deeds without waiting for repentance or apology. I quote, at this point, Richard Holloway, not a philosopher, but a retired Bishop: 'The mystery remains that this prodigal universe sometimes redeems its own pain through extraordinary souls who, from somewhere beyond all possibility, forgive the unforgivable.'[26] Such an individual human possibility does not necessarily, of course, involve the remission of punishment. For individuals do not punish. It is the state and the law that exact punishment. And, while a judge may indeed show mercy, he is bound by the constraints of justice to do so only within the limits of what the law prescribes. When we turn to the question of divine punishment and divine forgiveness, however, we have to ask ourselves whether God is to be thought of primarily by analogy with a judge or by analogy with, say, the father in the parable of the Prodigal Son.[27]

Where forgiveness is concerned, Marilyn McCord Adams's article, 'Forgiveness: A Christian Model',[28] offers a profound and detailed account of the way in which a Christian theological framework makes best sense of the possibilities of forgiveness in human relations. By setting both the offence perpetrated and the suffering caused in the context of God's love for both offender and victim, the latter is enabled to forgive, in the hope and trust that, in the end, truth will out, the wrong will be rectified, and both offender and victim will be transformed and reconciled.

The implications of this understanding of human forgiveness within a theistic framework for our understanding of God's own merciful love are very great. We shall be returning to this point again and again as we survey current theories of atonement. Suffice it to say here that, on Adams's view, there is no condoning of evil on God's part. After all, God in Christ 'paid horrendous suffering the ultimate compliment, by identifying Himself with it on the cross'. But, she insists, 'God is not interested in retribution, but in reform'.[29] We note again, in Adams as in MacKinnon, the stress on identification.

On such a view, the requirements of justice are not so much condemnation as a facing up to the truth about ourselves, the truth about what we have done, and the truth about where we are. Only so can reform begin. Only then can 'mercy go beyond justice', to quote Swinburne once again.

In the light of these considerations, we proceed to examine some examples of work on the Atonement by contemporary Christian philosophers.

6.3   Swinburne and his Critics

Swinburne's *Responsibility and Atonement* is the most substantial treatment of this chapter's subject matter to come from a philosopher working in the analytic tradition. Swinburne's method, here as elsewhere, is first to analyse in detail the human conceptuality involved in the topic under scrutiny, and then to spell out its theological application. Thus he begins by offering a detailed account of moral goodness, responsibility and freedom, merit and reward, guilt, atonement, punishment and forgiveness as they occur within purely human relations, before going on to examine their use in the case of God's way of dealing with human sin.

This method is not to be challenged as such. Human relations are bound to provide analogies for talk of God's relations with humankind, if our God-talk is to retain moral significance at all. But there are dangers. Any mistake in moral philosophy is liable to lead to magnified anomalies in the theological context. And the special case of our relation to our Maker may involve the need to bar at least some aspects of the purely human case from analogical extension.

Swinburne holds there to be four components in a purely human act of atonement, leading to the restoration of relations broken or disrupted by wrongdoing. There have to be repentance, apology, reparation and penance. We may agree that, even if forgiveness does not have to wait upon repentance and apology, restoration of relations cannot realistically be held to have occurred without acknowledgement of fault and expression of remorse. Moreover, in the purely human context, it is clear that, at least for serious cases of wrongdoing, repentance and apology are not enough.

The wrong done is often too great to be overcome simply by forgiveness, repentance and apology. In some cases reparation is indeed called for. Penance too may well be a mark of one's recognition of the seriousness of the wrong done. Sometimes, penance may replace reparation where the latter is impossible. In the human case, moreover, a penalty, imposed by law, may have to be paid, either in addition to, or in place of, reparation. Often, however, the something more, in addition to repentance and apology, required for genuine atonement, is not so much reparation or penance, let alone penalty, but amendment of life and the actual building up of the restored and renewed relationship that constitutes reconciliation. In many contexts, genuine costly forgiveness, leading not only to repentance and apology, but also to a process of amendment and reconciliation, may well involve the remission of penalty and the waiving of the right to reparation or of the offer of penance. The point to be stressed here is that in the purely human case we cannot insist on reparation and/or penance, any more than penalty, as necessary conditions of forgiveness and reconciliation.

Let us now consider the divine–human case. I have already commented on the implausibility of Swinburne's insistence that divine forgiveness requires *prior* repentance and apology. That seems to fly in the face of the whole Gospel story. I now stress the implausibility of what he says about reparation and penance in the context of our reconciliation with God. Swinburne holds that, such is the seriousness of sin, that repentance and apology plus forgiveness are not enough. There must be an equivalent of reparation and/or penance to mark the seriousness of the alienation to be overcome and the depth of our commitment to the process of reconciliation. And here he calls upon the sacrifice model as one that retains moral force and enables us to give the death of Christ on the cross something of its traditional role as a necessary, or central, element in the once-for-all act of atonement. Unable to make a sacrificial offering of our own sufficient to fulfil the necessary task of reparation and/or penance, we are to plead Christ's perfect, loving self-sacrifice, made for us on the cross. By associating with this, we are enabled to embrace the process of restoration with the slate wiped clean.

It has to be said that this is a somewhat forced rescue operation, on Swinburne's part, of an element that he mistakenly thinks to be essential to the Christianity of the creeds. It is surprising to find this element included in his quasi-credal list of the theological assumptions governing his whole approach.[30] Swinburne includes there the belief that Christ's life and death were openly intended by him as an offering to God to make expiation for human sin. This assumption (highly dubious as a piece of New Testament interpretation) seems deliberately designed to require what I called the forced view of atonement as including, necessarily, our offering Christ's sacrifice in place of our reparation and penance. Despite Swinburne's intriguing analogies from ways in which parents may help children to make reparation for wrongs which they have done by providing them with the means to do so, this is surely not a morally persuasive, let alone necessary, way of regarding Christ's death. The fact that Swinburne vacillates at this point between talking of our pleading Christ's sacrificial death and talking of our being associated with Christ's offering of a perfect human life to God the Father, is another indication of moral and theological insecurity in this way of articulating a theology of the Atonement. To speak of our being associated with Christ's offering of a perfect human life to God the Father is a much more plausible way into a theology of sanctification and of being conformed to Christ, as we shall see. But on that view, Christ's death is not going to play the role in atonement theory that Swinburne wants it to do. On that view, the something more, over and above repentance and apology, required for genuine at-one-ment, is not reparation and/or penance, but amendment of life and conformity to Christ through the sanctifying work of the Spirit.

Similar criticisms of Swinburne have been made by a number of philosophers. John Hick, for example, insists that God's forgiveness can no more be thought to be dependent on a sacrifice than on a ransom payment or a vicarious penalty. And, even where some reparation, or penance, is appropriate, in respect of wrongs done to our fellow humans, it is, says Hick, a 'category mistake' to treat the eternal God as just another individual equally subject to injury, and equally requiring redress. On Hick's view, God, being God, will freely forgive sinners who come 'in genuine penitence' and 'with a radically changed mind'.[31]

Lucas insists that 'the language of sacrifice only describes, and does not explain, Jesus' dying on the Cross'.[32] We can of course still speak of God's own self-sacrificial love there, in the life and death of the incarnate Son; but that was not a sacrifice made *to* anyone, least of all to God himself. It was simply done on our behalf, in order to win us back to God. We shall return to Lucas's view in the next section.

Philip Quinn, in another contribution to the Swinburne Festschrift,[33] tries to stay with an account of Christ's atonement in terms of sacrifice; but even he balks at the idea that Christ died on the cross in order to appease a wrathful God. Rather, he suggests, Christ's life and death are of such value to God that they enable or permit him to remit both penalty and the requirement of reparation, and to forgive the sins of repentant and apologetic sinners freely, whether or not they are in a position to plead Christ's sacrifice. This last point raises the question of the scope of God's act in

Christ, that is, the question whether it is effective only for those who consciously respond. This question will be considered later in this chapter. But Quinn's suggestion that the Passion and death of Christ permit God freely to forgive must surely strike the reader as somewhat bizarre. It makes little sense, in the context of an incarnational and trinitarian theology, for which the Passion and death of Christ are the act of God himself in the Person of his incarnate Son.

Eleonore Stump's review of Swinburne's book[34] raises a number of objections. First she asks, as Hick does, why an omnipotent, omniscient deity, who can hardly be harmed by human wrongdoing, should require some costly penance from sinners. Secondly, she asks why God should require a cruel death as reparation, when, as Swinburne himself allows, he is not obliged to require penance or reparation at all. Thirdly, again like Hick, she refers to the parable of the Prodigal Son, in which the father gladly forgoes the offer of reparation. Finally, she too points to the ambiguity in Swinburne's treatment as to whether it is really Christ's blameless life, or his death on the cross, that is supposed to constitute atonement.

One of the most extended and intriguing criticisms of Swinburne is to be found in an article by Richard Cross entitled 'Atonement Without Satisfaction'.[35] Cross rejects the view, held, as we noted, by both Hick and Stump, that God cannot objectively be harmed by human sin. Here, I think we have to agree with Cross. God is wronged by sin. Moreover, any serious theology of the Cross, that is, of the crucified God, is bound to recognize the cost to God himself of the world's sin and suffering, whatever one may want to say about God's ultimate metaphysical invulnerability. But even so, given his rejection of retributive theories of punishment, Cross finds no need to postulate more, in relation to God, than the need for repentance and apology, once repentance, apology and redress, where possible, have been accorded to the human victims of wrongdoing. Sacrifice (or satisfaction) simply has no moral point in respect of our relationship to God. Cross suggests replacing Swinburne's satisfaction theory of atonement with a merit theory of atonement. It is the sheer merit of Christ's life and death that persuades God to promise and perform the supererogatory acts of forgiveness and restoration.

I am bound to say that this too strikes me as a somewhat forced theory of atonement. If Christ is God incarnate, then his life and death do not persuade, any more than permit, God to do something he would or could not have done otherwise. They actually embody and enact God's forgiveness and mercy.

One advantage of Cross's theory, however (as of Quinn's) is that salvation does not depend on our knowledge of what Christ has done. Simply in virtue of Christ's merit, God's mercy is extended to all and, we may hope, will take effect universally, if not in this life, then in God's eternity. Much more needs to be said, of course, about the ways in which the divine Spirit actually achieves this restoration.

6.4   Quinn and Stump on Aquinas on Atonement

The different ways in which contemporary philosophers of religion have expounded and interpreted the writings of Thomas Aquinas on atonement throw further light on the problem before us, and may be illustrated from further articles by Quinn[36] and Stump.[37]

Quinn demonstrates the many-sidedness of Aquinas's treatment of atonement. He shows first how Aquinas breaks with a number of key elements in the Anselmian tradition. For Aquinas, the devil has no rights, and atonement cannot be thought of as a matter of paying the devil his dues. Again, Aquinas was clear that God could have restored human nature in some other way than through the Incarnation of his Son. Rather, this was the best or most fitting way of restoration. The benefits conveyed by the Incarnation are manifold, according to Aquinas, and making satisfaction for sin is only one of them. But Aquinas does insist that Christ's Passion and death satisfy the debt of punishment incurred by human sin. By incorporation into Christ's death by baptism we are set free from guilt and reunited with God.

Quinn himself recognizes the difficulties in this account. He admits that a different kind of remedy is required for those who have not had the opportunity of baptism. But this admission deprives Christ's Passion and death of their necessary role. Quinn is not prepared to abandon the doctrine of divine severity retained in Aquinas's account, a stance putting him at odds with the moral intuitions of Hick, Lucas, Adams and even Swinburne, as discussed above. But Quinn does see the difficulty in making moral sense of Aquinas's notion of vicarious satisfaction. At this point, Quinn is prepared to modify Aquinas's account (in a manner comparable to Cross's modification of Swinburne). God is merciful to sinners, not because their debt of punishment is paid by Christ's Passion and death; rather 'Christ's Passion works by prevailing upon God not to be severe in his dealings with sinners'.[38] Once again, I have to say that the trinitarian implications of this suggestion are highly implausible.

A rather different interpretation of Aquinas is provided by Stump. She points out, in the first of her two articles, that, for Aquinas, the function of satisfaction is to restore a sinner to a state of harmony with God. Sins are remitted when the soul of the offender is at peace with the one offended. It is possible for another to make satisfaction for us, provided we ally ourselves with the substitution. The satisfaction in question is Christ's humble, obedient love, as acted out in the suffering he endured for others' sake. And the transfer is effected by God's sanctifying grace, eliciting our response, as we commemorate Christ's passion in the Eucharist. It is interesting to observe that, although there is some sense of artificiality in the way in which the language of satisfaction is still employed in this account, the morally objectionable aspects of the sacrifice model are absent, if Aquinas is interpreted along these lines. For the transformation is entirely on our side, not God's. The sacrifice, with which, by a kind of substitution, we are associated, is characterized wholly in moral terms: a self-sacrificial offering of a life of obedient love. And the manner in which we are associated with this is described in moral, personal terms: God's own sanctifying grace eliciting the sacramentally based response of a life of faith, lived out in the Christian community.

In her own account, in the second of her articles, Stump stresses the same key elements, this time without the artificiality to be discerned in Aquinas's retention of the terminology of satisfaction. Stump argues that justification by faith is a matter of our free acceptance of God's transforming grace. While allowing, as any morally serious account must allow, that this transformation is a gradual process, Stump presses the question how God effects the initial change in our will that opens up the transforming possibilities, without any overriding of our free will. The wedge that cracks the heart and elicits conversion, she repeats, is Christ's sacrificial love in action, culminating in the way of the cross. This is what atonement means in relation to justification by faith. It is thus that God undermines resistance, enabling God to reform the heart without violating it, and that, presumably, is what atonement means in relation to sanctification. We shall return to the subject of justification and sanctification, and the relation between these two key elements in atonement theory, in a later section.

6.5   Identification

Lucas writes: 'A better account of the significance of the cross is available in terms of *identification*.'[39] (We have already encountered the notion of identification in discussing the work of MacKinnon and Adams.[40]) According to this view, the exchange at the heart of Christian soteriology is this: God identifies himself with us by incarnation, so that we may be identified with him by union with Christ. Lucas refers to the key affirmation taken up by the Eastern Orthodox tradition from the writings of Athanasius: 'for he [the divine Word] became man that we might become divine'.[41] Of course, the eastern doctrine of divinization or deification does not mean that we lose our creaturely status, ontologically speaking. It means that, by union with Christ, we are taken into the triune God and made immortal. (This latter point is one to which we shall be returning in the next chapter.)

Lucas points out that, while in fact God's incarnation meant suffering and a cruel death, it did not have to be like that. The depth and extent of the divine self-sacrificial love is indeed revealed, with effect, in the cross of Christ, but God's forgiveness did not depend on the cross. The life of Christ was such as to make such a fate virtually inevitable, but 'it was a human inevitability, not a necessitarian one'.[42]

A similar stress on identification as constituting the heart of Christian soteriology had already been expressed in the 1960s by Austin Farrer:

> What, then, did God do for his people's redemption? He came among them, bringing his kingdom, and he let events take their human course. He set the divine life in human neighbourhood. Men discovered it in struggling with it and were captured by it in crucifying it. What could be simpler? And what more divine?[43]

It is important to note that this view is more than a subjective or exemplarist view. The life of Christ and the way of the cross do, of course, provide a paradigmatic and morally compelling example. But that is not the whole story. It is God's own sacrificial act of self-involvement, through incarnation to the point of crucifixion, that, as it were, transmits God's forgiveness and God's love, and enables the divine Spirit, the Spirit of both God the Father and of Christ crucified, to penetrate human hearts and human society and begin the work of sanctification. These objective transactions are what are lacking in a purely exemplarist view. Hick appeals to eastern Christianity's idea of gradual transformation of the human by the divine Spirit,[44] and to that extent his view is objectively theistic, but having rejected eastern Christianity's incarnational Christology, he can only treat the work of Christ in exemplarist terms. And Hick is in no position to see the Spirit's work of sanctification as a matter of humanity being united with Christ crucified and risen, and taken into the triune life of God.

Lucas concludes his essay with these words:

> The concept of identification is itself sometimes unclear and often fuzzy-edged. But it can give us a way of expressing different explanations of the crucifixion at different levels, in a way, which reveals the force of traditional

theories and metaphors without committing ourselves to their unfortunate, and often unchristian, implications.[45]

6.6   Revelation and Response

According to both Stump and Lucas, the moral heart of any Christian doctrine of atonement lies in the way in which the Incarnation and the gift of the Spirit enable God's costly, forgiving love to penetrate and transform sinners and draw them into the triune life and energy of God. The question still arises, however, whether all this can only take effect where the revelation of God's love in Christ becomes the object of explicit response.

This was certainly the case on Swinburne's view: Christians are to plead Christ's sacrifice as a sufficient satisfaction for sin. Stump's talk of 'the wedge that cracks the heart', and Farrer's talk of our discovering the divine life through struggling with, and being captured by, the life and death of God incarnate, also seem to imply that the effectiveness of God's reconciling acts depends on our conscious response, as, of course, subjective or exemplarist theories too have always held to be the case.

I have already drawn attention to the way in which most earlier objective theories of atonement saw the scope of Christ's atoning work in much wider, even universal, terms. Admittedly, these theories often took morally unacceptable forms, as in traditional talk of ransom, penal substitution or expiatory sacrifice. But there was nothing morally unacceptable about the way in which the value or merit of Christ's life and death were held, by both Quinn and Cross, for example, to extend to repentant sinners everywhere, not just to those aware of what Christ had done. Similarly, something like Lucas's identification theory can be expressed in ways that do not restrict its effect to those with knowledge of Christ's work.

This is argued by Vernon White in his *Atonement and Incarnation*.[46] God's own self-involvement in the wicked world to the point of crucifixion gives God the right to forgive – there is no cheap grace here – but, for White, the incarnate Son's perfect response to the Father is not only revelatory but also constitutive of our salvation prior to our knowing about it. The stress here is on the Incarnation not only as God's identification of himself with humankind, but also as the taking of humanity into God. One way or another, the whole human race is destined to be taken into God by incorporation into Christ's risen life. And this is a process that can, at least initially and to some degree, be thought of as taking place in hidden ways, prior to our conscious recognition.

Similarly, Bruce Reichenbach argues for an inclusivist understanding of atonement, whereby God's grace, incarnate in Christ's life of self-sacrificial love, and effective through the work of the Spirit, can also be discerned in other religions and in purely human works of charity.[47] He refers to Karl Rahner's theory of 'anonymous Christians' and to C. S. Lewis's use, at the end of his Narnia series, of the Matthean parable of the sheep and the goats. (In Jesus' parable, the righteous did not know that, in caring for the poor, the sick and the prisoners, they had actually been responding to him.) Reichenbach even suggests that Swinburne's insistence on repentance, apology, reparation and penance can be given cash value in terms that do not include the explicit pleading of Christ's sacrifice.

Whereas traditional objective conceptions of the Atonement tended to ascribe universal effect to the death of Christ, more recent objectivists, such as Lucas, Cross, White and even Swinburne (at times), tend to place the emphasis on the whole story of the Incarnation and the Spirit's work in drawing repentant sinners, wherever they may be, into the loving arms of God. None of these writers goes as far as Hick's 'pluralist' position, which detaches God's salvific work from its key focus in the Incarnation. Salvation is still being thought of by these writers in terms of what God did in 'becoming man that we might become divine' (Athanasius again). But the emphasis has certainly shifted from the death of Christ to the whole story of the Incarnation and its aftermath.

6.7 Justification and Sanctification

The Christian doctrine of salvation was traditionally expressed in terms of justification and sanctification. Justification was understood as God's gracious acceptance of repentant sinners, either by imputing, or by imparting, righteousness to them. Sanctification was understood as the process whereby the faithful are refashioned, and made holy, by the indwelling Spirit of the crucified and risen Christ, into whose Body, the Church, they are incorporated by baptism. The two terms – justification and sanctification – are hardly separable. Certainly, where justification is understood as a matter of being made just, it already embraces sanctification. As we have seen, the eastern Church preferred the single term of divinization.

It is hard to recapture the force of medieval and Reformation disputes over these notions. Indeed, Christian theologians today have mostly reached agreement over their import.[48] There is no dispute about the priority of God's grace, both in the acceptance and also in the transformation of the sinner.

Philosophical reflection on this doctrine has also concentrated on these two facets of what God has done, and is doing, to reconcile the world to himself. The moral heart of the doctrine has been seen, first, in the way in which God's costly forgiveness and acceptance are demonstrated and conveyed in the life, passion and death of his incarnate Son. And, secondly, it is seen in the way in which God's enabling and transforming grace and love are experienced in the conversion and growth of Christians. This interpretation of the doctrine of salvation was persuasively expounded in Eleonore Stump's article 'Atonement and Justification', discussed above.[49]

What many traditionalists will find lacking in such philosophical presentations of the doctrine of salvation is the element of vicarious atonement that featured so centrally in objective theories such as those of Anselm and Aquinas. Again and again, in the present chapter, we have been confronted by moral objections to the ideas of vicarious punishment and vicarious satisfaction. Philip Quinn pinpoints the difficulty in his article, 'Christian Atonement and Kantian Justification': 'According to common sense moral thinking, moral credits and debits are neither transferable nor transmissible.'[50] Quinn argues that, while Kant's moral interpretation of justification, in *Religion with the Limits of Reason Alone*, is not open to the objections levelled against Anselm, it still retains an unacceptable element of vicariousness in holding that, in addition to our own moral conversion, we must also appropriate 'a righteousness not our own, which is offered to us as a gift of grace'.[51] But someone else's righteousness can no more be transferred than someone else's guilt or punishment or satisfaction. Quinn confesses himself puzzled by where this leaves the doctrine of Atonement. It would seem that Christ's perfect human life and his sacrifice on the cross are in no way necessary for our salvation.

Further reflection on the identification theory[52] will enable us to see what Quinn (and Kant) have failed to appreciate. It is not that Christ's righteousness is to be appropriated by us as a gift. Rather, we are so to be united with Christ crucified and risen that we are taken, forgiven and transformed, into the triune life of God. This is why Christ's life and death, and the gift of his Spirit, are necessary for our salvation. It is not that Christ's righteousness is transferred to us. Rather, we are made just, sanctified, by God himself through Christ and the Spirit.

Two further difficulties need to be faced. The scenario just sketched is still open to the accusations of exclusivism and excessive individualism.

We have already seen that a number of theologians and philosophers, sensitive to the so-called scandal of particularity, have come to realize that salvation is not confined to Christians. The scope of both justification and sanctification has been recognized to extend much more widely, through the hidden, anonymous work of Christ and the Spirit, throughout the human world. Moreover, the process of sanctification cannot be restricted to the transformation of individual persons into conformity with Christ. The structures of society and the world must also be seen, analogously, to be objects of the Spirit's penetration. It has to be admitted that reflection on this further aspect of the wider scope of sanctification is to be found, so far, at any rate, in the work, not so much of Christian philosophers, as of some Christian theologians and ethicists.[53] The understanding of salvation explored in the present chapter has concentrated on the way in which individuals are reconciled to God and drawn into the divine life. The theologians I now have in mind go on to speak further of the redemption of society and the sanctification of the world. It is to be hoped that Christian philosophers too will turn their attention to the way in which the Spirit of Christ crucified and risen penetrates the structures of society, and makes the whole human world conform more and more to the divine intention.

CHAPTER SEVEN

The Consummation of All Things

The religions of Semitic origin see the world process, in teleological terms, as leading to a final consummation beyond death and beyond history. The Christian creeds conclude with the affirmation of belief in the resurrection of the dead and the life of the world to come. There are many problems that exercise philosophers of religion reflecting on these apparently extravagant beliefs. Are there philosophical grounds for expecting survival? Does the notion of life after death make any sense? Is eternity itself to be thought of in temporal terms? Does belief in resurrection make better sense than belief in immortality? How are continuity and identity secured across the divide between this life and the next? Is there free will in the 'morally frictionless' environment of heaven? Further questions of philosophical and moral interest are raised by the specifically religious doctrines of heaven, hell and purgatory. In this chapter we shall survey and examine a selection – but only a selection – of recent work on these problems.

7.1   Is Death the End?

All living creatures on this planet are mortal. From the point of view of everyday experience and natural science, human beings, like all other animals, are born and die, each with a limited life span here on Earth. But, for large tracts of human history, all over the globe, most human beings have believed that they are more than biological organisms. Rather, they are composite creatures, made up of body and soul. In world cultures and world philosophies, east and west, the soul, the subject of consciousness and will, has been regarded as immortal, sometimes as pre-existing, more often as surviving, its period of embodiment. One need only mention, in the western tradition, the names of Plato, Descartes and Butler as prominent

defenders of the kind of mind–body dualism that lends itself to the formu-
lation of philosophical arguments for the immortality of the soul.[1]

Among the most persistent of such arguments is the argument that the
soul, being a simple substance, is not susceptible to dissolution and, as such,
is necessarily immortal. This argument is prominent in both Plato and
Butler. But it finds little favour in contemporary philosophy, even among
those philosophers sympathetic to the notion of survival. The main reason
for this is the widespread loss of confidence in mind–body dualism to be
found among both philosophers and theologians in the age of science. The
more we know about the dependence of the mental on the physical, in
humans as in other animals, the less easy it is to regard the soul as a separate,
indissoluble substance. This is not to say that the materialists, or physicalists,
have won the day. The philosopher John Searle has come up with powerful
arguments for taking consciousness and mind seriously as features of the
natural world.[2] But Searle's position is not a form of dualism. What he is
drawing attention to is the capacity of nature to evolve mind.

Even so, a number of strong arguments for dualism can still be found.
Karl Popper, together with the neurobiologist John Eccles, defended mind–
body dualism in their joint book, *The Self and its Brain*.[3] But there was no
question, at least in Popper's case, of deducing immortality from what he
called 'World 2', the world of the mind. And even philosophers of religion
such as H. D. Lewis and Richard Swinburne, both of them resolute
upholders of mind–body dualism, do not attempt to defend the idea of
the natural immortality of the soul.[4] For them, the soul, like the body, is a
finite, created substance, with a limited life span, unless sustained or recreated by God beyond death. So, even for these Christian dualist philosophers,
life after death is a theological, not a philosophical, postulate. Later in this
chapter we shall examine the Jewish-Christian preference for talk of resurrection rather than immortality; but, either way, survival is now regarded as
a matter of God's gift, not an inherent property.

The theological reasons for supposing that God does in fact bestow the
gift of life after death are quite easy to summarize. Restricting ourselves to
the Christian worldview, we may refer to the doctrine of Creation, discussed in chapter 3, and to the doctrines of Incarnation and Salvation,
discussed in chapters 4 and 6. Reflection on God's purposes in creation
and redemption, as revealed in the history of Israel and the story of Christ,
and that story's aftermath, shows that a future consummation to the whole
world process, involving a new creation in which at least God's personal
creatures are all to participate, is an integral aspect of the divine intention.[5]
Considerations of theodicy reinforce this view. We have already considered
briefly the problem of evil that afflicts Christian understanding of creation

and the love of God.[6] It is widely held that, at least where human beings are concerned, the creative project would not be worth the cost unless all life's victims, from every generation, can be assured of a place in God's ultimate future.[7] These considerations may be held to support the concluding affirmations of the Christian creed, whose primary foundation is, of course, Christ's Resurrection, recorded in the Gospels.

A small number of Christian philosophers have shown an interest in what they claim to be empirical evidence for survival of death, namely the alleged evidence of parapsychology or of reported near-death experiences. The contribution of parapsychology is discussed by John Hick, with intriguing reference to the Tibetan Book of the Dead, in his *Death and Eternal Life*,[8] which remains the major study of this whole subject area by a contemporary philosopher of religion. We shall be returning to Hick's book at various stages in this chapter. On the alleged evidence of parapsychology for survival of death, Hick remains pretty sceptical, given the possibility of alternative explanations in terms of telepathic impressions or even psychic traces, themselves of highly uncertain credibility. Accounts of near-death experiences have been collected by the Alister Hardy Research Institute, and discussed by Paul Badham and his colleagues.[9] These too are very intriguing, not least the extremely unexpected account of his own near-death experience by the atheist philosopher A. J. Ayer.[10] But again, the evidential value of such experiences, given the sheer difficulty of interpreting them in isolation from some prior psychological, philosophical or theological framework, is highly uncertain.

To sum up: the belief that death is not the end is best treated by philosophers of religion as something required by theology rather than by philosophy. Their main concern will be, not so much with philosophical reasons or empirical evidence for such belief, as with its coherence.

7.2 Does Life after Death Make Sense?

So far, in considering the question 'Is death the end?', the meaningfulness of the idea of survival has been presupposed. This was true whether we were thinking of philosophical arguments for immortality, theological arguments why God might or must raise the dead or empirical claims for some communication from beyond the grave. In turning to the question of the coherence of the idea of survival, we now examine challenges to this presupposition.

The suggestion that life after death is a contradiction in terms[11] need not detain us. The question at issue is whether sense can be made of the idea of a person's further life beyond the death of the biological organism that has been the vehicle of his or her life here on Earth. This question cannot be ruled out of court by definition.

Nor need we be deflected from our enquiry by D. Z. Phillips's suggestion that the religious power of talk of immortality or eternal life lies not in beliefs about survival but rather in the possibility of participation in the life of God here and now. 'Eternity is not *more* life, but this life seen under certain moral and religious modes of thought', writes Phillips.[12] As pointed out in chapter 1 (section 1.1), Phillips's Wittgensteinian analysis of religious language is a highly controversial matter. But one is bound to say that his treatment of the themes of death and immortality, as illustrated by the above quotation, gives some substance to the characterization of his work as non-cognitivist.

Most philosophers of religion prefer to treat the question of survival as a factual question, and to examine the specific difficulties involved in any attempt to spell out the meaning of life after death intelligibly. Examples of such treatment by a hostile critic may be found in the articles collected together as 'Part III: Immortality' of Antony Flew's book, *The Presumption of Atheism.*[13] We shall concentrate here on more sympathetic attempts to tackle the problems of identity and continuity that arise when one asks precisely what believers believe survives the death of the body, and precisely what ensures its being the same individual, now deceased, whose life is renewed under the radically changed conditions of God's new creation.

7.3   Time and Eternity

Before pursuing these reflections, we need to consider a more theological objection that has been raised to talk of a future life beyond death. Put crudely, the objection is this: if God's eternity is thought of in non-temporal terms, it does not make sense to think of our eternal life, that is, our participation in God's eternity, as life *after* death. For 'after' is undeniably a temporal term.

The question of how seriously, indeed how literally, we should take the word 'after' in talk of life after death is a highly controversial topic. Nicholas Lash and I debated this issue in several issues of *The Heythrop Journal* for 1978 and 1979.[14] According to Lash, resurrection and eternal life are best understood, not as a further, subsequent, unending span of temporal existence bestowed on us by God, but as our whole finite, contingent life story being affirmed, in all its inner transfigured significance, by God's creative love. Indeed, each finite life is held to be, eternally, an expression of God's creativity, and, as such, itself of eternal significance. Against this view I argued that, if eternal life means our bounded temporal existence being experienced from the standpoint of God's eternity, then we, as subjects, appear to slip out of the picture. There is no hope of our own conscious participation in the life of the world to come. I also pointed out that Lash's view contains no solace whatsoever for the millions of thwarted and truncated human lives that create such problems for theodicy. To this last point, Lash had little of substance to reply. To the first point he replied that he had not meant that, in resurrection, our earthly life is experienced eternally by God alone. Rather, it is experienced by us from God's eternal standpoint. But it was hard to conceive what this might mean if it could not be given cash value in terms of something new, something richer, something more rewarding for us than what had gone before. A fortiori, it was hard to make sense of Christ's Resurrection on such a view.

Lash's position was premised not only on the conviction of God's timeless eternity, but also on the conviction of the inherently bounded nature of our finite temporal life span. But Christian theology puts a question mark against both these premises. It challenges the kind of secular anthropology that confines human life within the boundaries of birth and death. And, as was shown in chapter 3, the doctrine of *God's* timelessness is itself the subject of criticism in much systematic and philosophical theology today.[15] In the *Heythrop Journal* debate, I concentrated on the point that, if God has created a temporally structured universe, he must relate himself to it in a mode appropriate to its temporality, not only now but in the future. On any view, the future of *creation* has to be reckoned with. But, if God's own eternity is itself to be rethought in terms of sempiternity or primordial temporality, then there is all the more reason to think in terms of a future consummation to his creative project.

It is strange that a number of leading process theologians, despite their conviction of the temporality of God, have tended to follow Whitehead in holding the future to consist in the retention of all value in the mind of God. Thus, for Charles Hartshorne and Norman Pittenger, immortality is God's remembrance of the achieved values of a person's life.[16] This involves a very strong and positive sense of God's 'memory'; but, even so, it is hard not to agree with Hick that this is hardly a doctrine of *our* new life beyond death.[17]

7.4 Immortality and Resurrection

We resume, then, the question of how the future life beyond death, promised in the Gospel, is best to be conceived. This brings us to the topics

of immortality and resurrection. In a wide sense, as when Christians speak of
'the hope of immortality', the word 'immortality' simply means unending
life and, as such, includes resurrection. But, more usually, 'immortality'
and 'resurrection' are contrasted, the former meaning the soul's non-
susceptibility to death, the latter meaning a divine act of reconstitution as
the sole source of life beyond death. But even here the contrast is not
absolute. Strictly speaking, only God is intrinsically immortal. Dualists who
believe in the immortality of the soul as a simple substance still, for the most
part (an exception being the atheist philosopher, McTaggart[18]) hold the
immortal soul to be a created substance, held in being by God both in this
life and the next. Its immortality, therefore, is contingent upon the creative
power and act of its Maker and Sustainer.

That the idea of the soul's immortality as a disembodied state beyond
death is not popular amongst Christian theologians or among Christian
philosophers today has already been acknowledged. It still has some attractive features, however. In particular, it avoids the difficulty, perhaps the
impossibility, of supposing that a person's deceased and decomposed or
cremated remains are somehow reassembled by a divine act of resurrection.
Increased scientific knowledge of the nature and fate of organisms like the
human body has undermined the credibility of that old view of resurrection.
And, if it is urged that resurrection does not mean the reassembly of
particles, but rather the raising and transforming of the deceased body,
that view, too, seems increasingly difficult not only to believe but also to
understand, the more we know about the actual constitution of organisms.
A dualist belief in the immortality of the soul can ignore these difficulties.

On the other hand, there are also grave difficulties in making sense of the
future life as a community of disembodied spirits. How could such finite,
immaterial, souls be identified? How could they experience anything? How
could they communicate? A widely discussed attempt to answer these
questions and to provide a coherent sketch of what a world of disembodied
spirits might be like was made by the philosopher H. H. Price.[19] According
to Price, this would consist of subjects of purely mental images existing in
something like a dream world – not a private world, however, but rather a
public world of shared images, in which many minds could communicate
and interact telepathically. Price's own account was somewhat ambiguous
between the notion of private image worlds formed from prior life experiences and life choices, and a common image world that at least the like-
minded would be able to share. The former notion did provide some
intimation of how a person could fashion their own private hell, but the
latter is what is required if the future life is to possess anything like the
character of a common world. On this view, much more needs to be said

about the exercise of God's omnipotence in coordinating the images that make up the future mental environment envisaged. Paul Badham, in developing Price's view in this direction, points out that such a divinely coordinated image world would be very much akin to what the idealist/phenomenalist philosopher, George Berkeley, held our present world to be.[20]

More will be said in the next section about what might secure personal identity in such a shared image world. Clearly, for Price, the soul or subject is not inextricably linked to the physical body that it leaves behind. But it must retain memories and character traits, as well as imaginative powers, not only in the sense of the productive imagination, but also of the power to receive the divinely coordinated images of the world to come.

Those of a more Aristotelian temper regard the soul not as a substance in its own right but as the form of the body, that is to say, the kind of subjectivity and life enjoyed by organisms of a particular kind. Human beings, on this view, are psychosomatic unities, and the idea of humans continuing as disembodied spirits after death makes no sense. Thus Peter Geach, in an essay on 'Immortality',[21] holds not only that personal identity depends on continuity of material conditions, but also that psychological concepts tend to collapse when their connections with non-psychological concepts are broken. To these points he adds a Wittgensteinian suspicion of purely private sensations and feelings, deprived of their bodily base. He allows, with Thomas Aquinas, the possibility of surviving mental remnants of thought and will, but asks whether their previous histories of separate embodied individuality would be enough to individuate them in their disembodied state. (Indeed, other cultures have held that liberated souls do lose their individuality when absorbed into the world soul.) Geach is not convinced that memory is enough for personal identity. How, without connection to bodily continuity, could genuine memories be distinguished from spurious ones?

The dualist is not necessarily refuted by these criticisms, as we shall see. But we can appreciate the force of Geach's conviction (which he shares with Thomas Aquinas[22]) that only at the General Resurrection will the individual person really live again.

We turn, then, to the idea of resurrection. A good starting point is Peter van Inwagen's short article 'Resurrection', in the *Routledge Encyclopedia of Philosophy*.[23] Van Inwagen's views, here and in a number of essays,[24] are of particular interest, since he is one of relatively few Christian philosophers who explore the notion of resurrection on the basis of metaphysical materialism. He is perfectly aware that resurrection cannot be a matter of the reassembly of atoms, since the animal organism that constitutes a person consists of different atoms at different stages of its life. But he takes the criterion of material and causal continuity even more seriously than Geach does, since, for van Inwagen, material continuity is the only criterion of personal identity. He cites St Paul's simile of the grain sown in the earth becoming wheat. The person who dies and is dissolved in earth or fire becomes, through God's act of transformation, a citizen of heaven. This is not an easy notion to grasp. But *some* light is thrown on the notion of such a transformation by Dean Zimmermann in an article in *Faith and Philosophy*.[25] Zimmermann suggests that resurrection can be thought of as a kind of fission brought about by God at an individual's death, whereby a life is continued in a new mode, notwithstanding the spatio-temporal gap of death and resurrection. All one needs is a theory of immanent causation that allows for causal continuity between life stages, irrespective of such gaps. The new stage certainly has to be causally related to the old stage. It is *this* dying organism that is the object of God's act of fission, and it is my present, and past, life stages that determine the identity and character of my new one. But the old stuff of my body, prior to fission, is left behind.

This intriguing suggestion is premised on the very plausible view that my resurrection cannot simply be a matter of God's creating a replica of me in another mode. The replica theory of resurrection is best known in the writings of John Hick.[26] For Hick, resurrection is to be thought of as the new creation of a 'replica' person in another spatio-temporal environment, endowed by God with just those memories and character traits that were associated with the previous earthly body. But, as van Inwagen and Zimmermann insist, a replica cannot seriously be regarded as the *same* person as the person who lived on earth before. And as Julius Lipner has rather nicely put the matter, in an article entitled 'Hick's Resurrection': 'While it is greatly to be desired that Professor Hick will be resurrected in due time, it seems clear that his rendering of the event cannot allow this. And we will not be satisfied with a resurrection Hickoid; we want the man himself.'[27]

One problem for Hick's replica theory and for Zimmermann's fission theory is the problem dubbed the 'if not two, then not one argument'.[28] For, on either view, it might seem logically possible for God to create two or more replicas or fission products, irrespective of causal continuity. No doubt God would not wish to do such a thing, but, it is suggested, the logical possibility of such multiplicity is enough to undermine any such notion of survival. Zimmermann is well aware of the problem, but he has an answer, at least where causal continuity is an essential part of the story. Were multiple fission to occur, the individual in question would simply cease to be. Two or more new individuals (with shared memories up to that point) would come into existence. For continuity of the *same* individual to be preserved, God would have to ensure that one, and only one, prime causal chain links the old life and the new. In other words, for the fission theory, there is not even the *logical* possibility of the same individual continuing in two or more equally split modes. This answer clearly would not work, where Hick's replica theory is concerned. But there the problem is redundant. *One* replica would not be the same individual anyway.

Van Inwagen cites, in the brief bibliography to his encyclopaedia article, John Polkinghorne's book, *The Faith of a Physicist*,[29] as containing a broadly materialist account of resurrection. The reason for this characterization of Polkinghorne's position is the latter's use of the software/hardware analogy (from computer science) for what resurrection might mean. However, to describe Polkinghorne as a materialist is hardly accurate. Certainly, he is not a dualist. He regards the human person as a psychosomatic unity, informed by a 'complex, dynamic, information-bearing pattern developing through-out . . . the course of <one's> life'.[30] The person is in every respect mortal and death constitutes its end. But the 'software' pattern that identifies the particular person will be recreated by God so as to inform the new 'hardware' resurrection body in the new creation of God's future. Polkinghorne acknowledges that the software/hardware analogy is 'crude and inadequate'; but we have to press the question whether an information-bearing pattern, especially if dissolved and then 're-created', can really do justice to the facts of human subjectivity and identity, let alone preserve that identity and the continuity of the same person across the gap between death and new creation. Polkinghorne's view certainly avoids the problem of material causal continuity that makes the views of van Inwagen, Zimmermann and even Geach so hard to follow. One may well have to abandon that element in the more or less traditional views of resurrection. But it is not clear that Polkinghorne escapes the criticism levelled at Hick. His admittedly more sophisticated computer analogy, surely, still leaves us with no more than a (theoretically multipliable) replica person in the new creation.

A defence of the more traditional view, premised on acceptance of soul-body dualism, whereby a period of temporary disembodiment is followed by reanimation of the transformed body at the general resurrection, is to be found in Stephen Davis's book, *Risen Indeed*.[31] For Davis, it is the disembodied soul that carries a person's identity from this life to the next, but the new body which it receives is 'materially related' to the old body.[32] The difficulty with this view of resurrection is twofold. Can we make sense of the notion of the transformation of *material* substance that it involves? And is such material continuity necessary, if it is the soul that sustains identity? Polkinghorne is far from being alone in thinking that modern science requires us to abandon the notion of *material* resurrection.

7.5   Identity, Continuity and the Soul

If resurrection consists in the new creation, not the renewal or even the transformation of the body, then it is clear that the bearer of continuity and identity across the divide between this life and the next must indeed be something like the soul as traditionally conceived, namely as an enduring spiritual substance, preserved by God's sustaining hand through death and resurrection, death being the loss of the old body, resurrection being the gift of a new, imperishable, immortal 'body'. The transformation involved is from the old embodiment to the new. The question now arises: does this bring us straight back, as Davis apparently believes, to unqualified soul–body dualism?

Before answering this question, let us review the criteria of personal identity, as they apply in our *present* existence. They are at least five in number: bodily continuity, memory, character, a particular life history of interpersonal relation, and awareness of being the person one is (even if suffering from amnesia). The last of these was tellingly stressed by H. D. Lewis in his writings, and certainly played a role in his defence of soul–body dualism.[33] The crucial point to note is that the last four of these criteria cannot simply apply to the body as a material, physical and biological organism. They all require a mental, indeed, spiritual *subject*: the subject of a life history, with its relationships and memories, and endowed with distinctive character traits. Admittedly, all these, including subjectivity itself, are, in the present life, inseparable from bodily continuity. They are, as Polkinghorne says, aspects of the psychosomatic unity that forms a person. But qua subject, a person is more than just a highly developed organism with a highly developed brain. It is not unreasonable to think of the subject as a spiritual substance, at present inextricably linked to a growing organism but not identifiable with it. It is this that leads us to retain the idea of the soul.

The least plausible aspect of Swinburne's otherwise plausible defence of dualism, in *The Evolution of the Soul*, is his treatment of the soul as a separately created spiritual substance, specially made to inform a biological organism at a crucial stage of its development.[34] It would be more plausible to think of the soul as an emergent spiritual substance that supervenes upon an organism at a certain stage of developed complexity. On this view, created matter possesses the God-given capacity to evolve spirit, which then can be sustained by God, past the death of the body, until it is re-housed in the resurrection body in the resurrection world. A more appropriate analogy than either the grain/wheat analogy endorsed by Zimmermann and Davis (following St Paul) or the software/hardware analogy endorsed by Polkinghorne would be the chrysalis/butterfly analogy. This allows for the discarding of the old body – the chrysalis – and the emergence, and then new life, of the soul – the butterfly. It is still, of course, a 'crude and inadequate' analogy. For an actual butterfly retains *material* causal continuity with the chrysalis, and indeed is still a biological organism. Certainly the soul retains causal continuity with its previous embodied life, but material continuity ceases. This entails a broader sense of 'cause', of course. But that is required anyway if matter is so created as to be able to evolve spirit, which itself can interact with matter, as when a child raises a hand to answer a question.

Let us consider how far the view just sketched differs from Geach's position, discussed above. It has more in common with Geach's Thomism than with his Aristotelianism. For it treats the soul in much more substantial terms than is allowed for by Geach's talk of 'mental remnants'. Moreover, it parts company with Thomas Aquinas, Geach and Davis in dispensing with *material* continuity between the present body and the resurrection body. Causal continuity is maintained, on this view, simply by the soul.

One other way of attempting to resolve the problem of soul–body dualism is suggested by Stephen Voss, drawing upon the work of David Wiggins.[35] Suppose both body and soul (or *anima*, as Voss calls the part of the human being essential to survival) are not two different substances, but rather aspects or modes of a human being. The dissolution of the body at death is then no more than the cessation of a mode of functioning that is not essential to the survival of the *anima*. This is certainly a line of thought worth pursuing.

7.6   The Tedium of Immortality

Before we proceed to examine the more specifically theological aspects of Christian hope, it is worth pausing to consider an objection to the notion of unending life after death that has exercised a number of philosophers. Bernard Williams, for example, cites the play, *The Makropoulos Case* (turned into a splendid opera by Janácek), in which, unknown to everybody else, the heroine has lived on and on, through one relationship after another, for 342 years, in order to bring out the utterly boring character of the notion of unending life.[36] But such a model of eternal life is hopelessly unimaginative and pedestrian. We cannot think of the life of the world to come simply in terms of an endless continuation of what we experience here on Earth. But there may well be hints in present experience of what life in the resurrection world will be like. Garth Hallett explores a number of such possible analogies in an article on this theme in *Faith and Philosophy*.[37] He is suspicious of the notion of timeless beatitude, for reasons comparable to those already given in section 7.3 of this chapter; but totally absorbed activity, ever deeper awareness and growth, mystical experience, eternal youthfulness and delight, and creative contentment all provide hints of what might become immortalizable. Hallett points out how mystical experience, though taking place in time, constitutes a kind of subjective timelessness, a state in which one ceases to be aware of the passage of time. However, that can only be one among several possibilities. An earlier philosopher, A. E. Taylor, insisted on the temporal aspects of eternal life:

> Even a heavenly life would still be a forward-looking life . . . the blessed would always have new discoveries awaiting them, more to learn than they had already found out of the unspeakable riches of God. . . . Heaven – if a heaven indeed there is – we may safely say, must be a land of delightful surprises, not a country of Lotus-eaters where it is always afternoon. And in the same way, if we are to think morally of Heaven, we should, I suggest, think of it as a land where charity *grows*, where each citizen learns to glow more and more with an understanding love, not only of the common King, but of his fellow citizens.[38]

We shall have reason to take up a number of points from this quotation in subsequent sections, but, to redress the balance yet again, let us reflect on the following quotation from a much earlier philosophical theologian, Thomas Aquinas: 'Nothing that is contemplated with wonder can be tiresome, since as long as the thing remains in wonder it continues to stimulate desire. But the divine substance is always viewed with wonder by any created intellect. So it is impossible for an intellectual substance to become tired of this vision.'[39]

The vision of God is one of the prime notions in terms of which the Christian tradition has tried to articulate the final destiny of God's human creatures. Kenneth Kirk's magisterial Bampton Lectures, with the title *The Vision of God*, remains the standard work on this central theme of eschatology.[40] But the idea of the vision of God captures only one aspect of the consummation of all things. Like the idea of survival itself, it focuses on the *individual's* future state. This must now be complemented by reflection on the two other key symbols in terms of which the Christian tradition has envisaged the ultimate end-state of creation: namely, the communion of saints and the kingdom of God. It has to be admitted that, with one exception, these more theological aspects of the resurrection world have received less attention from philosophers of religion than questions of individual destiny.

7.7   The Resurrection World

The communal aspect of the end state of God's new creation was stressed by Hick in the final chapter of his book, *Death and Eternal Life*.[41] He suggested there, with reference to eastern as well as western thought, that the over-coming of ego-centredness will lead to the transcendence of individuality and the transformation of personal existence into an interpersonal corporate life, reflecting the communal nature of the triune God. This latter point can be made all the stronger, the more we go along with the social analogy in trinitarian theology, as explained in chapter 5. Hick himself has grown less and less inclined to press this analogy, admittedly. But it is interesting to find him making the point in this relatively early work. There, he went on to illustrate the perfected community of mutually open centres of conscious-ness with a telling quotation from John Donne, in which the poet uses the metaphor of the book of life:

> All mankind is of one author, and is one volume; when one man dies, one chapter is not torn out of the book, but translated into a better language; and every chapter must be so translated: God employs several translators; some pieces are translated by age, some by sickness, some by war, some by justice; but God's hand is in every translation, and his hand shall bind up all our scattered leaves again, for that library where every book shall lie open to one another.[42]

The relation of this corporate consummation to Christian belief in the 'body' of the risen Christ will be discussed in the final section of this chapter.

That the resurrection world is not simply a communion of selves in relation to each other and to God has already led us to speak of the environment of heaven. Here we turn again to Austin Farrer, who discussed the matter briefly in the last chapter of his *Saving Belief*.[43] For Farrer, as for nearly all the authors mentioned here, resurrection is God's gift of grace, and the communion of saints is sustained solely in relation to God. But this must entail a created sphere in and through which God brings our story to its intended consummation. This new creation, including our resurrection 'bodies', can be 'as dimensional as it likes', says Farrer, without being spatially related to our present universe. For 'space is a web of interactions between material energies which form a system by interacting'. The 'stuff of glory' of which heaven is composed is not such as 'to interact with sticks and stones, with flesh and blood'.

I myself have offered, in an earlier book, *The Christian Hope*, some speculations about which aspects of creaturely life and existence are susceptible of translation into the imperishable condition of the world to come.[44] Some present goods are inherently perishable: a rose, a cathedral, a mountain. Many such goods could be retained only in memory and idea. Here, Process Theology's talk of the divine memory, in which we may hope to share, perhaps comes into play. Personal and interpersonal values, by contrast, including all creative and cultural values, are, no doubt, translatable into the new imperishable environment. But present experience of such values, as has already been said, offers no more than hints of what form their future, imperishable 'embodiment' will take.

7.8   Purgatory, Heaven and Hell

The one exception referred to above, that is to say, the one aspect of specifically Christian eschatology to have attracted a great deal of attention from philosophers of religion in recent years, is the question of hell. Hell does not feature in the Christian creeds; but it has been the dominant view in Christian doctrine down the ages that salvation in and through Christ is effective only for those who, explicitly or implicitly, accept God's forgiveness and open themselves up, in faith, to the Spirit's work of sanctification. Human God-given freedom, it is held, always leaves open the possibility of rejection of the divine love, and consequent alienation from the springs of eternal life. The *possibility*, in this sense, of everlasting damnation cannot be denied. And, to judge simply by the empirical evidence of peoples' lives and deeds in this life, much of the world remains unredeemed, and many souls do repudiate the love of God and find themselves in hell. The tradition suggests that this remains the case for ever.

The view that this is not the case, and that no one can resist the gentle pressure of the love of God for ever, is known as universalism. It is the view that, in the end, all will be saved. Very much a minority view in earlier centuries, universalism is widely held today by Christian theologians and philosophers, as we shall see.

Before examining the debate over hell and universalism, we need to consider the doctrine of purgatory. This is the view, premised upon the highly plausible conviction that few are ready, at death, for immediate translation to the life of heaven, that the vast majority of the faithful require a period of gradual reconstruction before they are fit for the beatific vision. The doctrine emerged in the early Church — it has at least some scriptural basis in I Corinthians 3: 15 — and had secured a firm place in medieval Christianity. It fell into disrepute at the Reformation, largely through the scandalous practice of the sale of indulgences, whereby time in purgatory was alleged to be reduced. But the doctrine itself survived this abuse, and it is widely held in, and beyond, Roman Catholic Christianity today. A dramatic and moving portrayal of its religious significance may be found in John Henry Newman's poem, *The Dream of Gerontius*, turned into a wonderful oratorio by Elgar. And, as Austin Farrer put it, with his characteristic light touch: 'It seems strange, indeed, that so practical and pressing a truth as that of purgatory should be dismissed, while so remote and impractical a doctrine as the absolute everlastingness of hell should be insisted on.'[45]

A salient feature of the traditional doctrine of purgatory was its restriction to those whose wills are already set, at the moment of death, in the direction of trust in God. For the most part, mainstream Christianity has held to the notion of the finality of death, that is to say, the belief that no further opportunities for repentance or conversion will be given in the life of the world to come. Purgatory will simply be a matter of cleansing or purification for those who already have at least some degree of faith in God when they die. This conviction is challenged by John Hick in his greatly expanded treatment of purgatory in *Death and Eternal Life*.[46] Its rejection enables us to give proper attention to what Hick calls 'pareschatology', the doctrine of intermediate stages between death and the final consummation. Hick himself, in accordance with his philosophy of religious pluralism, whereby the different faith traditions of world religion provide alternative and complementary paths to spiritual fulfilment, sees these future stages as disparate. People pass through many post-mortem 'worlds' before they reach the ultimate state, itself conceived of as multifaceted. In the final section of the present chapter, we shall see reason to think in much more unitary terms of growth towards a Christ-centred eschaton. But one thing we shall have to accept from Hick's position is his unqualified rejection of the finality of death. Only so can the case for Christian universalism be considered seriously. To the debate over universalism we now turn.

Philosophers of religion who have argued in favour of universalism include John Hick, the present author, Marilyn McCord Adams, Thomas Talbott and Eric Reitan.[47] Their opponents, defenders, that is, of the traditional doctrine of hell, include Peter Geach, Eleonore Stump, William Lane Craig, Michael Murray and Stephen Davis.[48] To illustrate this debate, I shall concentrate here on Talbott and Adams among the universalists, and Craig and Stump among the traditionalists, with little more than passing reference to the other scholars mentioned.

Talbott argues his case with great clarity and cogency. In a nutshell, the argument goes like this: it is simply inconsistent to hold, in the first place, that God is love and wills the salvation of everyone, in the second place, that God has the power to achieve his redemptive purpose for the world, and yet, in the third place, that some sinners will never be reconciled to God, but will remain in hell for ever. These three convictions are still incompatible, even if hell is understood as a state of alienation brought about by people's own perversity, rather than as unending punishment exacted by the Creator. The only view consistent with the first two convictions is that, in the end, one way or another, if not in this life then in the next, even the most obdurate sinners will be won over and made fit for heaven.

At least four objections to Talbott's case for universalism have been raised. Craig and Davis both support the view that the dominant thrust of the Christian scriptures suggests not only the possibility but also the reality of eternal loss. Secondly, they observe that Christian mission loses much of its motivation if all are to be saved in any case. In the third place – and this is of more philosophical interest – they and other critics, such as Murray, urge the point that significant human freedom would have to be overridden on the universalist hypothesis. (Connected with this is Gordon Knight's argument[49] that the greater good of *not* overriding human freedom may entail God's inability to achieve all his redemptive purposes.) In the fourth place, Murray also raises the question why, if universalism is true, God puts human creatures through all the trials and tribulations of earthly life. Why does he not create heaven directly?

Taking these four points in reverse order, let us consider how Talbott replies to his critics. His answer to Murray[50] is a development of Hick's 'soul-making theodicy',[51] whereby the conditions of our formation are necessary for the creation of finite personal beings. This point has already been noted in the course of our brief discussion of the problem of evil in chapter 3 (section 3. 2. 6). Heaven *cannot* be created directly. Only by being fashioned from below, in and through an ordered material universe, can creatures capable of being translated into the conditions of eternity be made.

The objection that universalism entails the overriding of creaturely freedom is the most serious problem from the point of view of philosophy. But clearly, for Talbott, God's power to achieve his redemptive purposes does not require compulsion. The love of God, revealed in Christ crucified, will eventually succeed in persuading and winning even the most obdurate. The tenability of this view depends, of course, on our abandoning the idea of the finality of death. And, as Adams makes clear,[52] it involves a high doctrine of divine resourcefulness. Her other reasons for refusing to accord priority to the rebelliousness of creatures will be considered shortly.

Talbott and Adams make short shrift of the argument that, without the danger of incurring hell, morality and mission lose their motivation. It is indeed hard to see this as a serious point. The moral and religious motivation for evangelization is no more and no less than the command and the desire to make known, and to share, the love of God revealed in Christ.

The question of scriptural authority for universalism or for the traditional view is not as easy to resolve as Craig and Davis make out. Texts can be cited on both sides of the debate. Philosophical interest in this question will take us back to the issues concerning the nature of revelation considered in chapter 2. Universalists will argue that doctrines cannot be based on details culled from parabolic imagery or from the perfervid imagery of the Book of Revelation. They agree that the general thrust of scripture should determine the development of Christian doctrine, but their evaluation of that general thrust is very different from Craig's and Davis's. Moreover, if we take seriously the arguments of David Brown (see chapter 2, section 2.6) about the way in which revelation goes on, precisely through the kind of wrestling with scripture that leads to revised and changing understandings of key elements in the Christian faith, we shall be the readier to accept the view that sinners can never put themselves beyond redemption.

Let us now consider, however, two ways in which the doctrine of hell has been defended by Christian philosophers. William Lane Craig has suggested that perhaps 'God has actualised an optimal balance between saved and unsaved, and those who are unsaved suffer from trans-world damnation'.[53] What does this mean? Craig argues that some, maybe many, possible people will freely reject God's grace in every possible world. They incur, that is, 'transworld damnation'. And the creation of a world of free persons who do accept God's grace, and are thus able to accept the gift of heaven, may only be possible at the cost of allowing there to be other persons who suffer from transworld damnation. Accepting the doctrine of God's middle knowledge (which we rejected in earlier chapters – see chapter 3, section 3.1.6, and chapter 4, section 4.5), Craig then suggests that God's omniscience enables him to create an actual world which achieves the optimal balance between the saved and the unsaved. There is no injustice in this, since the damned freely incur their own fate.

Quite apart from its reliance on the dubious doctrine of middle knowledge, this scenario is bound to strike the sensitive reader as morally outrageous. As Marilyn McCord Adams says in her essay, to be discussed below, 'Craig's picture is not only theoretically mistaken, but also pragmatically pernicious',[54] just because it would be impossible to love a God who was prepared to create a world destined for heaven at such a cost.

Eleonore Stump defends Thomas Aquinas's doctrine of hell on rather different grounds. For her, God's love for the damned is shown is his preserving them in being for ever.[55] Since being and goodness are equated in Thomistic metaphysics, this is the best God can do for them without overriding their freedom to reject his love.

Some philosophers, among them Richard Swinburne,[56] consider the possibility that the language of hell and damnation is better interpreted in terms of annihilation rather than being kept for ever in a state of alienation. But it is hard not to agree with Adams that Stump's and Swinburne's views of the nature of eternal loss are no more compatible with the goodness and the love of God than is the traditional doctrine of everlasting punishment.[57]

Adams's defence of universalism has a moral and religious depth and perspicacity that far exceed those of any other author considered in this section. She brings out the incommensurability between any view of *everlasting* loss or punishment and the evils, even the horrendous evils, perpetrated by finite creatures. She also shows the limitations on human freedom and responsibility necessitated by our rootedness in a nature and a culture not of our own making. Above all, she brings out the incompatibility between any view of hell (other than as temporary and remedial) and the goodness and the love of God revealed in Christ. I have already referred to her stress on the resourcefulness of the divine love in overcoming, without compulsion, even the most obdurate resistance. The moral seriousness of Adams's defence of universalism is a standing refutation of the view express by Stephen Davis that 'the wrath of God is our only hope because it teaches us the moral significance of our deeds and shows us how life is to be lived'.[58]

7.9   Is there Free Will in Heaven

The subject of human freedom was central to the debate over universalism and hell. But it also arises in connection with the doctrine of heaven. For the Christian tradition has, virtually without exception, held that the blessed in heaven are beyond temptation and beyond the possibility of falling into sin again. But does this mean that they cease to be free?

We have already seen, in the chapters on Creation and Incarnation, that freedom cannot be defined in terms of the choice between good and evil. God's freedom and Christ's freedom have to be understood as embracing the whole range of activity and creativity open to perfect goodness. It was pointed out in that connection that the blessed, in the morally frictionless environment of heaven, will have come to share in the divine attributes, not only of immortality, but also of impeccability. Only under the conditions of our formation here on Earth, the conditions in and through which we are drawn out of nature into spirit, does our freedom entail susceptibility to temptation.

The question whether there is freedom in heaven is discussed by James Sennett in an article in *Faith and Philosophy*,[59] which seems to get the matter partly right and partly wrong. Sennett is quite right to distinguish between freedom on earth and freedom in heaven. The former, he says, is a matter of libertarian freedom and is essential to the formation of character. But the latter, he suggests, is best understood in terms of compatibilism: in heaven, one's 'free' actions are determined by formed, or graced, character. What this account fails to make clear is, first, the fact that it is the conditions of our *formation* that render libertarian freedom on Earth open to temptation, and, secondly, the fact that formed, or graced, character only *determines* that whatever one does is good. Libertarian freedom is preserved in heaven in the sense of openness to endless good alternative possibilities. Some intimation of what this means is given in the passage by A. E. Taylor quoted in an earlier section of this chapter (p. 119).

7.10   Christ and the Consummation

Finally, we consider a central aspect of Christian eschatology, to which philosophers have accorded rather scant attention, but which theologians would deem so central that its neglect here might be held to vitiate the whole treatment of life after death in this chapter. This is the Christ-centred nature of the specifically Christian concept of heaven. To justify the relative neglect of this aspect I would refer back to what was said in chapter 1 about the relation between philosophical theology and systematic theology. Philosophers have tended to concentrate not so much on the fully rounded theological picture as on certain key elements or aspects presupposed in the full account. These have to be explored in respect of their meaning and coherence, if sense is to be made of Christian doctrine about the life of the world to come. But, in concluding this chapter, I have to go back to the point made in chapter 6 (section 6.6) about the way in which salvation through incarnation involves the taking of humanity into God by incorporation into the risen life of Christ. It is Christ and the Spirit who, in the end, will take us into God. In its ultimate consummation, that is to say, the whole creative process will be caught up into the inner relations of love given, love received and love shared still more, within the blessed Trinity.

CHAPTER EIGHT

Other Themes in Christian Doctrine

─────────────

The larger part of this final chapter will be devoted to a doctrine not explicitly mentioned in the creed, although it is clearly presupposed and exemplified throughout the creed, namely, the doctrine of providence or divine action. This is a doctrine to which a very great deal of philosophical attention has been paid, as was the case with that other non-credal, yet all-pervasive, doctrine, divine revelation, which formed the subject matter of chapter 2.

But, before concentrating on providence, I include short sections on two credal doctrines left out of consideration as we moved from salvation to the consummation of all things, namely Church and sacraments. For under-standable reasons, these have not been the objects of philosophical scrutiny to the same extent as the doctrines considered in chapters 3–7. But Church and sacraments are well worth philosophical reflection, not least in connec-tion with the philosophy of worship.

8.1 The Church

If this were a book on Christian ethics, there would be much food for reflection concerning Church and State, community, authority and the common good. These topics are of great interest to ethicists and moral philosophers. However, they are beyond the scope of the present volume. I will simply refer, in the notes, to two useful studies of the issues that arise.[1] But reflection on the doctrine of the Church as such, the doctrine known as 'ecclesiology', while grist to the mill for theologians,[2] is, as I say, largely neglected by contemporary philosophers of religion. This fact is lamented by Philip Quinn in an article in *Faith and Philosophy* on 'Kantian Philosoph-ical Ecclesiology',[3] the title of which shows that earlier philosophers, such as

Kant, did have something to offer on the subject of the Church. Kant's *Religion within the Boundaries of Mere Reason*[4] attempted to spell out the pure religion of reason that underlies all the doctrines of Christianity, including that of the Church. This means, primarily, showing the moral import of each doctrine. For Kant, a church is an ethical commonwealth under laws of virtue regarded as divine commands. I quote Quinn's summary:

> Considered merely as an ideal, such an ethical commonwealth may be thought of as the church invisible. An actual social union of humans that harmonizes with this ideal is a visible church, and 'the true (visible) church is that which exhibits the (moral) kingdom of God on earth so far as it can be brought to pass by men'.[5]

Quinn criticizes Kant's ecclesiology for its monolithic structure. He objects that 'practical reason is just not up to the task Kant assigns it in his ecclesiology'.[6] But, he suggests, if we proceed in a more piecemeal manner, we can agree that ecclesiastical arrangements and traditions can and should be reformed and checked in the light of basic moral beliefs. Indeed, he sees just such critiques taking place in the ecclesiology of Vatican II.

Quinn's article is something of a *tour de force*. Readers less sceptical than Kant himself about the purely religious aspects of church life and practice, while agreeing that these are certainly open to moral criticism, will surely deem it necessary for philosophical theology to explore other central aspects of the Church's role, not least as a worshipping community.

Even more radical than Kant's critique of the visible church was Kierkegaard's, as is shown in another article in *Faith and Philosophy*, by Bruce H. Kirmmse.[7] Indeed, Kirmmse's conclusion is that 'in the end it is doubtful whether he [Kierkegaard] viewed any form of earthly congregation as compatible with what he believed to be "the Christianity of the New Testament"'.[8] So we are unlikely to get much positive help from Kierkegaard on the topic of ecclesiology.

Much the most substantial and positive treatment of ecclesiology by a contemporary philosopher of religion is to be found in Keith Ward's book, *Religion and Community*.[9] This, like Ward's earlier volumes discussed in previous chapters, is a comparative study, this time of the forms of social life fostered in five religions – Judaism, Islam, Buddhism, Hinduism and Christianity – with some remarks on the secular state thrown in. Where Christianity is concerned, Ward devotes a major section of his book to an account of the Church as a spiritual community at once critical of the 'world' and at the same time world-transforming through its special vocation to embody and proclaim the power of God's love in the world. Ward explores four aspects of this understanding of the Church, with chapters entitled 'The Church as a Teaching Community', 'The Church as a Charismatic community', 'The Church as a Sacramental Community' and 'The Church as a Moral Community'. In the first of these, the Church is seen as responding to God's inspiration in the search for truth and understanding. In the second, it is seen as the vehicle of transformation through the Spirit's agency. In the third, it is seen as the medium through which the material world is transfigured by the creative Spirit. And in the fourth, it is seen as a community of inspired moral thought and practice, whereby the obstacles to human justice, love and personal flourishing are challenged, and in part overcome. As befits its context in a comparative study, Ward's picture of the Church is of a developing, cooperative, non-exclusive instrument of the divine love. What we do not get is a picture of the Church as a worshipping community.

8.2   The Sacraments

Ward's treatment of the Church as a sacramental community leads us to reflect briefly on the topic of the sacraments as such. These are not mentioned in the Apostles' Creed, and, in the Nicene Creed, it is 'one Baptism for the remission of sins' that alone finds acknowledgement. Baptism is the outward and visible sign of the appropriation of God's justifying and sanctifying work through Christ and the Spirit. What philosophical theology has had to say about this was surveyed and discussed in chapter 6 on salvation. The actual sacrament of baptism has been of more theological than philosophical interest.[10]

Where the Eucharist is concerned, the doctrine of Christ's real presence in the sacrament of the altar is of much more philosophical concern, given the Roman Catholic doctrine of transubstantiation, with its medieval background and the use, there, of the Aristotelian categories of substance and accident. (The idea was that, at consecration in the Mass, the bread and wine, while retaining their outward phenomenal properties, are in reality – in substance – changed into Christ's body and blood.) This doctrine received remarkable treatment by the philosopher Elizabeth Anscombe, in what was originally a Catholic Truth Society pamphlet, now reprinted in her *Collected Philosophical Papers*.[11] Anscombe defends the doctrine that, at consecration, the bread and wine *become* the body and blood of Christ. In receiving them, believers are united with their crucified and risen Lord and sustained in union and communion with him. Now clearly, as Anscombe herself allows, this sacramental eating and drinking are symbolic. Christians are not cannibals. But it is not a matter of the bread and the wine just symbolizing Christ's crucified and risen life, into which communicants are incorporated. The bread and wine actually *become*, as a consequence of the words of consecration, following Christ's own stipulation at the Last Supper, the vehicle of his presence and unitive act.

As is well known, Protestant theology rejected the doctrine of transubstantiation while, at least in its Lutheran and Anglican streams, retaining the idea of Christ's real presence in the Eucharist. Philosophical theologians may well ask whether there is much of a difference here. Let us drop the Aristotelian talk of substance and accident. That, after all, as Anscombe allows, was a distinction in the metaphysics of *matter*. But talk of substance is not restricted to material substance. In previous chapters we have seen the need to speak of spiritual substance and of divine substance. If the bread and the wine of the Eucharist become the outward and visible signs, and indeed the vehicles, of the inward and spiritual grace of Christ's *substantial* presence and action, then even the language of transubstantiation might be allowed.

Insightful consideration of the Eucharist may be found in an essay by Nicholas Wolterstorff,[12] who, like Quinn, expresses regret at the relative lack of philosophical reflection on such themes. Wolterstorff, as he himself acknowledges, concentrates on the *commemorative* dimension of the Christian Eucharist, contrasting it with the rituals of archaic religion, as studied by Mircea Eliade.[13] In the latter, the participants are taken out of historical time into either the primordial time of origins or an eternal present. In the Eucharist, by contrast, Christians imitate and repeat Christ's actions in historical time and, through their commemoration, it is held, God acts causally here and now. Somewhat frustratingly, Wolterstorff refrains from exploring the modality of God's special action here. He refers to the sacramental dimension, but is curiously diffident about bringing it within the purview of philosophical investigation. Indeed, at one point he writes: 'What exactly God does by way of our liturgical actions and then, more specifically, by way of our imitative/commemorative actions in the Eucharist, belongs to the theologians and not to philosophers.'[14] But two pages later, he virtually contradicts himself by saying: 'As to *how* God acts by way of our participation in the liturgy, that is a rich field waiting for exploration by philosophers.'[15] That the second rather than the first of these quotations from Wolterstorff should be endorsed will surely be agreed by any reader sympathetic to the aims of the present volume.

The theme of special divine action is more than implicit in these treatments of the sacraments. It is explicit in both Anscombe's and Wolterstorff's analyses. But there is only the occasional hint in these authors – and the same is true of Ward on the Church as a sacramental community – of the role of both Church and sacraments in lifting up the creation specifically and consciously to the Creator in worship.

8.3 The Philosophy of Worship

Reflection on the Godward aspect of the Church's role, that is to say, reflection on the concept of worship, is another theme crying out for philosophical treatment.

There is some brief reflection on the topic in Robert Adams's *Finite and Infinite Goods*,[16] where the centrality of worship in Christian ethics is stressed. As Adams puts it: 'A genuine love for the good can find in symbolic expression [i.e. in worship] an integration and completion that would otherwise be impossible.'[17] But what we look for are more extended studies along the lines of Ninian Smart's 1972 book, *The Concept of Worship*.[18] In accordance with his special expertise, Smart gives us a comparative, phenomenological sketch of the salient features of worship in world religion. Smart would agree with Peter Geach that 'worship' is an intentional verb; that is to say, it is necessarily aimed at something.[19] In Smart's terms, worship is relational. He calls its object the 'Focus' of the rituals that express it. In all developed religions where worship takes place, it comes to be held that nothing finite, only the transcendent, can be the appropriate object of worship. Worship of money, sex or one's car is inappropriate worship, idolatry. Smart borrows from Rudolf Otto the term 'numinous' to characterize the kind of conscious states experienced where appropriate religious worship takes place.[20]

Where God is recognized as the Focus of human worship, the question arises whether the same Focus is to be discerned as lying at the heart of all theistic faiths. Here, Smart and Geach differ. For Smart (and Ward and, a fortiori, Hick[21]), since there can only be *one* ultimate transcendent reality, this must be the true object of all theistic worship, in however distorted a form. But, for Geach, the arrow of worship may miss its mark entirely, if its object is sufficiently falsely conceived. This is a debate inviting much further philosophical reflection.

The importance of incorporating a philosophy of worship within one's whole worldview lies in the fact that, for theists, including Christian theists, the universe as God's creation is specifically designed to evolve conscious, rational, spiritual beings capable of felt and articulated response to God. Finite being is, in this sense, open to the transcendent and cannot be fully understood apart from this inbuilt propensity.

What is special about Christian worship was briefly treated in chapters 6 and 7 on salvation and the consummation of all things. For Christians, worship involves not simply the Church's response of prayer and praise to the Creator. Nor are the sacraments simply signs and vehicles of God's grace. In both cases, it is held, the processes whereby God's human creatures are taken into the triune life of God are already under way. Much more work is called for from philosophical theologians on this aspect of the Creator–creature relation.

8.4   The Doctrine of Providence

We turn finally to the second of the two major, non-credal doctrines which underlie all the actual doctrines of the creed, namely, the doctrine of providence. This, as I say, has received a very great deal of attention from philosophers of religion and philosophical theologians in recent decades. Not that the concepts of providence and divine action simply coincide. Creation is *par excellence* God's action, and as such was discussed in chapter 3 (see especially section 3.1). But the act of creation itself is to be differentiated from the acts of God within creation and, in particular, within human history. It is the latter that constitute the field of providence. And of course they are supremely exemplified, for Christians, by the acts of God, culminating in the Incarnation and its sequel, to which the Bible bears witness and which the creeds summarize. But the sphere of providence is not restricted to the 'mighty acts of God' that constitute the story of our redemption. Christian believers, and indeed believers in other theistic faith traditions, claim to see God at work in innumerable ways in history and in individual lives, through vocation, inspiration, guidance and in answer to prayer.

To distinguish between creation and providence in this way is really to distinguish between creation and *special* providence. For, as was the case with revelation, there is a distinction between general and special providence. General providence is a matter of the structural regularities and inbuilt propensities, including the laws of nature and the moral law, which enable God's creation to fulfil its intended goals without divine intervention. In this sense it is possible to blur the distinction between creation and providence. But the issue that particularly concerns both theologians and philosophers is the question of specific acts of God within these divinely ordained structures – the question, that is, of special providence.

It is a happy fact that recent work on the topic of special divine action has already been surveyed and assessed in a book, with precisely that title, by

Paul Gwynne.[22] The existence of that book enables me to be even more selective than before in my own discussion of the key issues.

8.4.1 Special providence under attack

Three factors in particular have led a number of theologians, as well as many philosophers, to question the idea of special providence: namely, the problem of evil, the rise of modern science and the rise of modern historical-critical sensibility. There is so much evil and suffering in God's world that the course of human lives and of human societies often appears anything but providential. And our increasing scientific and historical knowledge of the structures of creation, and of the way things work in the world, leaves less and less scope for postulation of the hand of God behind what happens. These are the main reasons why the theologian Maurice Wiles (whose views on revelation were discussed in chapter 2, section 2.2), has attempted to dispense with the whole idea of special providence.[23] Instead, he see the whole world, with its God-given powers, including human freedom, as one great divine creative act. Wiles's God is not an absent God, like the God of the deists. God's immanent presence is universal. The divine Spirit pervades everything and can, as it were, be latched on to by human beings in many different specific ways. But the particularity is all on our side. What may look like the effects of special providence are better understood as particular effects of general providence, the all-pervasive presence and pressure of the divine. Thus salvation history is better understood as the response of Israel and the Church to God's universal will and purpose than as the mighty acts of God. Personal conversion and growth in sanctity are better understood in terms of people's own response and the retrospective light this throws on their life story than in terms of 'arbitrary election, implausible disposition of external circumstance and unacceptable manipulation of inner life'.[24] That quotation sums up most trenchantly Wiles's objections to the notion of special providence.

It is interesting to compare what we might call Wiles's reduction of special providence to general providence with two other attempts to provide a non-arbitrary theory of providence that at first sight look very different indeed. I refer to Paul Helm's 'no-risk' view of creation and providence, already mentioned in chapter 3,[25] and Vernon White's *The Fall of a Sparrow.*[26]

Helm's 'no-risk' view of creation and providence sees the whole story of creation from start to finish as providentially ordained in all its detail, including human actions and God's specific responses to what humans do.

From God's angle this is indeed one single non-temporal act, and to that extent Helm's position is like that of Wiles. But from our angle, God does come to meet us in innumerable special ways. It is just that these divine acts too are part of the whole story which God ordains. We shall return to this view when we consider the issue of prayer and providence in the final section of this chapter. As pointed out in chapter 3, Helm is unusually frank in admitting that there is no room for libertarian freedom on the part of humans in his 'no-risk' view.

Vernon White's position appears to be at the very opposite end of the spectrum of views of divine providence from that of Wiles. For where Wiles does away with the notion of special providence, White sees special providence at work in everything that happens and in everything that is done in God's world. This seems more like Helm's view. But it differs in at least two respects. White does not deny human freedom. Our free acts are themselves elements in the providential pattern being woven by God, as is, of course, what God himself makes of them. In the second place, White is more ready than Helm to explore the notion of divine temporality, a temporality out of which God adapts his action in the world to the world's temporality. On the other hand, White's, like Helm's, is a 'no-risk' view of creation and providence. From God's perspective there is no such thing as chance or accident.

All three views are highly problematic. We may ask, of Wiles, whether personal theism can survive the restriction of particularity to the human side alone. This does not begin to do justice to the reciprocity of personal relation, however asymmetrical, which Christian spirituality and incarnational religion make possible and show to be real. And it is clear that, for Wiles, both the Incarnation and the Resurrection have to be demythologized. We may ask, of Helm, whether freedom is not of the essence of personality and of any gracious personal relation. We must also ask whether Helm really succeeds in absolving God from responsibility for evil, when he says that evil is indeed ordained by God, not *as* evil, but rather as a necessary element in an overall good. And we may ask, of White, whether ascribing everything to God's special providence really differs from ascribing everything to God's general providence. Moreover, it is far from clear that White succeeds, any more than Helm does, in detaching evil from God's direct responsibility.

Where freedom is concerned, we know where Wiles and Helm stand. Wiles affirms it. Helm denies it. White's position is ambiguous. Does he or does he not allow our libertarian freedom its genuine autonomy? The notion of our free acts being at the same time God's acts in and through us is a topic to which we shall return in section 8.4.4 below.

Divine intervention has no place in the worldview of any of these three authors. This is quite clear in the case of Wiles. For him, the world has its own God-given autonomy, with many opportunities for human response to the divine Spirit, but that is all. In Helm's case, natural and historical happenings are only aspects of a much larger world story that includes many particular divine acts, but these can hardly be thought of as divine interventions, since they are parts of the whole God-ordained story. And, in White's case, God is at work in everything that happens; so again we can hardly speak of intervention.

8.4.2 Providence, predestination and foreknowledge

The most difficult issue for any theory of providence is that of God and time. Readers will recall that, in chapter 3 (sections 3.1.8 and 3.2.5), it was suggested that divine eternity is better conceived in terms of sempiternity than timelessness, and that an open-futured world, including genuine alternative possibilities, is a greater creative project on the part of God than a fore-ordained whole such as Helm appears to envisage. It was pointed out that, on such a view, even omniscience cannot know the future in all its details. Rather, God acts and responds appropriately to what his creatures do, and weaves the results of both free choice and accident into the tapestry of his providence. Only the eventual outcome of the whole story is predestined and foreknown, not the precise paths by which that future goal is eventually to be attained. Peter Geach compares this view of providence and the future to the way in which a chess Grand Master will indubitably win a whole number of games, whatever moves his amateur opponents make.[27]

In an essay in *A Companion to Philosophy of Religion*,[28] Thomas P. Flint distinguishes four positions on providence and predestination. He calls them determinist traditionalism, compatibilist traditionalism, libertarian traditionalism and libertarian revisionism. The first three views all enable one to maintain divine foreknowledge and thus God's overall control of everything. That is why Flint calls all three of them forms of traditionalism.

On the first view, determinist traditionalism, everything is simply determined by God, and freedom is an illusion. Flint claims that this view lacks contemporary support, though surely Helm's 'no-risk' view falls within this category. (Flint cites Helm in his bibliography, but appears to classify him as a compatibilist; but that ignores Helm's explicit rejection of free will.)

On the second view, compatibilist traditionalism, which Flint holds to be the mainstream view (as found in Aquinas and many others), human freedom, like all other forms of created causality, falls under God's supervenient governance. There is no incompatibility between God's primary causality and what God enables creatures themselves to do. This compatibilist view Flint deems implausible philosophically, and, if God's governance is indeed understood deterministically, he is surely right about this. (Compatibilism is the view that freedom and determinism are perfectly compatible, provided you define freedom as lack of external constraint. But, clearly, that is not what freedom really means.) Whether the mainstream view attributed to Aquinas is, in fact, a version of compatibilism may well be doubted (see section 8.4.4 below).

On the third view, libertarian traditionalism, human beings are given true libertarian freedom; but God, through his middle knowledge, is able infallibly to know what any free creature will do, and thus what has to be allowed, if their freedom is not to be overridden. This is the view that Flint himself prefers. Accepting the view that God has middle knowledge, Flint is able to defend divine omniscience in its strongest sense, while at the same time accepting libertarian freedom. But middle knowledge, as argued in chapter 3 (p. 55), is a deeply incoherent notion. Recall the objections raised against it: not even omniscience could possibly know precisely what a genuinely free creature will do, let alone would have done in other circumstances. And, in any case, the idea that God could simply actualize individuals who would freely act only in certain ways makes no sense at all. Free creatures cannot just be actualized fully formed. A free person is the result of a whole history of interpersonal relationships. Only in and through such a history can God himself relate to his free creatures. Nor does it make any sense to suppose that God could simply actualize only those situations in which free creatures would act one way rather than another. Supporters of middle knowledge fail utterly to reckon with the logical constraints on what can be actualized just like that. (Readers are referred to articles and books by William Hasker[29] and by Robert Adams[30] for further arguments against middle knowledge.)

On the fourth view, libertarian revisionism (which denies the possibility of middle knowledge), God cannot know the future in all its details, but does know all possibilities and what he will do whatever creatures do. Flint mocks this view for reducing God's omniscience to little more than probabilistic guesswork. Hence his preference for libertarian traditionalism and middle knowledge. But, if middle knowledge is impossible, we ought surely to look more closely at the view outlined in chapter 3 (section 3.2.5), whereby the limitations on God's foreknowledge, *logically* entailed by his creation of an open-futured universe, do not deprive the Creator of overall control.

I sketched a libertarian revisionist view along these lines in an earlier article, 'Some Reflections on Predestination, Providence and Divine Foreknowledge' and defended it against criticism of Geach's Grand Master chess analogy by Patrick McGrath. McGrath wrote: 'if God does not have knowledge of future free actions, it means that he is constantly acquiring new knowledge; and such a being cannot be either infinite or unchanging'.[31] I replied:

> But such an objection does not take seriously the logic of creation. We cannot consider notions such as omniscience or omnipotence in abstraction from the situation set in motion by God's free decision to create. Creation is an act of God's omnipotence, but in order to relate himself to the creatures he has made, he must limit himself in a manner appropriate to the nature of what he has made.... [But of course] the creation does not escape the purview of God's omniscience. He knows every past and present fact, and every future possibility. Nothing takes him by surprise.[32]

Much more, of course, needs to be said about the way in which God's providence works in such an open-futured world, drawing the threads together and ensuring that its ultimate destiny is realized, whatever free creatures do. This is indeed the key issue in the doctrine of special providence, whatever one's views on divine foreknowledge.[33]

Geach's Grand Master chess analogy certainly captures something of the libertarian revisionist view. But I have to admit to parting company with Geach over God's immutability. Geach tries to combine his view of omniscience and the future with the traditional view of God himself not being subject to change. He suggests that it is only the creature who changes, thus making statements true of the creature's relation to God which were previously false, but not ascribing real change to God himself. But, if God does not know my next move in the game of chess until I make it, then his knowledge of my move when I have made it *is* something new in the divine mind. The same point has to be made about God's action in the world in response to what his creatures freely do. Defenders of divine immutability have not reckoned with the self-limitations logically involved in the creation of an open-futured world. God subjects himself to change, in knowledge and action alike, in making a changing universe.[34]

8.4.3 Providence and miracle

The question immediately arises whether God's special providential action both prior to and in response to what his free creatures do necessarily involves miraculous intervention. Ludwig Feuerbach declared, without any qualification: 'Belief in providence is belief in miracle.'[35] But it depends what you mean by 'miracle'. If, with David Hume, we define miracle as 'a transgression of a law of nature by a particular volition of the Deity',[36] then clearly not all acts of special providence are miracles. Believers generally hold that God acts in the world in many ways in and through events and words which in no way involve transgression of the laws of nature. A particular vocation, for example, may come to someone through a sermon heard. That natural event becomes the vehicle of God's call, God's act, in the believer's life. Revelation, as discussed in chapter 2, consists of many acts of God, mediated through events, books and prophets. Moreover, many combinations of events in people's lives may well, in retrospect, be deemed providential, without involving miracles. So we can distinguish between miraculous intervention, whereby God brings something about which goes beyond any possible natural explanation (turning water into wine, for example) and providential intervention, whereby God brings something about which could be given a naturalistic explanation, but which, nevertheless, would not have occurred without God's intervention, working in and through nature, history and human words (the call of the Apostles, for example).

Miraculous intervention, in the sense defined, is a perfectly intelligible notion, given a theistic world view, as Swinburne shows in an early book, *The Concept of Miracle*.[37] On the question of evidence for miracles having taken place, both Swinburne and Houston (whose treatment of this theme was mentioned in chapter 4[38]) are agreed that Hume's notorious argument against reported miracles has no force at all. What normally happens has no bearing whatsoever on the question whether or not, for some exceptional reason, God has miraculously intervened.

A prima facie case for scepticism about miracles may be found in Hume's subsidiary arguments, first, that miracle stories tend to come from relatively primitive and unsophisticated milieux, and tend to proliferate wildly in relation to any remarkable religious innovator, and, secondly, that the presence of miracle stories in all the religions of the world tends to undermine the credibility of any one religion's reported miracles.[39] These are by no means decisive arguments, however. Even if many miracle stories are suspect, one cannot rule out the possibility of an occasional miracle being given, say, as a sign of God's unique presence by incarnation. And one could construct a theory of the genesis and growth of religion the whole world over which allows for some miraculous interventions in all the world's religions. This suggestion finds tentative support in the writings of Keith Ward.[40]

There is no denying the fact that the rise of modern science has made us more and more sceptical about miracles. This is really the converse point to the one about miracle stories proliferating in pre-scientific, relatively ignorant cultures. In a later section we shall consider the bearing of modern science on theories of divine providence. But even miracle cannot be ruled out of court by a scientific worldview. For scientific explanations and predictions only work *ceteris paribus* (other things being equal). And on the hypothesis of theism, other things are not equal. God may be intervening.

The most compelling arguments against miracles – though even these do not rule them out – are thoroughly theological arguments, coming from within a developed theistic worldview. The first argument stems from considerations of theodicy. In order to make even minimal sense of the presence of so much evil and suffering in God's world, it is necessary to suppose that God has to respect the structures of his creation, if his purpose of fashioning a world of finite persons out of an evolving world, and in a regularly structured predictable environment that secures their relative independence and personhood, is to be achieved. Even occasional miraculous interventions could upset the whole story. The second argument, touched on in our reflections on the Incarnation (pp. 67f), concerns the theological implausibility of treating God's action as one cause among others at the same level, and of supposing that God has to override the structures of creation in order to act within them.

The present structures of creation are indeed overridden with the Resurrection of Jesus Christ from the dead. But, as Farrer pointed out in *Saving Belief*, 'the Resurrection is not a miracle like any other. It is a unique manifestation within this world of the transition God makes for us out of this way of being into another'.[41] So it would be a mistake to draw general conclusions about miracle from the Resurrection.

For these reasons, many theologians and philosophers of religion now try to spell out a non-miraculous view of God's providential action in and though what is said and done, and in and through what happens, at the creaturely level. We shall survey and comment on such theories of 'double agency' in the next section.

Before we leave the topic of miracle, however, it is worth asking whether the language of divine intervention should be retained in respect of such non-miraculous, mediated agency. David Brown, whose work on the topics of Revelation, Incarnation and Trinity was discussed in chapters 2, 4 and 5 (see pp. 30–2, 61–3 and 81–8) was keen in his early book, *The Divine Trinity*, to defend the idea of divine intervention against all forms of deism, and against Wiles's reduction of special providence to general providence.[42] But later, in *Tradition and Imagination*, Brown says of his earlier book, 'use of the term "intervention" to describe God's action in the world was unfortunate, since it could so easily be taken to imply that God was absent except where he was intervening'. He goes on to say that, in later work, he had attempted to correct this by substituting the term 'interaction', and insisting that most divine action in the world had no need to be brought under the rubric of 'miracle'.[43] While agreeing with this last point, we may not share the fear that 'intervention' necessarily has the implications stated. There is no need to equate divine intervention with miracle, nor to suppose that talk of special interventions implies God's absence elsewhere.

8.4.4 Double agency

Let us then consider the notion of 'double agency' involved in the view that God acts in and through the acts of creatures. The philosophical theologian most closely associated with this notion is Austin Farrer. It is the leading theme of the four short books that Farrer wrote towards the end of his life.[44]

Farrer's recognition of the difficulty of ascribing the same event or act to two agents, divine and human, is reflected in his talk of the paradox of double agency;[45] but a paradox is not a contradiction. It is only when we treat divine and human agency as two causal factors operating at the same level that it makes no sense to speak of double agency, except in mundane terms, say, of delegation. The notion remains paradoxical, but only because, as Farrer admits, the modality of divine action is strictly inaccessible to us. 'The hand of God is perfectly hidden.'[46] We do not have access to the 'causal joint' between the supernatural and the natural.

Where the natural is concerned, Farrer seeks to do full justice to the reality of creaturely causality and agency at every level. 'God not only makes the world, he makes it make itself.'[47] But, in and through the events of nature, history and human action, the providence of God is at work. Moreover, says Farrer, 'God's agency must actually be such as to work omnipotently on, in, or through creaturely agencies without either forcing them or competing with them.'[48] God lets things follow their own bent, and yet 'without faking the story or defying probability at any point he pulls the history together into the patterns we observe'.[49]

One of Farrer's most powerful analogies is the author analogy already cited in chapter 3 (p. 41). It will be recalled that Farrer compared the Creator to 'the good novelist who has the wit to get a satisfying story out of the natural behaviour of the characters he conceives'.[50]

The hand of God may be perfectly hidden, but the effects of God's action are far from hidden. Anyone who has experienced the grace of God at work in their life will know that grace and free will are not rivals. I am most myself, most truly free, as I embrace the divine will, and yet I am, at the same time, most conscious of God's working in me. As Farrer puts it: 'We know that the action of a man can be the action of God in him.'[51] This becomes the paradigm case, for Farrer, of double agency. But, contrary to John Polkinghorne's criticism,[52] Farrer by no means restricts the scope of the notion to God's interaction with persons. Rather, he uses the paradox of grace as a clue to the way God acts throughout the created order. The whole story of nature and history, as well as of individual lives, is a matter of God's agency working in and through creaturely agency. This goes for the effects of evolution.[53] And it goes, especially, for the history of Israel, culminating in the Incarnation, which, Farrer says, has a providential intelligibility not elsewhere evident, because nowhere else is the goal of God's purpose so clear. But, of course, Farrer returns to the personal in the end. The interaction of human and divine, he observes, is most clearly evident in 'Christ's ability to play his part, with a mental furniture acquired from his village rabbi'.[54]

The notion of double agency has been followed up and developed by a number of philosophers of religion, examples of whose work may be seen in the volume which came out of the fourth International Conference on the Theology of Austin Farrer held in Baton Rouge, Louisiana, in 1986.[55] Of particular interest is the essay by Thomas Tracy, enlarging on his own earlier book, *God, Action and Embodiment*.[56] Tracy suggests 'that we think of God as continuously shaping the direction of each individual's self-determination by contributing to the network of influences that condition our actions from moment to moment throughout our histories'.[57] Tracy's critics, we may note, have expressed some doubts about this account.[58] Does he avoid the danger of treating God as just one force among many others? But at least he does not confuse God's special acts in and through what his creatures do with God's basic act of creating and empowering everything. This confusion, sadly, is to be found in Keith Ward's dismissal of Farrer's 'paradox' of double agency in his own book, *Divine Action*.[59] According to Ward, this 'is not really a paradox ... if one spells out the way in which particular states are brought about by natural causes, while the whole system of causal powers is held in being by God's action'. That is simply not the point. What Farrer is talking about is the way in which, over and beyond that 'holding in being', God acts in *specific* ways in and through what Ward refers to here as 'natural causes'.

Double agency in this sense presupposes that the created world is open or flexible enough to permit such mediated divine influence or persuasion. This leads us to reflect on the question of science and providence.

8.4.5   Science and providence

A good starting point for reflection on this theme is John Polkinghorne's *Science and Providence*.[60] Polkinghorne, a former professor of mathematical physics, is well placed to expound our new understanding, in quantum physics and chaos theory, of the physical universe as a non-determined, open environment, productive of, and hospitable to, freedom and creativity. On this, by contrast with his critical remarks on double agency, already noted, Polkinghorne is prepared to endorse what Farrer wrote: 'The grid of causal uniformity does not (to any evidence) fit so tight upon natural processes as to bar the influence of an over-riding divine persuasion.'[61] Philosophers had already appealed to the openness of a non-deterministic universe in order to account for the possibility of freewill in the *human* world. In her inaugural lecture at Cambridge, Elizabeth Anscombe observed that 'there is nothing unacceptable about the idea that "physical" haphazard should be the only physical correlate to human freedom of action'.[62] In philosophical theology, the same openness or flexibility of structure is held to make intelligible the possibility of divine action in and through the contingencies of nature and history. The central chapters of Keith Ward's book, *Divine Action*, explore this in some detail.[63] Ward is particularly interesting on the constraints of creation, the parameters within which divine action takes place and has to take place if the structures of creation are to be respected. These constraints include those of probability, and we are reminded again of what Farrer wrote about God's mediated providence not defying probability. It must always be possible to give an account of what the believer sees as providential in terms of coincidence, however unlikely, its unlikeliness as coincidence suggesting interpretation as providential.

One of the factors reckoned with by Farrer, Polkinghorne and Ward is that of chance. Unlike the 'no-risk' view of creation and providence, the view under scrutiny here allows not only for freedom but also for chance elements at all levels, material and interpersonal, within the non-deterministic structures of creation. This aspect of providence in an open universe is the subject of the book, *God of Chance*, by the statistician, D. J. Bartholomew.[64]

There is much controversy over the question of the location of the 'causal joint' between divine and creaturely agencies. Ward is more inclined than Polkinghorne to see scope for divine action at the quantum level, interpreted indeterministically.[65] Polkinghorne himself prefers to think of the macro-level at which chaos theory operates as giving scope to the operations of God's providence.[66] He draws the analogy with our own 'top-down' agency, which exploits just such openness and unpredictability in order freely to realize our purposes in the physical world.

Such suggestions are discussed, with special reference to Polkinghorne's work, by Steven Crain in an article in *Faith and Philosophy*.[67] Among other things, Crain defends the idea of miraculous intervention against Polkinghorne's restriction of divine special action to mediated providence. But he also expresses scepticism about any attempt to locate a specific feature of the world that God is supposed to exploit in acting within it. Since God is the transcendent creator, the 'causal joint' between God's action and the world is, in the nature of the case, *meta*physical, and not to be located or identified in inner-worldly terms.

This point is helpful in reminding us that God's action cannot be treated as one causal factor among others operating at the same level, and simply at locatable points in the world story. But Ward and Polkinghorne, and indeed Farrer, are perfectly well aware of this. God's action informs the world process and influences its outcome from another dimension, as it were. But it remains 'top-down' agency, by analogy with our agency. And there is still a case for attempting to spell out the nature of the openness or flexibility within the world process that permits it. And, to borrow Anscombe's phraseology, there is nothing unacceptable about the idea that 'physical haphazard' should be the correlate of divine special providence.

8.4.6   *Prayer and providence*

In the opening chapter of this book I made a case for the legitimacy of philosophical reflection on the theoretical aspects and implications of religious belief and practice. In conclusion, I illustrate this again with some reflections on prayer and God's answer to prayer.

Ward defines prayer as 'the conscious turning of the mind and will to God'.[68] This raises no problems as far as meditation, contemplation, praise, thanksgiving and penitence are concerned. These are all aspects of the creation's response to its Creator referred to above in connection with the philosophy of worship; although, again, it should be noted that these are not simply matters of creaturely response. Christians hold that the divine Spirit is active in human hearts and communities precisely as they turn to God in prayer. But the chief problems for the philosophical theologian regarding prayer and answers to prayer concern petition and intercession.

The first difficulty reflects the intuition that God is bound to do what is for the best in any case. What, then, is the point of petitionary or intercessory prayer? A clear and convincing response to this difficulty is provided by Ward, who argues that, if personal theism means that human beings are called into a gracious personal relation with their Maker, then that can only be realized through the reciprocities of prayer and answer to prayer. In other words, it is better that some things should occur as a result of prayer and God's answer to prayer than that God should bring them about in any case. As Ward puts I: 'What is best if we do not pray might well be different from what is best if we do pray. So it is a feeble argument that, since God will do what is best anyway, we need not bother to pray.'[69]

The second difficulty takes us back to the question of God's immutability. Are prayers and answers to prayers themselves changelessly predestined? It looks as if Thomas Aquinas, at the end of the day, thought so: 'We do not pray in order to change the decree of divine providence; rather we pray in order to acquire by petitionary prayer what God has determined would be obtained by our prayers.'[70] As we saw, Helm's 'no-risk' view states this even more explicitly. The trouble with this view, as Ward says, is that, while in a sense it allows for our prayers to have real effects, in that God has decreed the whole story, including our prayers and his own response, 'the suspicion remains that, in such a case, our prayers are not really freely made, and God does not really respond to them in new and creative ways'.[71]

Much better sense can be made of prayer and answer to prayer, if we adopt the theology of mediated, non-manipulative providence, sketched above. If God can be thought of as acting freely and creatively, in and through each aspect of the whole world story, not as one agent among others at the same level, but rather as the all-pervading Spirit, guiding, calling, inspiring and drawing good out of evil, then it becomes possible to see prayer and answer to prayer as central aspects of an open world process, now conscious of its source and rendering itself explicitly instrumental to the divine activity.

It is worth remembering, at this point, the way in which Farrer sought to extend his view of mediated providence from the paradigm case of grace and freedom to every level of creation. An open-structured, flexible world process does not only allow for the operation of the hidden hand of providence in response to prayer. Nor is response to prayer necessarily restricted solely to God's interaction with human hearts and minds.

These and other problems about petitionary prayer are discussed perceptively by Eleonore Stump in her contribution to Blackwell's *A Companion to the Philosophy of Religion*.[72] She has wise words to say about heartfelt prayer and appropriate prayer. Petitionary prayer undertaken in an experimental frame of mind could not possibly constitute a genuine response to the love of God. Believers have to learn, too, what it is that is religiously appropriate and inappropriate in the matter of prayer. But Stump's attempt to combine her sensitive understanding of Christian prayer with the classical doctrines of divine atemporality and immutability does not convince. According to Stump:

> Although an atemporal God does not frame his response to a prayer *after* the prayer any more than he determines it in advance of a prayer, he can still act *simultaneously* with prayer (where simultaneity has to be understood in a more sophisticated way than temporal co-occurrence) and nothing in the nature of simultaneity keeps God's action from being a *response* to the prayer, a divine action done because of the petition in the prayer.[73]

This notion of simultaneity seems hardly intelligible. Again, it makes much greater sense to follow Farrer and Ward in thinking of God's special providence, including his answers to prayer, in temporal terms, as responses to, and interactions with, free creatures – and other creaturely energies – in a manner appropriate to their God-given nature.

Notes

CHAPTER 1   PHILOSOPHY OF RELIGION AND THEOLOGY

1 A. G. N. Flew, 'Theology and Falsification', in A. Flew and A. MacIntyre (eds.), *New Essays in Philosophical Theology* (London: SCM Press, 1955).

2 Ludwig Wittgenstein, *Lectures and Conversations on Aesthetics, Psychology and Religious Belief* (Oxford: Blackwell, 1966).

3 E.g., D. Z. Phillips, *Faith and Philosophical Enquiry* (London: Routledge & Kegan Paul, 1970).

4 Don Cupitt, *The Sea of Faith* (London: BBC, 1984).

5 Ninian Smart, *Dimensions of the Sacred* (London: Harper Collins, 1996), and *World Philosophies* (London: Routledge, 1999).

6 John Hick, *An Interpretation of Religion* (London: Macmillan, 1989).

7 Austin Farrer, *Saving Belief* (London: Hodder and Stoughton, 1964).

8 Richard Swinburne, *The Coherence of Theism* (Oxford: Clarendon Press, 1977; revised edn. 1993); *The Existence of God* (Oxford: Clarendon Press, 1979; revised edn. 1991); *Faith and Reason* (Oxford: Clarendon Press, 1981).

9 Richard Swinburne, *The Evolution of the Soul* (Oxford: Clarendon Press, 1986).

10 Richard Swinburne, *Responsibility and Atonement* (Oxford: Clarendon Press, 1989); *Revelation* (Oxford: Clarendon Press, 1992); *The Christian God* (Oxford: Clarendon Press, 1994); *Providence and the Problem of Evil* (Oxford: Clarendon Press, 1998).

11 R. H. Popkin, 'Pascal, Blaise', in P. Edwards (ed.), *The Encyclopedia of Philosophy*, vol. 6 (New York: Macmillan and Free Press, 1967), p. 52.

12 G. D. Kaufman, 'Evidentialism: A Theologian's Response', *Faith and Philosophy* 6 (1989), pp. 35–46.

13 E. Stump and N. Kretzmann, 'Theologically Unfashionable Philosophy', *Faith and Philosophy* 7 (1990), pp. 329–39.

14 J. A. Keller, 'On the Issues Dividing Contemporary Christian Philosophers and Theologians', *Faith and Philosophy* 10 (1993), pp. 68–78.

15   W. Hasker, 'Can Philosophy Defend Theology? A Response to James Keller', *Faith and Philosophy* 11 (1994), pp. 272–8.

16   J. A. Keller, 'Should Christian Theologians become Christian Philosophers? A Reply to William Hasker', *Faith and Philosophy* 12 (1995), pp. 260–8.

17   Maurice Wiles, *A Shared Search. Doing Theology in Conversation with One's Friends* (London: SCM Press, 1994).

18   Thomas F. Torrance, *Theological Science* (Oxford University Press, 1969), ch. 5.

19   Wolfhart Pannenberg, 'History and Meaning in Bernard Lonergan's Approach to Theological Method', in Patrick Corcoran (ed.), *Looking at Lonergan's Method* (Dublin: The Talbot Press, 1975), pp. 88–100: p. 98.

20   Wolfhart Pannenberg, *Ethics* (Philadelphia: The Westminster Press, 1977), ch. 2, *and Basic Questions in Theology*, vol. 2 (London: SCM Press, 1971), ch. 4.

21   Dennis Nineham, *Christianity, Mediaeval and Modern* (London: SCM Press, 1993).

22   From the Preface to Anselm's *Proslogion*.

23   Alasdair MacIntyre, *Whose Justice, Which Rationality?* (London: Duckworth, 1988).

24   Hans Küng, *A Global Ethic for Global Politics and Economics* (London: SCM Press, 1997).

25   See Thomas Luckmann, *The Invisible Religion* (London: Macmillan, 1971).

26   W. Alston, 'Some Reflections on the Early Days of the Society of Christian Philosophers', *Faith and Philosophy* 15 (1998), p. 142.

27   M. L. Peterson, 'A Long and Faithful Journey', *Faith and Philosophy* 15 (1998), p. 157.

28   Alvin Plantinga, *Warranted Christian Belief* (New York: Oxford University Press, 2000).

29   Austin Farrer, *Faith and Speculation* (London: A. and C. Black, 1967).

30   John Macquarrie, *An Existentialist Theology* (London: SCM Press, 1955).

31   Martin Heidegger, *Discourse on Thinking* (New York: Harper and Row, 1966).

32   Michel Foucault, *Power/Knowledge. Selected Interviews and Other Writings 1972–1977* (New York: The Harvester Press, 1980).

33   E.g. by Michael Buckley, *At the Origins of Modern Atheism* (New Haven, CT: Yale University Press, 1987).

34   Gerard J. Hughes (ed.), *The Philosophical Assessment of Theology. Essays in Honour of Frederick C. Copleston* (Tunbridge Wells: Search Press, 1987). Mitchell's essay is reprinted in his own collection, *How to Play Theological Ping Pong. Collected Essays on Faith and Reason* (London: Hodder and Stoughton, 1990).

35   Basil Mitchell, *Faith and Criticism* (Oxford: Clarendon Press, 1994).

36   Ibid., p. 88.

37   Diogenes Allen, *Philosophy for Understanding Theology* (London: SCM Press, 1985).

38   Ibid., p. 269.

39 'Christian Philosophy at the End of the Twentieth Century', in J. F. Sennet (ed.), *The Analytic Theist. An Alvin Plantinga Reader* (Grand Rapids, MI: Eerdmans, 1998), pp. 140, 141.
40 Wolfhart Pannenberg, *Theology and the Philosophy of Science* (London: Darton, Longman and Todd, 1976).
41 Ingolf Dalferth, *Theology and Philosophy* (Oxford: Blackwell, 1988).
42 Christof Schwöbel, *God: Action and Revelation* (Kampen: Kok Pharos, 1992).
43 Wolfhart Pannenberg, *Systematic Theology*, vol. 1 (Edinburgh: T. and T. Clark, 1991), p. 410.
44 Robert Jenson, *Systematic Theology. Vol. 1: The Triune God* (New York: Oxford University Press, 1997), ch. 1.
45 Ibid., p. 218.
46 Ibid., p. 211. John of Damascus spoke of God as 'above Being', Jean-Luc Marion of God 'without Being'. For references, see Jenson, *Systematic Theology*, vol. 1.
47 Robert Jenson, *Systematic Theology. Vol. 2: The Works of God* (New York: Oxford University Press, 2000), p. 21.
48 Alvin Plantinga, *God, Freedom and Evil* (London: George Allen and Unwin, 1975), and *Warranted Christian Belief*.
49 Alvin Plantinga, *Does God Have a Nature?* (Milwaukee: Marquette University Press, 1980).
50 In *Faith and Philosophy* 1 (1984), pp. 253–71.
51 Ronald J. Feenstra and Cornelius Plantinga Jr. (eds.), *Trinity, Incarnation and Atonement. Philosophical and Theological Essays* (Notre Dame, IN: University of Notre Dame Press, 1989).
52 Ibid., p. 2.

CHAPTER 2   REVELATION

1 Thomas Aquinas, *Summa Theologiae* 1a.2.2 and 1a.1.2.
2 Psalm 19: 1.
3 Alvin Plantinga, *Warranted Christian Belief* (New York: Oxford University Press, 2000).
4 See, e.g., Brand Blanshard, *Reason and Belief* (London: George Allen and Unwin, 1974).
5 Cf. Immanuel Kant, *Critique of Practical Reason* (1788), Conclusion.
6 H. H. Farmer, *Revelation and Religion. Studies in the Theological Interpretation of Religious Types* (London: Nisbet & Co., 1954), ch. 1.
7 Brian Hebblethwaite, *The Problems of Theology* (Cambridge: Cambridge University Press, 1980), p. 79.
8 James Barr, *Biblical Faith and Natural Theology* (Oxford: Clarendon Press, 1993), p. 126.

9   Wolfhart Pannenberg et al., *Revelation as History* (London: Sheed and Ward, 1969).

10 Joseph Butler, *The Analogy of Religion Natural and Revealed to the Constitution and Course of Nature* (1736), Part II, ch. 3.

11 Basil Mitchell and Maurice Wiles, 'Does Christianity Need a Revelation? A Discussion', *Theology* lxxxiii (1980), pp. 103–14. The discussion was followed up by Mitchell in his contribution, 'Revelation Revisited', to the Festschrift for Maurice Wiles: see S. Coakley and D. A. Pailin (eds.), *The Making and Remaking of Christian Doctrine. Essays in Honour of Maurice Wiles* (Oxford: Clarendon Press, 1993), pp. 177–91.

12 'Does Christianity Need a Revelation?', p. 109. This point would, of course, lead us to put a question mark against the idea of general revelation, or at least to see general revelation as involving a wider notion of revelation than is envisage in respect of special revelation.

13 'Revelation Revisited'.

14 Ibid., p.188.

15 George Mavrodes, *Revelation in Religious Belief* (Philadelphia: Temple University Press, 1988).

16 William James, *The Varieties of Religious Experience* (New York: Modern Library, 1902).

17 Nicholas Wolterstorff, *Divine Discourse. Philosophical Reflections on the Claim that God Speaks* (Cambridge: Cambridge University Press, 1995).

18 Ibid., ch. 2.

19 See J. L. Austin, *How to Do Things with Words* (Oxford: Clarendon Press, 1962).

20 Karl Barth, *Church Dogmatics I.1* (Edinburgh: T. & T. Clark, 1936; new trans. 1975), ch. 1, para. 4.

21 See Austin Farrer, *Faith and Speculation. An Essay in Philosophical Theology* (London: Adam and Charles Black, 1967).

22 William J. Abraham, *The Divine Inspiration of Holy Scripture* (Oxford: Oxford University Press, 1981), and *Divine Revelation and the Limits of Historical Criticism* (Oxford: Oxford University Press, 1982).

23 *Divine Revelation*, p. 224.

24 Richard Swinburne, *Revelation* (Oxford: Clarendon Press, 1992).

25 See also Richard Swinburne, *Responsibility and Atonement* (Oxford: Clarendon Press, 1989); *The Christian God* (Oxford: Clarendon Press, 1994); *Providence and the Problem of Evil* (Oxford: Clarendon Press, 1998).

26 *Revelation*, p. 224.

27 Peter Byrne, 'A Defence of Christian Revelation', *Religious Studies* 29 (1993), pp. 381–94.

28 See John Baillie, *The Idea of Revelation in Recent Thought* (New York: Columbia University Press, 1956).

29 Abraham, *Divine Revelation*, ch. 3.

30 Pannenberg et al., *Revelation as History*.

31   E.g.: 'Redemptive Event and History', in Wolfhart Pannenberg, *Basic Ques-
     tions in Theology*, vol. 1 (London: SCM Press, 1970); and *Systematic Theology*,
     vol. 1 (Edinburgh: T. & T. Clark, 1991), ch. 4.
32   Wolfhart Pannenberg, *Jesus, God and Man* (London: SCM Press, 1968).
33   Søren Kierkegaard, *Philosophical Fragments* (Princeton: Princeton University
     Press, 1936), ch. 2.
34   See above p. 23 and chapter 8 below.
35   See above p. 19.
36   Keith Ward, *Religion and Revelation. A Theology of Revelation in the World's
     Religions* (Oxford: Clarendon Press, 1994).
37   Ibid., p. 342.
38   Austin Farrer, *The Glass of Vision* (Westminster: Dacre Press, 1948). See also
     Farrer's response to criticism in his essay, 'Inspiration: Poetical and divine', in
     Interpretation and Belief (London: SPCK, 1976), pp. 39–53.
39   In Basil Mitchell (ed.), *Faith and Logic. Oxford Essays in Philosophical Theology*
     (London: George Allen and Unwin, 1957), pp. 84–107.
40   Ibid., p. 99.
41   Brian Hebblethwaite, 'The Communication of Divine Revelation', in Alan
     Padgett (ed.), *Reason and the Christian Religion. Essays in Honour of Richard
     Swinburne* (Oxford: Clarendon Press, 1994), p.159.
42   David Brown, *The Divine Trinity* (London: Duckworth, 1985).
43   David Brown, 'God and Symbolic Action', in Brian Hebblethwaite and
     Edward Henderson (eds.), *Divine Action. Studies Inspired by the Philosophical
     Theology of Austin Farrer* (Edinburgh: T. & T. Clark, 1990), pp. 103–22.
44   David Brown, *Tradition and Imagination. Revelation and Change* (Oxford:
     Oxford University Press, 1999), and *Discipleship and Imagination. Christian
     Tradition and Truth* (Oxford: Oxford University Press 2000).
45   See Ingolf Dalferth, *Theology and Philosophy* (Oxford: Blackwell, 1988), Part
     III; and Christoph Schwöbel, *God: Action and Revelation* (Kampen: Kok Pharos,
     1992), Part II.
46   William P. Alston, *Perceiving God. The Epistemology of Religious Experience*
     (Ithaca and London: Cornell University Press, 1991).
47   John Hick, *Faith and Knowledge*, 2nd edn. (Ithaca and London: Cornell Univer-
     sity Press, 1966; paperback edn. Glasgow: Collins Fontana Books, 1979).
48   Ibid., p. 29 (Fontana edition).
49   John Hick, *The Fifth Dimension. An Exploration of the Spiritual Realm* (Oxford:
     Oneworld, 1999).
50   Ibid., p. 78.
51   Philip Almond, 'John Hick's Copernican Theology', and John Hick, 'The
     Theology of Pluralism', *Theology* lxxxvi (1983). Hick's piece is reprinted in his,
     Problems of Religious Pluralism (Basingstoke and London: Macmillan, 1985).
52   Hick, *Problems of Religious Pluralism*, pp. 97f.
53   K. Satchidananda Murty, *Revelation and Reason in Advaita Vedanta* (Waltair:
     Andhra University, 1961), pp. 320f.

54 Ward, *Religion and Revelation*; *Religion and Creation* (Oxford: Clarendon Press, 1996); *Religion and Human Nature* (Oxford: Clarendon Press, 1998); *Religion and Community* (Oxford: Clarendon Press 2000).
55 Swinburne, *Responsibility and Atonement*; *Revelation*; *The Christian God*; *Providence and the Problem of Evil*.
56 Ward, *Religion and Revelation*, p. 324.

CHAPTER 3   CREATION

1 Thomas Aquinas, *Summa Contra Gentiles*, Books I and II, translated, with an Introduction and Notes, by Anton C. Pegis (Notre Dame: University of Notre Dame Press, 1975).
2 Norman Kretzmann, *The Metaphysics of Theism. Aquinas's Natural Theology in Summa Contra Gentiles I* (Oxford: Clarendon Press, 1997), and *The Metaphysics of Creation. Aquinas's Natural Theology in Summa Contra Gentiles II* (Oxford: Clarendon Press, 1999).
3 *The Metaphysics of Theism*, p. 113.
4 Thomas V. Morris, *Anselmian Explorations* (Notre Dame: University of Notre Dame Press, 1987).
5 Anselm, *Proslogion* II
6 Morris, *Anselmian Explorations*, p.12.
7 Plato, *Timaeus* 27d following.
8 Plato, *Republic* Book VI.
9 Ibid., VI, 508
10 Augustine, *Confessions* VII, §14.
11 George Gamow, *The Creation of the Universe* (New York: Viking Press, 1952; revised edn., 1961).
12 Keith Ward, *Rational Theology and the Creativity of God* (Oxford: Basil Blackwell, 1982).
13 See ibid., pp. 223–7.
14 Aquinas, *Summa Theologiae* Ia.46.2.
15 Morris, *Anselmian Explorations*, pp. 151ff. See also Bertrand Russell, *The Analysis of Mind* (London: George Allen & Unwin Ltd, 1921), p. 159.
16 Richard E. Creel, *Divine Impassibility. An Essay in Philosophical Theology* (Cambridge: Cambridge University Press, 1986), ch. 4.
17 Jonathan L. Kvanvig and Hugh McCann, 'Divine Conservation and the Persistence of the World', in Thomas V. Morris (ed.), *Divine and Human Action. Essays in the Metaphysics of Theism* (Ithaca and London: Cornell University Press, 1988), pp. 13–49.
18 See N. Malebranche, *Dialogues on Metaphysics and Religion*, ed. N. Jolley and D. Scott. Cambridge Texts in the History of Philosophy (Cambridge: Cambridge University Press, 1997).

19   Philip L. Quinn, 'Divine Conservation, Secondary Causes and Occasionalism', in Morris (ed.), *Divine and Human Action*, pp. 50–73.

20   See, e.g., *Romans* 9: 21.

21   J. R. R. Tolkien, *The Silmarillion* (London: George Allen and Unwin, 1977), pp. 13–22.

22   Austin Farrer, *A Science of God?* (London: Geoffrey Bles Ltd, 1966), pp. 76ff. The American edition of this book was given a different title: *God is not Dead* (Wilton, CT: Morehouse-Barlow, 1966).

23   Hans Urs von Balthasar, *Theodrama. Theological Dramatic Theory*, vol. II (San Francisco: Ignatius Press, 1990), p. 269.

24   See p. 36 above and *The Metaphysics of Theism*, pp. 223ff.

25   Keith Ward, *Religion and Creation* (Oxford: Clarendon Press, 1996).

26   Gottfried Wilhelm Leibniz, *Discourse on Metaphysics* (1686), §6.

27   François-Marie Arouet de Voltaire, *Candide* (1759).

28   Richard Swinburne, *Providence and the Problem of Evil* (Oxford: Clarendon Press, 1998), pp. 8ff.

29   Robert Merrihew Adams, *The Virtue of Faith and Other Essays in Philosophical Theology* (New York; Oxford University Press, 1987), ch. 4.

30   Thomas V. Morris, 'Perfection and Creation', in Eleonore Stump (ed.), *Reasoned Faith* (Ithaca and London: Cornell University Press, 1993), pp. 234–47.

31   Balthasar, *Theodrama*.

32   Thomas V. Morris, *Our Idea of God. An Introduction to Philosophical Theology* (Notre Dame: University of Notre Dame Press, 1991), ch. 8.

33   Plato, *Timaeus* 38.

34   Richard Swinburne, *The Coherence of Theism* (Oxford: Clarendon Press, 1977), ch. 12.

35   Ward, *Religion and Creation*, ch. 11.

36   See Austin Farrer, *Faith and Speculation* (London: Adam & Charles Black, 1967), ch. 11.

37   See Paul Helm, *The Providence of God* (Leicester: Inter-Varsity Press, 1993), ch. 2.

38   Morris, *Our Idea of God*, ch. 7.

39   Paul Helm, *Eternal God. A Study of God without Time* (Oxford; Clarendon Press, 1988).

40   See, e.g., Brian Davies, *Thinking about God* (London: Geoffrey Chapman, 1985), ch. 5, and Eleonore Stump and Normann Kretzmann, 'Absolute Simplicity', in *Faith and Philosophy* 2 (1985), pp. 353–82.

41   See Swinburne, *The Coherence of Theism*, pp. 220ff.

42   Morris, *Anselmian Explorations*, p. 122.

43   Morris, *Our Idea of God*, p. 124.

44   Alfred N. Whitehead, *Process and Reality* (New York: Macmillan, 1929).

45   See, e.g., Charles Hartshorne, *A Natural Theology for our Time* (La Salle IL: Open Court, 1967); David Griffin, *A Process Christology* (Philadelphia: The Westminster Press, 1973); and Norman Pittenger, *The Lure of Divine Love*.

Human Experience and Christian Faith in a Process Perspective (New York: The Pilgrim Press, 1979).

46 Farrer, *Faith and Speculation*.

47 In Austin Farrer, *Reflective Faith. Essays in Philosophical Theology* (London: SPCK, 1972), pp. 178–91.

48 Thomas F. Torrance, *Divine and Contingent Order* (Oxford: Oxford University Press, 1981).

49 Wolfhart Pannenberg, *Toward a Theology of Nature. Essays on Science and Faith* (Louisville, KY: Westminster/John Knox Press, 1993).

50 In G. E. M. Anscombe and P. T. Geach, *Three Philosophers* (Oxford: Basil Blackwell, 1961).

51 See Russell's debate with F. C. Copleston, reprinted in John Hick (ed.), *The Existence of God* (New York: Macmillan, 1964), pp. 167–91.

52 See Ayer's debate with Copleston, reprinted in A. J. Ayer, *The Meaning of Life and Other Essays* (New York: C. Scribner's Sons, 1990).

53 Brian Hebblethwaite, *The Ocean of Truth* (Cambridge: Cambridge University Press, 1988), pp. 88f.

54 See Charles Gugnon (ed.), *The Cambridge Companion to Heidegger*, (Cambridge: Cambridge University Press, 1993), ch. 7.

55 Austin Farrer, *Finite and Infinite. A Philosophical Essay*, 2nd edn. (Westminster: Dacre Press, 1959), p. 299 (1st edn. 1943).

56 Stephen Hawking, *Black Holes and Baby Universes and Other Essays* (London: Bantam Press, 1993), ch. 9.

57 See p. 39 above.

58 William Lane Craig and Quentin Smith, *Theism, Atheism and Big Bang Cosmology* (Oxford: Clarendon Press, 1993).

59 Compare Hawking, *Black Holes*, p. 99, with Stephen Hawking, *A Brief History of Time* (London: Bantam Press, 1988), p. 141.

60 John Polkinghorne, *Science and Christian Belief. Theological Reflections of a Bottom-up Thinker* (London: SPCK, 1994), p. 73.

61 Ward, *Religion and Creation*, pp. 296–9.

62 Richard Swinburne, *The Existence of God*, revised edn. (Oxford: Clarendon Press, 1991), pp. 300–22.

63 John D. Barrow and Frank Tipler, *The Anthropic Cosmological Principle* (Oxford: Clarendon Press, 1986).

64 John Gribbin and Martin Rees, *The Stuff of the Universe. Dark Matter, Mankind and the Coincidences of Cosmology* (London: Heinemann, 1990).

65 John Leslie, *Universes* (London and New York: Routledge, 1989).

66 See Creel, *Divine Impassibility*.

67 Thomas V. Morris, 'Absolute Creation', in *Anselmian Explorations*, pp. 161–78.

68 *Faith and Philosophy* 4 (1987), pp. 365–82.

69 See E. Bréhier, 'The Creation of the Eternal Truths in Descartes's System', in W. Doney (ed.), *Descartes* (London: Macmillan, 1968), pp. 192–208.

70 See above p. 46.

71 *Religion and Creation.* The relevant chapter is entitled 'God and Time'.

72 Ibid., pp. 270f.

73 G. E. M. Anscombe, *Metaphysics and the Philosophy of Mind.Collected Philosophical Papers, vol.* II (Oxford: Basil Blackwell, 1981), p.146.

74 Polkinghorne, *Science and Christian Belief,* pp. 24–8.

75 J. R. Lucas, *The Freedom of the Will* (Oxford: Clarendon Press, 1970).

76 J. R. Lucas, *The Future* (Oxford: Basil Blackwell, 1989).

77 Ibid., p.233.

78 In addition to Lucas's work, we may mention A. N. Prior, 'The Formalities of Omniscience', in his *Papers on Time and Tense* (Oxford: The Clarendon Press, 1968), ch. 3; Nelson Pike, *God and Timelessness* (London: Routledge & Kegan Paul, 1970); Swinburne, *The Coherence of Theism,* ch. 12; Anthony Kenny, *The God of the Philosophers* (Oxford: Clarendon Press, 1979), ch. 4; Peter Geach, *Providence and Evil* (Cambridge: Cambridge University Press, 1977), ch. 3; and Brian Hebblethwaite, 'Some Reflections of Predestination, Providence and Divine Foreknowledge', in *Religious Studies* 15 (1979), pp. 433-48.

79 The theory is associated particularly with Luis de Molina (1535–1600).

80 William Hasker, *God, Time and Knowledge* (Ithaca: Cornell University Press, 1989).

81 See, e.g., W. Hasker, 'Anti-Molinism is Undefeated!' *in Faith and Philosophy* 17 (2000), pp. 126–31, and references given there.

82 Genesis 1: 10, etc.

83 Robert Merrihew Adams, *Finite and Infinite Goods. A Framework for Ethics* (New York: Oxford University Press, 1999).

84 Mark Wynn, *God and Goodness. A Natural Theological Perspective* (London: Routledge, 1999).

85 See, e.g., Austin Farrer, *Love Almighty and Ills Unlimited* (London: Collins, 1962); John Hick, *Evil and the God of Love* (London: Macmillan, 1966); Alvin Plantinga, *God, Freedom and Evil* (London: George Allen & Unwin, 1974); Brian Hebblethwaite, *Evil, Suffering and Religion,* revised edn. (Oxford: Oneworld, 2000); Marilyn McCord Adams and Robert Merrihew Adams (eds.), *The Problem of Evil* (Oxford: Oxford University Press, 1990); Swinburne, *Providence and the Problem of Evil.*

86 See Augustine, *Confessions* VII.

CHAPTER 4   INCARNATION

1 Peter van Inwagen, 'Incarnation and Christology', in *Routledge Encyclopedia of Philosophy,* vol. 4 (London and New York: Routledge, 1998), pp. 725–32.

2 See *The Modern Churchman* 11 (1921–2).

3 John Hick (ed.), *The Myth of God Incarnate* (London: SCM Press, 1977).

4   John Hick, *An Interpretation of Religion. Human Responses to the Transcendent* (London: Macmillan, 1989).

5   John Hick, *The Metaphor of God Incarnate* (London: SCM Press, 1993).

6   Thomas Aquinas, *Summa Theologiae* 1a.13.5.

7   Ibid., 1a.13.3.

8   Michael Green (ed.), *The Truth of God Incarnate* (London: Hodder and Stoughton, 1977).

9   Maurice Wiles, 'Myth in Theology', in John Hick (ed.), *The Myth of God Incarnate* (London: SCM Press, 1977), p. 161.

10 John Hick, 'Jesus and the World Religions', in id. (ed.), *The Myth of God Incarnate* (London: SCM Press, 1977), p. 178.

11 *The Metaphor of God Incarnate*, p. 105.

12 Brian Hebblethwaite, 'Incarnation – The Essence of Christianity?', in *Theology* lxxx (1977), reprinted as ch. 1 of *The Incarnation. Collected Essays in Christology* (Cambridge: Cambridge University Press, 1987).

13 David Brown, *The Divine Trinity* (London: Duckworth, 1985).

14 In *Oriel Review* (1986), pp. 41f.

15 Thomas V. Morris, *The Logic of God Incarnate* (Ithaca and London: Cornell University Press, 1986).

16 'The Metaphysics of God Incarnate', in Ronald J. Feenstra and Cornelius Plantinga, Jr. (eds.), *Trinity, Incarnation and Atonement. Philosophical and Theological Essays* (Notre Dame: University of Notre Dame Press, 1989), pp. 110–27.

17 For a defence of kenotic Christology, see Stephen T. Davis, *Logic and the Nature of God* (London: Macmillan, 1983), ch. 3.

18 'The Metaphysics of God Incarnate', p. 121.

19 Morris, *The Logic of God Incarnate*, pp. 161ff.

20 *The Metaphor of God Incarnate*, ch. 5.

21 Richard Swinburne, *The Christian God* (Oxford: Clarendon Press, 1995).

22 *Faith and Philosophy* 3 (1986), pp. 27–53.

23 Peter van Inwagen, *God, Knowledge and Mystery. Essays in Philosophical Theology* (Ithaca and London: Cornell University Press, 1995).

24 'Incarnation and Christology'.

25 *The Logic of God Incarnate*, p. 65.

26 Romans 8: 17.

27 Matthew 1: 18 and Luke 1: 31–5.

28 Karl Barth, *Church Dogmatics IV.1* (Edinburgh: T. & T. Clark, 1956), p. 207.

29 *The Divine Trinity*, ch. 6.

30 *The Christian God*, p. 234.

31 *God, Faith and the New Millennium. Christian Belief in an Age of Science* (Oxford: Oneworld, 1998), pp. 175f.

32 J. Houston, *Reported Miracles. A Critique of Hume* (Cambridge: Cambridge University Press, 1994).

33 *The Metaphor of God Incarnate*, pp. 56ff.

34 *The Logic of God Incarnate*, pp. 146–53.
35 Harry Frankfurt, 'Alternate Possibilities and Moral Responsibility', *Journal of Philosophy* 66 (1969), pp. 829–39.
36 *The Christian God*, p. 205n.
37 Ibid., pp. 203–9.
38 Thomas Flint, '"A Death He Freely Accepted": Molinist Reflections on the Incarnation', *Faith and Philosophy* 18 (2001), pp. 3–20.
39 Alvin Plantinga, *God, Freedom and Evil* (London: George Allen & Unwin, 1974). See also James E. Tomberlin and Peter van Inwagen (eds.), *Alvin Plantinga* (Dordrecht: D. Reidel, 1985), pp. 36–55.
40 Austin Farrer, *Saving Belief. A Discussion of Essentials* (London: Hodder & Stoughton, 1964), p. 112.
41 *The Christian God*, p. 220.
42 Brian Hebblethwaite, 'Jesus Christ – God and Man: The Myth and Truth Debate', in William R. Farmer (ed.), *Crisis in Christology. Essays in Quest of Resolution* (Livonia, MI: Dove Booksellers, 1995), pp. 1–11.
43 *The Christian God*, p. 218.
44 In Eleonore Stump and Thomas P. Flint (eds.), *Hermes and Athena. Biblical Exegesis and Philosophical Theology* (Notre Dame: University of Notre Dame Press, 1993), p. 19.
45 *Warranted Christian Belief*, ch. 12.
46 *The Divine Trinity*, ch. 3.
47 *The Christian God*, ch. 10.
48 Austin Farrer, *Faith and Speculation* (London: Adam & Charles Black, 1967), chs. 1–3. See also Brian Hebblethwaite, 'The Experiential Verification of Religious Belief in the Theology of Austin Farrer', in Jeffrey C. Eaton and Ann Loades (eds.), *For God and Clarity. New Essays in Honor of Austin Farrer* (Allison Park, Pennsylvania: Pickwick Publications, 1983), pp. 163–76.
49 See Brown, *The Divine Trinity*, pp. 126–45, and Richard Swinburne, 'Evidence for the Resurrection', in Stephen Davis, Daniel Kendall and Gerald O'Collins (eds.), *The Resurrection* (Oxford: Oxford University Press, 1997), pp. 191–212.
50 E. P. Sanders, *The Historical Figure of Jesus* (London: Allen Lane, The Penguin Press, 1993), p. 280.
51 See Hick, *An Interpretation of Religion*, passim.
52 *Warranted Christian Belief*, pp. 43–63.
53 Geoffrey Parrinder, *Avatar and Incarnation* (London: Faber and Faber, 1970).
54 Ninian Smart, *Reasons and Faiths* (London: Routledge & Kegan Paul, 1958), ch. 4.
55 *God, Faith and the New Millennium*, p. 164.
56 See Julius Lipner, 'Avatara *and* Incarnation?', in David Scott and Israel Selvanayagam (eds.), *Re-Visioning India's Religious Traditions* (Delhi: SPCK, 1996).
57 H. H. Farmer, *Revelation and Religion* (London: Nisbet & Co., 1954), p. 196.

58 See Ward, *God, Faith and the New Millennium*, p. 162, and Morris, *The Logic of God Incarnate*, p. 183.

59 Brian Hebblethwaite, 'The Impossibility of Multiple Incarnations', *Theology* civ (2001), pp. 323–34.

60 Ibid., p. 333.

CHAPTER 5   TRINITY

1 See Maurice Wiles, *Working Papers in Doctrine* (London: SCM Press, 1976), and Geoffrey Lampe, *God as Spirit* (Oxford: Clarendon Press, 1977).

2 Karl Barth, *Church Dogmatics I.1* (Edinburgh: T. & T. Clark, 1936; new translation, 1975), ch. 2, part 1; Karl Rahner, *The Trinity* (London: Burns & Oates, 1970); Bernard Lonergan, *The Way to Nicea. The Dialectical Development of Trinitarian Theology* (London: Darton, Longman and Todd, 1976).

3 Walter Kasper, *The God of Jesus Christ* (London: SCM Press, 1984), Part III.

4 Wolfhart Pannenberg, *Systematic Theology*, vol. 1 (Edinburgh: T. & T. Clark, 1991), ch. 5; Jürgen Moltmann, *The Trinity and the Kingdom of God. The Doctrine of God* (London: SCM Press, 1981); Robert Jenson, *Systematic Theology*. Vol. 1: *The Triune God* (New York: Oxford University Press, 1997); T. F. Torrance, *The Christian Doctrine of God. One Being, Three Persons* (Edinburgh: T. & T. Clark, 1996).

5 See, e.g., Vladimir Lossky, *Orthodox Theology. An Introduction* (Crestwood, NY: St Vladimir's Seminary Press, 1978).

6 See, e.g., Thomas Aquinas, *Summa Contra Gentiles* 1.14.2.

7 See chapter 4, p. 60 above.

8 Wolfhart Pannenberg, 'History and Meaning in Bernard Lonergan's Approach to Theological Method', in Patrick Corcoran (ed.), *Looking at Lonergan's Method* (Dublin: The Talbot Press, 1975), pp. 98. See also p. 5 above.

9 Norman Kretzmann, 'Trinity and Transcendentals' in Ronald J. Feenstra and Cornelius Plantinga, Jr. (eds.), *Trinity, Incarnation and Atonement. Philosophical and Theological Essays* (Notre Dame: University of Notre Dame Press, 1989), pp. 79–109.

10 See D. M. MacKinnon, 'Aristotle's Conception of Substance', in Renford Bambrough (ed.), *New Essays on Plato and Aristotle* (London: Routledge & Kegan Paul, 1965), pp. 97–119.

11 Peter Geach, *The Virtues* (Cambridge: Cambridge University Press, 1977), p. 77.

12 See B. L. Hebblethwaite, 'God and Truth', *Kerygma und Dogma* 40 (1994), pp. 2–19.

13 See Patrick Sherry, *Spirit and Beauty. An Introduction to Theological Aesthetics* (Oxford: Clarendon Press, 1992).

14 William P. Alston, 'Substance and Trinity', in Stephen T. Davis, Daniel Kendall SJ, and Gerald O'Collins SJ (eds.), *The Trinity. An Interdisciplinary*

Symposium on the Trinity (Oxford: Oxford University Press, 1999), pp. 179–201.

15 See above, p. 45.

16 Donald MacKinnon, 'The Relation of the Doctrines of the Incarnation and the Trinity', in Richard W. A. McKinney (ed.), *Creation, Christ and Culture. Studies in Honour of T. F. Torrance* (Edinburgh: T. & T. Clark, 1976), pp. 92–107.

17 Richard Cross, 'Two Models of the Trinity?', *The Heythrop Journal* 43 (2002), pp. 275–94

18 *The Metaphysics of Theism. Aquinas's Natural Theology in Summa Contra Gentiles I* (Oxford: Clarendon Press, 1997), pp. 238–50.

19 C. J. F. Williams, 'Neither Confounding the Persons nor Dividing the Substance', in Alan Padgett (ed.), *Reason and the Christian Religion. Essays in Honour of Richard Swinburne* (Oxford: Clarendon Press, 1994), pp. 227–43.

20 Ibid., p. 238.

21 *The Virtues.*

22 Ibid., p. 75.

23 Ibid., p. 76.

24 Richard Swinburne, *The Christian God* (Oxford: Clarendon Press, 1994), pp. 177–9.

25 Richard of St Victor, *De Trinitate* III. Richard's views are presented and discussed succinctly in Edmund J. Fortman, *The Triune God. A Historical Study of the Doctrine of the Trinity* (London: Hutchinson & Co. Ltd., 1972), pp. 191–4.

26 Thomas Aquinas, *Summa Theologiae* 1a.31.3.ad 1 (Blackfriars edn., vol. VI, London: Eyre and Spottiswoode, 1965), pp. 94f.

27 Stephen T. Davis, *Logic and the Nature of God* (Grand Rapids, MI: William B. Eerdmans, 1983), pp. 132ff.

28 Swinburne, *Revelation* (Oxford: Clarendon Press, 1992), pp. 136f.

29 *The Christian God*, p. 191.

30 'The Relation of the Doctrines of the Incarnation and the Trinity'.

31 Ibid., p. 104.

32 David Brown, *The Divine Trinity* (London: Duckworth,, 1985), pp. 159–213.

33 See his review in *The Times*, 21 November 1985, p. 13.

34 Kenneth Surin, 'The Trinity and Philosophical Reflection. A Study of David Brown's *The Divine Trinity*', *Modern Theology* 3 (1986), pp. 235–56.

35 David Brown, 'Wittgenstein against the "Wittgensteinians": A Reply to Kenneth Surin on *The Divine Trinity*', *Modern Theology* 3 (1986), pp. 257–76.

36 Ibid., pp. 266–71.

37 Thomas V. Morris, *Our Idea of God. An Introduction to Philosophical Theology* (Notre Dame: University of Notre Dame Press, 1991), pp. 174–84.

38 Ibid., p. 183.

39 Richard Swinburne, 'Could There Be More Than One God?', *Faith and Philosophy* 5 (1988), pp. 225–41.

40   Peter van Inwagen, 'Trinity', in *Routledge Encyclopedia of Philosophy*, vol. 9 (London/New York: Routledge, 1998), pp. 457-61.
41   Brown, *The Divine Trinity*, ch. 7.
42   Ibid., p. 289.
43   Graham Greene, *Monsignor Quixote* (London: The Bodley Head, 1982).
44   Peter van Inwagen, 'And Yet They Are Not Three Gods But One God', in *God, Knowledge and Mystery. Essays in Philosophical Theology* (Ithaca and London: Cornell University Press, 1995), pp. 222-59.
45   'Two Models of the Trinity?'
46   Ibid., p. 288.
47   Ibid., p. 290.
48   Keith Ward, *Religion and Creation* (Oxford: Clarendon Press, 1996), pp. 321-9.
49   See Pannenberg, *Systematic Theology*, vol. 1, p. 321.
50   Ward, *Religion and Creation*, p. 324.
51   Ibid., p. 325.
52   Rahner *The Trinity* p. 176.
53   Ward, *Religion and Creation*, p. 328.
54   Sarah Coakley, ' "Persons" in the "Social" Doctrine of the Trinity: A Critique of Current Analytic Discussion', in Stephen T. Davis, Daniel Kendall SJ, and Gerald O'Collins SJ (eds.), *The Trinity. An Interdisciplinary Symposium on the Trinity* (Oxford: Oxford University Press, 1999), pp. 123-44.
55   Brian Leftow, 'Anti Social Trinitarianism', in Stephen T. Davis, Daniel Kendall SJ, and Gerald O'Collins SJ (eds.), *The Trinity. An Interdisciplinary Symposium on the Trinity* (Oxford: Oxford University Press, 1999), pp. 202-49.
56   Ibid., p. 204.
57   David Brown, 'Trinitarian Personhood and Individuality', in Ronald J. Feenstra and Cornelius Plantinga, Jr. (eds.), *Trinity, Incarnation and Atonement. Philosophical and Theological Essays* (Notre Dame: University of Notre Dame Press, 1989), pp. 48-78
58   Ibid., p. 49.
59   Cornelius Plantinga, 'Social Trinity and Tritheism', in Ronald J. Feenstra and Cornelius Plantinga, Jr. (eds.), *Trinity, Incarnation and Atonement. Philosophical and Theological Essays* (Notre Dame: University of Notre Dame Press, 1989), pp. 21-47.
60   Ibid., p. 28.
61   Ibid., p. 37.
62   See Thomas Aquinas, *Summa Theologiae* 1a.28.
63   Williams, 'Neither Confounding the Persons nor Dividing the Substance'.
64   Ibid., pp. 242f.
65   C. Stephen Layman, 'Tritheism and the Trinity', *Faith and Philosophy* 5 (1988), 291-8.
66   John Macnamara, Marie La Palma Reyes and Gonzalo E. Reyes, 'Logic and the Trinity', *Faith and Philosophy* 11 (1994), pp. 3-18.

67   E. Feser, 'Has Trinitarianism been Shown to be Coherent?', *Faith and Philosophy* 14 (1997), pp. 87–97.

68   Richard Cartwright, 'On the Logical Problem of the Trinity', in Richard Cartwright, *Philosophical Essays* (Cambridge, MA: MIT Press, 1987).

69   T. W. Bartel, 'Could There be more than One Lord?', *Faith and Philosophy* 11 (1994), pp. 357–78.

70   Swinburne, 'Could There Be More Than One God?', pp. 230f.

CHAPTER 6   SALVATION

1   See J. Ramsey McCallum, *Abelard's Christian Theology* (Merrick, NY: Richwood Pub. Co., 1976).

2   Hastings Rashdall, *The Idea of Atonement in Christian Theology* (London: Macmillan and Co., 1919).

3   Anselm of Canterbury, *Cur Deus Homo?*, in *St Anselm: Basic Writings*, trans. Sidney Norton Deane (La Salle, IL: Open Court, 1961).

4   Gustav Aulen, *Christus Victor* (London: SPCK, 1931).

5   In F. G. Healey (ed.), *Prospect for Theology. Essays in Honour of H. H. Farmer* (Welwyn: James Nisbet & Co. Ltd., 1966), pp. 167–82.

6   Ibid., p. 181.

7   Richard Swinburne, *Responsibility and Atonement* (Oxford: Clarendon Press, 1989).

8   J. R. Lucas, 'Reflections on the Atonement', in Alan G. Padgett (ed.), *Reason and the Christian Religion. Essays in Honour of Richard Swinburne* (Oxford: Clarendon Press, 1994), pp. 265–75.

9   C. S. Lewis, *The Lion, the Witch and the Wardrobe* (London: Geoffrey Bles, 1950).

10   Charles Taliaferro, 'A Narnian Theory of the Atonement', *Scottish Journal of Theology* xli (1988), pp. 75–92.

11   'Reflections on the Atonement', p. 267.

12   John Hick, 'Is the Doctrine of the Atonement a Mistake?', in Alan G. Padgett (ed.), *Reason and the Christian Religion. Essays in Honour of Richard Swinburne* (Oxford: Clarendon Press, 1994), pp. 247–63.

13   Ibid., pp. 256f.

14   Austin Farrer, *Saving Belief* (London: Hodder and Stoughton, 1964), p. 88.

15   *Responsibility and Atonement*, p. 124.

16   Ibid., pp. 137–47.

17   William J. Wainwright, 'Original Sin', in Thomas V. Morris (ed.), *Philosophy and the Christian Faith* (Notre Dame: University of Notre Dame Press, 1988), pp. 31–60.

18   Michael J. Langford, *A Liberal Theology for the Twenty-First Century. A Passion for Reason* (Aldershot: Ashgate 2001).

19   Ibid., p. 181.

20 Merold Westphal, 'Taking St Paul Seriously: Sin as an Epistemological Category', in Thomas P. Flint (ed.), *Christian Philosophy* (Notre Dame: University of Notre Dame Press, 1990), pp. 200–26.
21 Paul W. Gooch, *Partial Knowledge. Philosophical Studies in Paul* (Notre Dame: University of Notre Dame Press, 1987).
22 *Responsibility and Atonement*, p. 139.
23 Ibid., ch. 6.
24 J. R. Lucas, *Responsibility* (Oxford: Clarendon Press, 1995), ch. 6.
25 *Responsibility and Atonement*, p. 99.
26 Richard Holloway, *On Forgiveness* (Edinburgh: Canongate, 2002), p. 88.
27 Luke 15: 11–32.
28 In *Faith and Philosophy* 8 (1991), pp. 277–304.
29 Ibid., p. 297.
30 *Responsibility and Atonement*, p. 122.
31 Hick, 'Is the Doctrine of the Atonement a Mistake?', p. 255.
32 Lucas 'Reflections on the Atonement', p. 269
33 Peter Quinn, 'Swinburne on Guilt, Atonement, and Christian Redemption', in Alan G. Padgett (ed.), *Reason and the Christian Religion. Essays in Honour of Richard Swinburne* (Oxford: Clarendon Press, 1994), pp. 277–300.
34 In *Faith and Philosophy* 11 (1994), pp. 321–8.
35 Richard Cross, 'Atonement Without Satisfaction', *Religious Studies* 37 (2001), pp. 397–416.
36 Philip L. Quinn, 'Aquinas on Atonement', in Ronald J. Feenstra and Cornelius Plantinga, Jr. (eds.), *Trinity, Incarnation and Atonement. Philosophical and Theological Essays* (Notre Dame: University of Notre Dame Press, 1989), pp. 153–77.
37 Eleonore Stump, 'Atonement according to Aquinas', in Thomas V. Morris (ed.), *Philosophy and the Christian Faith* (Notre Dame: University of Notre Dame Press, 1988), pp. 61–91; and 'Atonement and Justification', in Ronald J. Feenstra and Cornelius Plantinga, Jr. (eds.), *Trinity, Incarnation and Atonement. Philosophical and Theological Essays* (Notre Dame: University of Notre Dame Press, 1989), pp. 178–209.
38 Quinn, 'Aquinas on Atonement', p. 174.
39 Lucas, 'Reflections on the Atonement', p. 269.
40 See above, pp. 92 and 97.
41 Athanasius, *De Incarnatione* 54.
42 Lucas, 'Reflections on the Atonement', p. 271.
43 Farrer, *Saving Belief*, p. 99.
44 Hick, 'Is the Doctrine of the Atonement a Mistake?', p. 249.
45 Lucas, 'Reflections on the Atonement', p. 275.
46 Vernon White, *Atonement and Incarnation* (Cambridge: Cambridge University Press, 1991).
47 Bruce Reichenbach, 'Inclusivism and the Atonement', *Faith and Philosophy*, 16 (1999), pp. 43–54.

48   See, for example, the Report of the Second Anglican–Roman Catholic International Commission, *Salvation and the Church* (London: Church House Publishing and the Catholic Truth Society, 1987).

49   See above p. 102.

50   Philip Quinn, 'Christian Atonement and Kantian Justification', *Faith and Philosophy* 3 (1986), pp. 440–62.

51   Ibid., p. 455.

52   Discussed above, pp. 102f.

53   See, for example, Hendrikus Berkhof, *Christian Faith. An Introduction to the Study of the Faith* (Grand Rapids, MI: William B. Eerdmans Publishing Company, 1979), pp. 507–20; Oliver O'Donovan, *The Desire of the Nations. Rediscovering the Roots of Political Theology* (Cambridge: Cambridge University Press, 1996), pp. 243–84; and Enda McDonagh, *The Gracing of Society* (Dublin: Gill and Macmillan, 1988).

CHAPTER 7   THE CONSUMMATION OF ALL THINGS

1   For Plato's view see, especially, the *Phaedo*, most easily accessible in the Penguin collection, *The Last Days of Socrates*, trans. and with an Introduction by Hugh Tredennick (Harmondsworth: Penguin Books Ltd, 1954). For Descartes, see *Meditations on the First Philosophy in which the Existence of God and the Distinction between Mind and Body are Demonstrated* (1641). For Butler, see Joseph Butler, *The Analogy of Religion to the Constitution and Course of Nature* (1736), Part I, ch. 1.

2   John R. Searle, *The Rediscovery of the Mind* (Cambridge, MA: MIT Press, 1992).

3   Karl R. Popper and John C. Eccles, *The Self and Its Brain. An Argument for Interactionism* (New York: Springer International, 1977).

4   H. D. Lewis, *The Elusive Mind* (London: George Allen & Unwin, 1969), and *The Self and Immortality* (London: Macmillan, 1973); Richard Swinburne, *The Evolution of the Soul* (Oxford: Clarendon Press, 1986), and his article 'Soul: Nature and Immortality of the', in *Routledge Encyclopedia of Philosophy*, vol. 9 (London/New York: Routledge, 1998), pp. 44–8.

5   Brian Hebblethwaite, *The Christian Hope* (Basingstoke: Marshall Morgan & Scott, 1984).

6   See chapter 3, pp. 55f. above, and the literature cited in note 85 to that chapter.

7   See, also, Brian Hebblethwaite, 'The Problem of Evil', in Geoffrey Wainwright (ed.), *Keeping the Faith. Essays to Mark the Centenary of Lux Mundi* (Philadephia: Fortress Press, 1988), pp. 54–77.

8   John Hick, *Death and Eternal Life* (London: Collins, 1976; reissued 1985), pp. 129–46.

9   See Paul Badham and Paul Ballard (eds.), *Facing Death* (Cardiff: University of Wales Press, 1996), and, especially, Christopher Cherry, 'Are Near-Death

Experiences Really Suggestive of Life after Death?', in Dan Cohn-Sherbok and Christopher Lewis (eds.) *Beyond Death. Theological and Philosophical Reflections on Life After Death* (London: Macmillan, 1995), pp. 145–63.

10 See Ben Rogers, *A. J. Ayer. A Life* (London: Chatto & Windus, 1999), ch. 22.

11 This seems to be Lionel Blue's opinion in his introductory reflections to the Cohn-Sherbok/Lewis collection, p. 1 (see note 9).

12 See D. Z. Phillips, *Death and Immortality* (London: Macmillan, 1970), p. 49.

13 Antony Flew, *The Presumption of Atheism and other philosophical essays on God, Freedom and Immortality* (London: Elek/Pemberton, 1976).

14 Nicholas Lash, 'Life "after" Death?', *The Heythrop Journal* xix (1978), pp. 271–84; Brian Hebblethwaite, 'Time and Eternity and Life "after" Death', *The Heythrop Journal* xx (1979), pp. 57–62; Nicholas Lash, 'Time and Eternity and life "after" Death. A Comment', *The Heythrop Journal* xx (1979), pp. 63–4; Brian Hebblethwaite, 'A Further Comment of Life "after" Death', *The Heythrop Journal* xx (1979), pp. 187–8.

15 See chapter 3, section 3.1.8 (pp. 44–6).

16 Charles Hartshorne, *The Logic of Perfection* (Lasalle, IL: Open Court, 1962); Norman Pittenger, *After Death, Life in God* (London: SCM Press, 1980).

17 See Hick's discussion in *Death and Eternal Life*, pp. 217–21.

18 John McTaggart Ellis McTaggart, *Some Dogmas of Religion* (London: Edward Arnold, 1906), ch. 3. On McTaggart's philosophy, see P. T. Geach, *Truth, Love and Immortality. An Introduction to McTaggart's Philosophy* (London: Hutchinson, 1979).

19 H. H. Price, *Essays in the Philosophy of Religion* (Oxford: The Clarendon Press, 1972), especially ch. 6.

20 Paul Badham, *Christian Beliefs about Life after Death* (London: Macmillan, 1976).

21 Peter Geach, *God and the Soul* (London: Routledge & Kegan Paul, 1969), ch. 2.

22 See, e.g., Thomas Aquinas, *Summa contra Gentiles*, Bk. 4, ch. 79., para. 10.

23 *Routledge Encyclopedia of Philosophy*, vol. 8 (London and New York: Routledge, 1998), pp. 294–6.

24 E.g., Peter van Inwagen, 'The Possibility of Resurrection', *International Journal for Philosophy of Religion* 9 (1978), pp. 114–21; and 'Dualism and Materialism: Athens and Jerusalem?', *Faith and Philosophy* 12 (1995), pp. 475–88.

25 Dean W. Zimmermann, 'The Compatibility of Materialism and Survival: The "Falling Elevator" Model', *Faith and Philosophy* 16 (1999), pp. 194–212.

26 See *Death and Eternal Life*, ch. 15.

27 Julius Lipner, 'Hick's Resurrection', *Sophia* 17 (1979), pp. 22–34.

28 See the discussion in Hick, *Death and Eternal Life*, pp. 290–2.

29 John Polkinghorne, *The Faith of a Physicist. Reflections of a Bottom-up Thinker* (Princeton: Princeton University Press, 1994). This book, in its English edition, has a slightly different title: *Science and Christian Belief. Theological reflections of a bottom-up thinker* (London: SPCK, 1994).

30 Ibid., p. 163.

31   Stephen T. Davis, *Risen Indeed. Making Sense of the Resurrection* (London: SPCK, 1993).

32   Ibid., p. 93.

33   See, especially, H. D. Lewis, *The Elusive Self* (London: Macmillan, 1982).

34   *The Evolution of the Soul*, p. 199.

35   Stephen Voss, 'Understanding Eternal Life', *Faith and Philosophy* 9 (1992), pp. 3–22.

36   Bernard Williams, 'The Makropoulos Case; Reflections on the Tedium of Immortality', in *The Problems of the Self. Philosophical Papers 1956–1972* (Cambridge: Cambridge University Press, 1973), pp. 82–100.

37   Garth E. Hallett, 'The Tedium of Immortality', *Faith andPhilosophy* 18 (2001), pp. 279–91.

38   A. E. Taylor, *The Faith of a Moralist, Gifford Lectures Delivered in the University of St Andrews, 1926–1928*, Series I (London: Macmillan & Co., 1930), pp. 420f.

39   Thomas Aquinas, *Summa Contra Gentiles*, Bk. III, ch. 62.

40   K. E. Kirk, *The Vision of God. The Christian Doctrine of the Summum Bonum* (London: Longmans, Green and Co., 1931).

41   Hick, *Death and Eternal Life*, pp. 459–63.

42   John Donne, *Devotions*, Meditation 17, quoted in Hick, ibid., pp. 463f.

43   Austin Farrer, *Saving Belief* (London: Hodder and Stoughton, 1964), pp. 144–6.

44   Hebblethwaite, *The Christian Hope*, pp. 207–11.

45   *Saving Belief*, pp. 154f.

46   *Death and Eternal Life*, pp. 236–40.

47   Ibid., ch. 13; Hebblethwaite, *The Christian Hope*, pp. 215–220; Marilyn McCord Adams, 'The Problem of Hell: A Problem of Evil for Christians', in Eleonore Stump (ed.), *Reasoned Faith* (Ithaca: Cornell University Press, 1993), pp. 301–27; Thomas Talbott, 'The Doctrine of Everlasting Punishment', *Faith and Philosophy* 7 (1990), pp. 19–42, and 'Three Pictures of God in Western Theology', *Faith and Philosophy* 12 (1995), pp. 79–94; Eric H. Reitan, 'Universalism and Autonomy: Towards a Comparative Defense of Universalism', *Faith and Philosophy* 18 (2001), pp. 222–40.

48   Peter Geach, *Providence and Evil* (Cambridge: Cambridge University Press, 1977), ch. 7; Eleonore Stump, 'Dante's Hell, Aquinas's Moral Theory, and the Love of God', *Canadian Journal of Philosophy* 16 (1986), pp. 181–98; William Lane Craig, ' "No Other Name": A Middle Knowledge Perspective on the Exclusivity of Salvation through Christ', *Faith and Philosophy* 6 (1989), pp. 172–88; Michael J. Murray, 'Three Versions of Universalism', *Faith and Philosophy* 16 (1999), pp. 55–68; Davis, *Risen Indeed*, ch. 8.

49   Gordon Knight, 'Universalism and the Greater Good: A Response to Talbott', *Faith and Philosophy* 14 (1997), pp. 98–103.

50   Thomas Talbott, 'Universalism and the Supposed Oddity of our Earthly Life: Reply to Michael Murray', *Faith and Philosophy* 18 (2001), pp. 102–9.

51   John Hick, *Evil and the God of Love* (London: Macmillan, 1966); pp. 289–97.

52   Adams, 'The Problem of Hell', p. 325.

53 Craig, '"No Other Name"', p. 184.
54 Adams, 'The Problem of Hell', p. 319.
55 Stump, 'Dante's Hell', pp. 196f. Stump's view is defended by Michael Potts in his 'Aquinas, Hell and the Resurrection of the Damned', *Faith and Philosophy* 15 (1998), pp. 341–51.
56 Swinburne, *Responsibility and Atonement* (Oxford: Clarendon Press, 1989), pp. 182–4
57 Adams, 'The Problem of Hell', pp. 320–3.
58 Davis, *Risen Indeed*, p.166.
59 James F. Sennett, 'Is there Freedom in Heaven?', *Faith and Philosophy* 16 (1999), pp. 69–82.

CHAPTER 8   OTHER THEMES IN CHRISTIAN DOCTRINE

1 See, e.g., David Fergusson, *Community, Liberalism and Christian Ethics* (Cambridge: Cambridge University Press, 1998), and Raymond Plant, *Politics, Theology and History* (Cambridge: Cambridge University Press, 2001).
2 E.g. Hans Küng, *The Church* (Tunbridge Wells: Search Press, 1968).
3 Philip L. Quinn, 'Kantian Philosophical Ecclesiology', *Faith and Philosophy* 17 (2000), pp. 512–34.
4 Kant's work (dating from 1793) may be found, in English translation, in the volume of the Cambridge Edition of the Works of Immanuel Kant, entitled *Religion and Rational Theology*, ed. and trans. Allen Wood and George Giovanni (Cambridge: Cambridge University Press, 1996).
5 Quinn, 'Kantian Philosophical Ecclesiology', p. 515. (The Kant quotation may be fund, in another translation, on p. 135 of the Cambridge Edition cited in note 4).
6 Ibid., p. 524.
7 Bruce H. Kirmmse, 'The Thunderstorm: Kierkegaard's Ecclesiology', *Faith and Philosophy* 17 (2000), pp. 87–102.
8 Ibid., p. 87 (summary).
9 Keith Ward, *Religion and Community* (Oxford: Clarendon Press, 2000).
10 See, e.g. Geoffrey Lampe, *The Seal of the Spirit* (London: Longmans, 1951).
11 G. E. M. Anscombe, *Ethics, Religion and Politics. Collected Philosophical Papers Volume III* (Oxford: Basil Blackwell, 1981), pp. 107–12.
12 Nicholas Wolterstorff, 'The Remembrance of Things (Not) Past: Philosophical Reflections on Christian Liturgy', in Thomas P. Flint (ed.), *Christian Philosophy* (Notre Dame: University of Notre Dame Press, 1990), pp. 118–61.
13 See, e.g., Mircea Eliade, *The Myth of the Eternal Return* (Princeton: Princeton University Press, 1974).
14 Wolterstorff, 'The Remembrance of Things (Not) Past', p. 153.
15 Ibid., p. 155.

16   Robert Merrihew Adams, *Finite and Infinite Goods. A Framework for Ethics* (New York: Oxford University Press, 1999), pp. 225–8.

17   Ibid., p. 227.

18   Ninian Smart, *The Concept of Worship* (London: Macmillan, 1972).

19   See Peter Geach, 'On Worshipping the Right God', in his *God and the Soul* (London: Routledge & Kegan Paul, 1969), pp. 100–16.

20   See Rudolf Otto, *The Idea of the Holy* (Oxford: Oxford University Press, 1923).

21   See, e.g., John Hick, *God has Many Names* (London: Macmillan, 1980).

22   Paul Gwynne, *Special Divine Action. Key Issues in the Contemporary Debate* (Rome: Gregorian University Press, 1996).

23   Maurice Wiles, *God's Action in the World* (London: SCM Press, 1986).

24   Ibid., p. 81.

25   Section 3.1.8. Details of Helm's book are given in note 37 to that chapter.

26   Vernon White, *The Fall of a Sparrow. A Concept of Special Divine Action* (Exeter: the Paternoster Press, 1985).

27   P. T. Geach, *Providence and Evil* (Cambridge: Cambridge University Press, 1977), p. 58.

28   Thomas P. Flint, 'Providence and Predestination', in Philip L. Quinn and Charles Taliaferro (eds.), *A Companion to Philosophy of Religion* (Oxford: Blackwell, 1997), pp. 569–76.

29   See William Hasker, *God, Time and Knowledge* (Ithaca: Cornell University Press, 1989) and 'Anti-Molinism is Undefeated!' in *Faith and Philosophy* 17 (January 2000), pp. 126–31, and references given there.

30   Robert M. Adams, 'An Anti-Molinist Argument', *Philosophical Perspectives* 5 (1991), pp. 343–53, and 'Middle Knowledge and the Problem of Evil', *American Philosophical Quarterly* 14 (1977), reprinted in Robert M. Adams, *The Virtue of faith and Other Essays in Philosophical Theology* (New York: Oxford University Press, 1987), pp. 77–93.

31   Patrick McGrath, 'Professor Geach and the Future', *New Blackfriars* 54 (1973), pp. 497–504: pp. 503f.

32   Brian Hebblethwaite, 'Some Reflections on Predestination, Providence and Divine Foreknowledge', *Religious Studies* 15 (1979), pp. 433–48: p. 440.

33   Other aspects of the debate over divine foreknowledge are discussed by David Hunt and his critics in *Faith and Philosophy* 10 (1993), pp. 394–438: see David P. Hunt, 'Divine Providence and Simple Foreknowledge'; Tomis Kapitan, 'Providence, Foreknowledge, and Decision Procedures'; David Basinger, 'Simple Foreknowledge and Providential Control'; and David P. Hunt, 'A Reply to my Critics'.

34   See chapter 3, section 3.1.8.

35   Ludwig Feuerbach, *The Essence of Christianity* (1841), Eng. trans. by George Eliot (1854), ed. Harper Torchbook (New York: Harper and Row, 1957), p. 113.

36 David Hume, *An Enquiry Concerning Human Understanding*, section X (*Hume's Enquiries*, ed. L. A. Selby-Bigge, Oxford: The Clarendon Press; 2nd edition, 1902), p. 115n.

37 Richard Swinburne, *The Concept of Miracle* (London: Macmillan, 1970).

38 See p. 68 above.

39 Hume, *An Enquiry Concerning Human Understanding*, pp. 116–22.

40 See Keith Ward, *Divine Action* (London: Collins, 1990), ch. 10.

41 Austin Farrer, *Saving Belief. A Discussion of Essentials* (London: Hodder and Stoughton, 1964), p. 83.

42 David Brown, *The Divine Trinity* (London: Duckworth, 1985), ch. 1.

43 David Brown, *Tradition and Imagination. Revelation and Change* (Oxford: Oxford University Press, 1999), p. 277.

44 Austin Farrer, *Love Almighty and Ills Unlimited* (London: Collins, 1962); *Saving Belief*; *A Science of God?* (London: Geoffrey Bles, 1966; American edn. entitled, *God is not Dead* (Wilton, CT: Morehuse-Barlow, 1966)); *Faith and Speculation* (London: Adam & Charles Black, 1967).

45 *Faith and Speculation*, p. 104.

46 *Love Almighty and Ills Unlimited*, p. 95

47 *Saving Belief*, p. 51.

48 *Faith and Speculation*, p. 62.

49 *A Science of God?, p.* 78.

50 *A Science of God?*, p. 76.

51 *Faith and Speculation*, p. 66.

52 John Polkinghorne, *Science and Providence. God's Interaction with the World* (London: SPCK, 1989), p. 12.

53 *A Science of God?*, chs. 3 and 4.

54 *Faith and Speculation, p.* 103.

55 Brian Hebblethwaite and Edward Henderson (eds.), *Divine Action. Studies Inspired by the Philosophical Theology of Austin Farrer* (Edinburgh: T. & T. Clark, 1990).

56 Thomas F. Tracy, *God, Action and Embodiment* (Grand Rapids MI: William B. Eerdmans, 1984). Tracy's essay in *Divine Action* is entitled 'Narrative Theology and the Acts of God', pp. 173–96.

57 'Narrative Theology and the Acts of God', p. 186.

58 See Hebblethwaite and Henderson (eds.), *Divine Action*, pp. 16f.

59 Keith Ward, *Divine Action*. The reference to Farrer is on p. 51.

60 See also John Polkinghorne, 'The Metaphysics of Divine Action', in Robert John Russell, Nancey Murphey and Arthur Peacocke (eds.), *Chaos and Complexity. Scientific Perspectives on Divine Action* (Vatican City: Vatican Observatory, 1995), pp. 147–56.

61 Farrer, *Faith and Speculation*, p. 62.

62 G. E. M. Anscombe, *Metaphysics and the Philosophy of Mind.Collected Philosophical Papers*, vol. II (Oxford: Basil Blackwell, 1981), p. 146.

63 Ward, *Divine Action*: ch. 4 'The Integral Web'; ch. 5 'The Death of the Closed Universe'; ch. 6 'The Enfolding Spirit'; ch. 7 'The Constraints of Creation'.

64 D. J. Bartholomew, *God of Chance* (London: SCM Press, 1984).

65 See Ward, *Divine Action*, pp. 98f., and Polkinghorne, *Science and Providence*, pp. 27f.

66 *Science and Providence*, pp. 28ff.

67 Steven D. Crain, 'Divine Action in a World Chaos: An Evaluation of John Polkinghorne's Model of Special Divine Action', *Faith andPhilosophy* 14 (1997), pp. 41–61.

68 Ward, *Divine Action*, p. 158.

69 Ibid., p. 161.

70 Thomas Aquinas, *Summa Theologie* 2a2ae.83.ad 2.

71 Ward, *Divine Action*, p. 160.

72 Eleonore Stump, 'Petitionary Prayer', in Philip L. Quinn and Charles Taliaferro (eds.), *A Companion to Philosophy of Religion* (Oxford: Blackwell, 1997), pp. 577–83. See also Stump's earlier article, 'Petitionary Prayer', *American Philosophical Quarterly* 16 (1979), pp. 81–91.

73 Stump, 'Petitionary Prayer', in Quinn and Taliaferro (eds.), p. 581.

A Brief Guide to Further Reading

———————————

The large number of notes necessitated by a survey of this kind, give plenty of references, enabling interested readers to follow up the material discussed in this book. But it might be helpful if I select just three titles for further reading on the subject matter of each of the foregoing chapters:

CHAPTER 1   PHILOSOPHY OF RELIGION AND THEOLOGY

Basil Mitchell, *Faith and Criticism* (Oxford: Clarendon Press, 1994).
Thomas V. Morris, *Our Idea of God. An Introduction to Philosophical Theology* (Notre Dame: University of Notre Dame Press, 1991).
Austin Farrer, *Faith and Speculation. An Essay in Philosophical Theology* (London: Adam and Charles Black, 1967).

CHAPTER 2   REVELATION

William J. Abraham, *Divine Revelation and the Limits of Historical Criticism* (Oxford: Oxford University Press, 1982).
Richard Swinburne, *Revelation. From Metaphor to Analogy* (Oxford: Clarendon Press, 1992).
Keith Ward, *Religion and Revelation* (Oxford: Clarendon Press, 1994).

CHAPTER 3   CREATION

Norman Kretzmann, *The Metaphysics of Creation. Aquinas's Natural Theology in Summa Contra Gentiles II* (Oxford: Clarendon Press, 1999).

John Polkinghorne, *Science and Creation. The Search for Understanding* (London: SPCK, 1988).
Keith Ward, *Religion and Creation* (Oxford: Clarendon Press, 1996).

CHAPTER 4   INCARNATION

Brian Hebblethwaite, *The Incarnation. Collected Essays in Christology* (Cambridge: Cambridge University Press, 1987).
Thomas V. Morris, *The Logic of God Incarnate* (Ithaca and London: Cornell University Press, 1986).
Geoffrey Parrinder, *Avatar and Incarnation* (London: Faber and Faber, 1970).

CHAPTER 5   TRINITY

David Brown, *The Divine Trinity* (London: Duckworth, 1985).
Stephen T. Davis, Daniel Kendall SJ and Gerald O'Collins SJ (eds.), *The Trinity. An Interdisciplinary Symposium on the Trinity* (Oxford: Oxford University Press, 1999).
Richard Swinburne, *The Christian God* (Oxford: Clarendon Press, 1994).

CHAPTER 6   SALVATION

Richard Swinburne, *Responsibility and Atonement* (Oxford: Clarendon Press, 1989).
Ronald J. Feenstra and Cornelius Plantinga, Jr. (eds.), *Trinity, Incarnation and Atonement. Philosophical and Theological Essays* (Notre Dame: University of Notre Dame Press, 1989).
Vernon White, *Atonement and Incarnation. An Essay in Universalism and Particularity* (Cambridge: Cambridge University Press, 1991).

CHAPTER 7   THE CONSUMMATION OF ALL THINGS

Brian Hebblethwaite, *The Christian Hope* (Basingstoke: Marshall Morgan & Scott, 1984).
John Hick, *Death and Eternal Life* (London: Collins, 1976).
H. D. Lewis, *The Self and Immortality* (London: Macmillan, 1973).

CHAPTER 8   OTHER THEMES IN CHRISTIAN DOCTRINE

Paul Gwynne, *Special Divine Action. Key Issues in the Contemporary Debate (1965–1995)* (Rome: Gregorian University Press, 1996).
Paul Helm, *The Providence of God* (Leicester: Inter-Varsity Press, 1993).
Keith Ward, *Divine Action* (London: Collins, 1990).

Index

Abelard, Peter, 91
Abraham, William, 20, 24, 27
Adams, Marilyn McCord, 96–7, 101, 102, 122–5
Adams, Robert Merrihew, 43, 55, 131, 136
alienation, 94–5, 98, 121, 123, 125
Allen, Diogenes, 13
Almond, Philip, 33
Alston, William, 2, 20, 32, 77
analogy, 4, 7, 12, 31, 40–1, 42, 43, 45, 50, 59, 61–2, 64, 76, 80, 82, 87, 90, 96, 97, 116, 118, 140, 143
analytic tradition, the, 2–3, 9–12, 13, 97
anima mundi, 47
Anscombe, G. E. M., 54, 129–30, 142, 143
Anselm, 36, 70, 91, 101, 106
anthropic principle, 51–2
Apollinarianism, 62
apologetics, 15, 72
Arianism, 86, 89
Aristotle, 6, 89, 114, 117, 129
Athanasian Creed, 57
Athanasius, 103, 105
atheism, 8, 11, 50, 110, 113
Atonement, 25, ch. 6 *passim*
Augustine, 37, 55, 83, 86, 94
Aulen, Gustav, 91
Austin, J. L., 21
authority, 17–18, 26, 27–8, 30, 81, 127

avatar, 73–4
Ayer, A. J., 49, 110

Badham, Paul, 110, 114
Balthasar, Hans Urs von, 41, 43
baptism, 101, 105, 129
Barr, James, 18
Barrow, John, 52
Bartel, T. W., 90
Barth, Karl, 5, 22–3, 27, 67, 75
Bartholomew, D. J., 142
Berkeley, George, 114
Bible, the, 12, 17, 18, 19, 21–5, 26, 28–9, 31, 40, 44, 47, 57, 59, 67, 71, 79, 80, 81–2, 88, 110, 121, 123–4, 128, 132
Brown, David, 29, 30–2, 34, 61–3, 64, 67, 72, 81–2, 83–4, 87–8, 124, 139–40
Buddhism, 33, 128
Bultmann, Rudolf, 9
Butler, Joseph, 18, 108–9
Byrne, Peter, 26

Calvin, John, 24, 94–5
Cartwright, Richard, 90
Chalcedon, 57, 62, 64, 68
chance, 142
chaos theory, 142–3
Church, the, 25, 57, 60, 76, 91, 105, 121, 127–9, 131
Coakley, Sarah, 85–6, 87
consciousness, 62–3, 108

contingency, 47–9, 53, 55, 75, 89, 111, 142
Copleston, Frederick, 12
cosmological arguments, 48–9
Craig, William Lane, 50, 122–4
Crain, Stephen, 143
creation, 8, 15, 18, ch. 3 *passim*, 59, 64, 67–8, 75, 80, 85, 89, 92, 109, 111, 116, 123–4, 125–6, 131–2, 133, 135–6, 137, 139, 140, 142, 143–4
Creel, Richard, 39, 52
Cross, Richard, 78, 84, 86, 100–1, 104, 105
Cupitt, Don, 2

Dalferth, Ingolf, 14, 32
Davis, Stephen, 81, 116, 117–18, 122–5
death, 101, 106, 108–11, 112–16, 117–18, 121, 122
deism, 39, 133, 139
Descartes, René, 53, 108
design arguments, 48–9, 51–2
devil, the, 93, 101
divine action, 18–19, 21–4, 26, 27–30, 37, 38, 39, 44–6, 47, 49, 59, 64, 67–8, 88, 91, 99, 125, 127, 130, 132–45
divinization, 103, 105
Donne, John, 120
double agency, 23, 28, 139, 140–3
dualism, 109, 113, 116, 117–18
Dummett, Michael, 72

Eccles, John, 109
Edwards, Jonathan, 94
Eliade, Mircea, 130
emanation, 38
Enlightenment, the, 6, 10–11
epistemology, 15, 24, 32, 73
eschatology, 27, 74, ch. 7 *passim*
eternity, 14, 44–5, 56, 58, 66, 78, 82, 101, 108, 111–12, 118, 123, 135
ethics, 8, 10, 55, 92, 127, 131
Eucharist, the, 102, 129–30
evidence, 71–3, 110, 138, 142
evil, the problem of, 1, 14, 31, 43, 52, 55–6, 68, 70, 71, 109, 123, 133, 139

evolution, 48–9, 52, 139, 141
exemplarist theories, 91–2, 94, 103, 104
existentialism, 9
experience, 4, 16, 20–1, 27, 32–4, 68, 72, 82, 83, 108, 110, 113, 119, 131
expiation, 98

faith, 7–8, 12–13, 20, 24, 30, 32, 58, 102, 121, 122, 132
fall, the, 95
Farmer, Herbert H., 17, 74, 92
Farrer, Austin, 2, 9, 14, 23, 28, 29–31, 41, 45, 47, 50, 70, 72, 94, 103, 104, 120, 122, 139, 140–3, 144, 145
Feenstra, R. J., 15, 63, 87
Feuerbach, Ludwig, 138
fideism, 2
finitude, 49–50, 75
Flew, Antony, 1, 111
Flint, Thomas P., 69, 135
foreknowledge, 135
forgiveness, 27, 58, 92, 94–7, 99, 100, 103, 105, 121
Foucault, Michel, 10, 95
Frankfurt, Harry, 69
Freddoso, Alfred J., 61, 63, 65
free will, 31, 40, 41, 43, 45–6, 54, 55–6, 64, 65, 68–70, 97, 108, 121, 123–6, 134, 135–6, 141, 142, 144–5
Frege, Gottlob, 77
Freud, Sigmund, 95

Gamow, George, 38, 40
Geach, Peter, 48–9, 77, 78–9, 83, 86, 89, 114–15, 117, 122, 131, 135, 137
Gooch, Paul, 95
goodness, 36, 42–4, 55–6, 68, 69–70, 72, 76, 77, 78–80, 92, 97, 125, 127, 131
grace, 28, 41, 53, 60, 62, 102, 104–5, 106, 124, 126, 134, 140–1, 144
Greene, Graham, 84
Gregory of Nyssa, 85–6
Gribbin, John, 52
Griffin, David, 46
guilt, 94–5, 97, 101, 106
Gwynne, Paul, 133

Hallett, Garth, 118–19
Hartle, Jim, 50
Hartshorne, Charles, 46, 112
Hasker, William, 2, 4–5, 55, 136
Hawking, Stephen, 50–1
heaven, 108, 115, 119, 120, 125–6
Hebblethwaite, Brian, 17–18, 30, 61, 71, 74, 120–1, 122, 137
Hegel, Georg Wilhelm Friedrich, 9, 13, 27, 38
Heidegger, Martin, 9–10, 13, 50
hell, 108, 113, 121–5
Helm, Paul, 45–6, 53, 133–4, 135, 144
Hick, John, 2, 27, 32–4, 58–60, 64, 68–9, 73, 93–4, 99, 100, 101, 103, 105, 110, 112, 116, 115–16, 120, 122, 123, 131
Hinduism, 33, 45, 73–4, 128
history, 4, 6–7, 17, 24, 27–9, 32, 34, 54, 58, 59, 71–3, 74, 81, 108, 109, 117, 130, 132, 133, 135, 136, 140–1, 142
Holloway, Richard, 96
Holy Spirit, the, 19, 24, 26, 38, 45, 73, 75, 78, 80–2, 83, 86, 87, 89, 99, 101, 103, 104–5, 106–7, 121, 126, 129, 133, 135, 143, 144
hope, 118
Houston, J., 68, 138
Hume, David, 68, 138

identification, 92–3, 97, 102–4, 106
identity, 62–3, 64, 66, 84, 108, 111, 113, 114, 117–18
image of God, the, 7, 59
imagination, 29–32, 41, 114
immanence, 39
immortality, 108–9, 112–16, 117, 118–19, 125
immutability, 46, 77, 137, 144–5
impassibility, 77
impeccability, 69, 125
Incarnation, 4, 11, 17, 19, 25, 26, 27, 29, 30, 33–4, 37, 45, ch. 4 passim, 75, 77–8, 80–2, 83, 87, 94, 99–100, 101, 102, 104–5, 106, 109, 125–6, 132, 134, 138, 139, 141

inspiration, 19, 26, 27, 30–1, 53, 63, 82, 92, 129, 132, 144
Islam, 35, 45, 86, 128

James, William, 20
Jenson, Robert, 14, 75
Jesus, 25, 26, 27, 30, ch. 4 passim, 91, 105
John of Damascus, 14
Judaism, 27, 35, 45, 57, 80, 86, 92, 128
judgement, 57, 92, 94–7
Julian of Norwich, 49
justification, 102, 105–7, 129

Kant, Immanuel, 1, 9, 106, 127–8
Kasper, Walter, 75
Kaufman, George, 3–4, 19
Keller, James, 4
kenosis, 62–3, 66, 67
Kierkegaard, Søren, 9, 28, 128
Kirk, Kenneth, 119
Kirmmse, Bruce H., 128
Knight, Gordon, 123
Kretzmann, Norman, 35–7, 42, 76, 7
Kvanvig, Jonathan, 39

Langford, Michael, 95
Lash, Nicholas, 82, 111–12
Layman, C. Stephen, 90
Leftow, Brian, 86–7
Leibniz, Gottfried Wilhelm, 42–3, 66
Leslie, John, 52
Lewis, C. S., 93, 105
Lewis, H. D., 109, 117
liberalism, 3–5, 11, 25, 58
linguistic philosophy, 7, 12, 13
Lipner, Julius, 74, 115
logic, 9, 31, 53, 59, 60, 61–7, 90, 115–16, 136
logical positivism, 1, 11, 12–13
Lonergan, Bernard, 75
love, 29, 36, 42, 44, 47, 59, 71, 78–80, 82, 83, 85, 86–7, 88–90, 91, 92, 96, 99, 102, 103, 104–5, 106, 109, 111, 119, 121, 123–5, 128, 129, 131

Lucas, John, 54, 93, 96, 99, 101, 102–4, 105
Luther, Martin, 65, 94, 130

McCann, Hugh, 39
McGrath, Patrick, 137
MacIntyre, Alasdair, 8, 10–11
MacKinnon, Donald, 77–8, 81, 83, 92–3, 97, 102
Macnamara, John, 90
Macquarrie, John, 9
McTaggart, J. M. E., 113
Malebranche, Nicolas, 40
Marion, Jean-Luc, 14
Marx, Karl, 95
materialism, 109, 114, 116
Mavrodes, George, 2, 20–1, 22, 24, 27, 32
memory, 112, 114, 117, 121,
Menzel, Christopher, 53
metaphor, 58–61
metaphysics, 10, 11, 12, 14, 19, 36, 46, 48–9, 50, 52, 57, 59, 61–7, 76, 77–8, 84, 100, 114, 130, 143
middle knowledge, 55, 69, 124, 136
miracle, 66–7, 137–40, 143
Mitchell, Basil, 4f., 12–13, 19–20, 21–2, 24, 29, 31
modalism, 89
Modern Churchmen's Union, 58
Moltmann, Jürgen, 75
Morris, T. V., 2, 36–7, 39, 43, 44, 45–6, 47, 50, 52, 62, 63–4, 66, 68–9, 74, 83
Mozart, Wolfgang Amadeus, 41, 43, 54
Murray, Michael, 122–3
Murty, K. Satchidananda, 33
mysticism, 82, 88–9, 119
myth, 58–61, 62, 67, 134

natural theology, 5, 17–18, 32, 35, 37, 55, 76
necessity, 36, 41–2, 48–9, 52–3, 75, 76, 78, 80, 83, 85, 87, 89, 95, 98–9, 103, 134
Nestorianism, 62
Newman, John Henry, 122
Newton, Isaac, 53
Nineham, Denis, 6

omnipotence, 14, 36, 63, 66, 75, 90, 100, 113, 137
omnipresence, 66
omniscience, 14, 36, 54–5, 63, 66, 69, 75, 100, 124, 135, 136, 137
Otto, Rudolf, 13

Pannenberg, Wolfhart, 5, 6, 9, 14, 18, 27–8, 48, 75, 85
parapsychology, 110
Parrinder, Geoffrey, 73
Pascal, Blaise, 3
Paul, St, 80, 82, 94, 95, 114, 117
penal substitution, 93, 104
perichoresis, 88
person, 62–6, 74, 77, 78–9, 80, 81–4, 85–6, 87–90, 109, 114, 115, 117, 124, 134, 135, 139, 140–1, 144
phenomenology, 6, 8, 131
Phillips, D. Z., 1f., 111
Pittenger, Norman, 46, 112
Plantinga, Alvin, 2, 3, 9, 14–15, 16, 20, 24, 26, 35, 70, 72, 73, 95
Plantinga, Cornelius, 15, 63, 87, 88–9
Plato, 1, 6, 10, 13, 36–7, 44, 52, 108–9
politics, 8, 11
Polkinghorne, John, 51, 54, 116, 117, 141, 142–3
Popper, Karl, 109
postmodernism, 10
prayer, 132, 134, 143–5
preaching, 21, 22
predestination, 135, 144
Price, H. H., 113
probability, 72, 142
Process Theology, 46–7, 112, 121
providence, 28, 29, 42, 45, 67–8, 69, 127, 132–45
punishment, 95–6, 97, 100, 101, 106, 123, 125
purgatory, 108, 121–2

Quakerism, 58
Quinn, Philip, 40, 99–100, 101, 104, 106, 127–8, 130

Rahner, Karl, 75, 85–6, 105
Rashdall, Hastings, 91
rationality, 4, 5, 7–9, 10, 11, 13, 17, 18, 34, 76, 81, 95
realism/anti-realism, 2
reason, 12–13, 17, 18
reconciliation, 17, 91–2, 96, 98, 105
Rees, Martin, 52
Reitan, Eric, 122
Reformation, the, 105, 121, 130
Reichenbach, Bruce, 105
reincarnation, 62
relative identity, 66–7, 84, 90
religious pluralism, 2, 3, 32–4, 73, 105, 122
reparation, 98–9, 100, 105
repentance, 95, 97–8, 100, 104, 105, 122
resurrection, 25, 26, 27, 28, 58, 68, 72–3, 74, 108–9, 110, 111–16, 117–18, 119–21, 134, 139
revelation, 5, ch. 2 passim, 76, 80–2, 83, 87, 104–5, 124–5, 127, 138, 139
Reyes, Gonzalo E., 90
Reyes, Mary La Palme, 90
Richard of St Victor, 79, 87
Rublev, Andrei, 87–8
Russell, Bertrand, 39, 46, 49

sacrament, 73, 127, 129–31
sacrifice, 92–3, 98–9, 100, 103, 104–5, 106
salvation, 57, 58, 66–7, 70, 73, 74, ch. 6 passim, 109, 121, 123–5, 132, 133
sanctification, 99, 102, 103, 105–7, 121, 129
Sanders, E. P., 73
Sartre, Jean-Paul, 9
satisfaction, 100, 102, 104, 106
Schwöbel, Christoph, 14, 32
science, 8, 10, 17, 19, 23, 28, 50–2, 109, 113, 133, 139, 141–3
Searle, John, 109
Sennett, James, 126
simplicity, divine, 36, 44–6, 89
sin, 68–70, 91, 94–7, 99–100, 101, 104, 105, 123–4, 125

Smart, Ninian, 2, 73, 131
Smith, Quentin, 50
soul, 108, 113–16, 117–18
Stump, Eleonore, 3, 6, 100–2, 104, 106, 122, 124–5, 144–5
substance, 77–8, 87, 90, 109, 113, 117, 118, 119, 129–30
Surin, Kenneth, 82
Swinburne, Richard, 2, 3, 4, 7, 25–7, 31, 33, 43, 45–6, 47, 51, 62, 63, 64–7, 69–71, 72, 73, 79, 81, 83–4, 85, 86, 87, 90, 93, 94, 95, 96, 97–101, 104, 105, 109, 117, 125, 138

Talbott, Thomas, 122–4
Taliaferro, Charles, 93
Taylor, A. E., 119, 126
temptation, 65, 68–70, 125–6
testimony, 18
Thomas Aquinas, St, 6, 16, 35, 37, 38, 40, 48, 51, 59, 62, 74, 76, 78, 80, 89, 101–2, 106, 114, 117, 119, 125, 135, 144
time, 14, 38, 40, 44–6, 50–1, 53–5, 66, 77, 78, 108, 111–12, 118–19, 130, 134, 135–7, 145
Tipler, Frank, 52
Tolkien, J. J. R., 41
Torrance, Thomas F., 5, 7, 48, 75, 77
Tracy, Thomas, 141
tradition, 4, 12, 26, 27, 28, 29–32, 34, 76, 119, 125, 135
transcendence, 39, 81, 87, 131, 143
transcendentals, 76–7
transubstantiation, 129–30
Trinity, 4, 11, 25, 42, 47, 57, 58, 62, 64, 71, ch. 5 passim, 100, 101, 103, 106, 120, 126, 132, 139
Troeltsch, Ernst, 72
truth, 4, 6, 7, 9, 11, 14, 19, 24, 25–7, 28, 31, 58–61, 72, 76–7, 92, 129

Unitarianism, 58, 75
universalism, 121–5

van Inwagen, Peter, 57, 61, 63, 66–7, 83, 85, 114–16

Vatican II, 128
vision of God, 119, 121
virgin birth, 67–8
vocation, 138
Voltaire, François-Marie Arouet, 43
Voss, Stephen, 118

Wainwright, William, 2, 95
Ward, Keith, 5, 27, 29, 33, 38, 42, 45, 47, 51, 53, 67, 73, 74, 85, 128–9, 130, 131, 138, 141, 142–3, 144–5
Westphal, Merold, 95
White, Vernon, 104, 105, 133–4
Whitehead, A. N., 9, 13, 46, 112

Wiggins, David, 118
Wiles, Maurice, 4–5, 7, 12, 19–20, 60, 133–4, 139
Williams, Bernard, 118
Williams, C. J. F., 78, 86–7, 89
Wittgenstein, Ludwig, 1, 82, 111, 114
Wolterstorff, Nicholas, 2, 3, 20, 21–4, 26, 95, 130
worldview, 7, 10, 17, 18, 19, 48, 109
worship, 72, 127, 128, 129, 131–2, 143
Wynn, Mark, 55

Zimmermann, Dean, 115–16, 117